W9-CCH-156

31st edition

The Good Retirement Guide 2017

Everything you need to know about health, property, investment, leisure, work, pensions and tax

Edited by
Frances Kay and Allan Esler Smith

Publisher's note
Every possible effort has been made to ensure that the information contained in this book is accurate at the time of going to press, and the publishers and authors cannot accept responsibility for any errors or omissions, however caused. No responsibility for loss or damage occasioned to any person acting, or refraining from action, as a result of the material in this publication can be accepted by the editor, the publisher or the author.

This 31st edition published in Great Britain and the United States in 2017 by Kogan Page Limited

Apart from any fair dealing for the purposes of research or private study, or criticism or review, as permitted under the Copyright, Designs and Patents Act 1988, this publication may only be reproduced, stored or transmitted, in any form or by any means, with the prior permission in writing of the publishers, or in the case of reprographic reproduction in accordance with the terms and licences issued by the CLA. Enquiries concerning reproduction outside these terms should be sent to the publishers at the undermentioned addresses:

2nd Floor, 45 Gee Street
London
EC1V 3RS
United Kingdom

c/o Martin P Hill Consulting
122 W 27th St, 10th Floor
New York NY, 10001
USA

4737/23 Ansari Road
Daryaganj
New Delhi 110002
India

www.koganpage.com

© Kogan Page, 2013, 2014, 2015, 2016, 2017

The right of Allan Esler Smith to be identified as the author of Chapter 4 'Super Saturday, scams and complaints' and Chapter 7 'Starting your own business' has been asserted by him in accordance with the Copyright, Designs and Patents Act 1988.

The right of Kogan Page to be identified as the author of this work has been asserted by them in accordance with the Copyright, Designs and Patents Act 1988.

ISBN 978 0 7494 7867 4
E-ISBN 978 0 7494 7868 1
ISSN 2397-1967

British Library Cataloguing-in-Publication Data

A CIP record for this book is available from the British Library.

Typeset by Graphicraft Limited, Hong Kong
Print production managed by Jellyfish
Printed and bound by CPI Group (UK) Ltd, Croydon CR0 4YY

CONTENTS

01 Your future, your money, your life: Doing the sums! 1

Pre-retirement planning 4
The power of the 'grey pound' 5
Doing the sums 5
Estimating income 6
Estimating expenditure 7
Balancing the books 9
How to go about it 10
A final word on doing the sums 11
Other possible ways of increasing your retirement income 11

02 Pensions, savings and financing your retirement: The 'treacle' chapter 13

The importance of pensions and investment planning 15
Understand your State Pension entitlement 16
Defined contribution pensions 19
Beware of predators stalking your pension 26
Other help and advice 26
Protection for pension scheme members 28
Other sources of help in retirement – benefits 28
Equity release (selling off part of your home) 29
Savings as part of your retirement planning 30
Sources of investable funds 33
General investment strategy 33
Annuities 34
National Savings and Investments (NS&I) 36
Variable interest accounts 37
Fixed interest securities 39
Equities and some other investments 39
Investing for your grandchild 44
Long-term lock-ups 46
Investor protection 51

03 Tax 53
But it's all so complicated – and what about Betty down the road? 56
Self-assessment 56
Income Tax 57
Tax allowances 58
Tax relief 60
Tax-free income 60
Income tax on savings and investments 62
Mistakes by HMRC 64
Tax rebates 65
Capital Gains Tax 66
Inheritance Tax and wills 68
Retiring abroad 75
Further information 76
Useful reading 77

04 Super Saturday, scams and complaints 78
Super Saturday defeats over-charging 79
Protecting yourself from the scammers 81
Some common scams 83
Keeping safe from telephone cold calls, email scammers and online fraud 86
Professional advisers 92
Other types of advisers 94
Complaints and 'how to complain' 97
Further reading 100

05 Your home 101
Future proofing your home 103
What to do if staying put 104
Moving to a new home 105
Living in leasehold 108
Other options 108
Practical suggestions for reducing your energy bills 109
Structural repairs and improvements 111
Safety in the home 113
Home security 114
Insurance 115

Earning money from your home 117
Benefits and taxes 119

06 Health 121
Keeping fit 123
Organized activities 124
Healthy eating 125
How to keep healthy in the heat 126
Food safety 127
Drink (alcohol) 128
Smoking 129
Accident prevention 129
Aches, pains and other abnormalities 130
Health insurance 130
Long-term care insurance 132
Income protection 133
Health screening 133
National Health Service 133
Complementary and alternative medicine 136
Eyes 137
Feet 137
Hearing 138
Sleep/insomnia 138
Teeth 139
Personal relationships 140
Depression 141
Some common disorders 141
Disability 147

07 Starting your own business 148
Start a small business – in one page 149
The secret ingredient 150
Some of the differences between starting a small business and employment 151
Why bother with a plan? 152
What goes into a plan? 153
Practical and emotional tips 155
Keep on top of the paperwork 155
Paying tax and National Insurance 158

Marketing tips to fill your diary 162
Trading formats 165
Alternative ways of getting started 168
Operational and other issues 170
Insurance 172
Property investment 173
Further help, advice and training 174
Useful reading 175
Starting and running a business – checklist 175

08 Working for others: Volunteering and paid work 179
Volunteering opportunities 181
Citizens Advice – now there's a thought, and maybe an opportunity for you! 183
Choosing the right voluntary work 185
Animals 186
The elderly 187
Armed and ex-services 187
Bereavement 188
Children and young people 188
Conservation 188
Family 189
Health and disability 189
Heritage 189
Politics 190
Social welfare 190
Long-term and overseas volunteering 190
Searching for paid employment 191
Training opportunities 194
Employment ideas 194

09 Hobbies and holidays 200
Arts and culture 202
Coach and rail holidays 206
Cruising 207
Education at home and learning holidays 209
Gardens and gardening 211
Heritage, history and related holidays 211
Sport 213

Hobbies and holidays for people with disabilities 220
Hobbies and holidays that can be done on your own 221
3G holidays 222
Home-swapping holidays 223
Travel insurance 223
When things go wrong 225
General information 226

10 Taking care of elderly parents and relatives 229
Maintaining independence 232
Key voluntary organizations 237
Getting around 238
Holidays 239
Lasting power of attorney 239
When help becomes necessary 240
Emergency care for pets 242
Practical help for carers 242
Benefits and allowances 243
Financial assistance 245
Special accommodation for the elderly 246

11 No one is immortal 253
Wills 255
Provision for dependent adult children 259
Money and other worries – and how to minimize them 259
Funeral plans 259
State benefits and tax 262
Organizations that can help 264

Useful resources and contacts 265
Index 280

Chapter One
Your future, your money, your life
Doing the sums!

'Life is like riding a bicycle. To keep your balance, you must keep moving.'
ALBERT EINSTEIN

Welcome to your very shrewd purchase – if you pick up on just two or three of the suggestions in our book it will have more than paid for itself. But we are confident you will find lots of nuggets so please don't restrict yourself to just two or three.

And now for the even better news. Did you know that a recent Office for National Statistics study suggests that people age 65 to 79 are 'happiest of all'? If you are approaching the age of 65, perhaps you already feel the exciting anticipation of this euphoria? If you are in your 50s then you not only have the happiest days to look forward to, but you actually have even more of that vital ingredient – time. Time to take some action and plan your steps, and really make the days ahead some of the happiest of your life.

The Office for National Statistics carried out this research last year, having surveyed more than 300,000 adults across the United Kingdom. It found that life satisfaction, happiness and feeling life was worthwhile all peaked in that age bracket, but declined as we grow older. However, the survey also found that the 45–59 age group had the lowest levels of satisfaction and the highest levels of anxiety (BBC News, 2 February 2016, **www.bbc.co.uk/news/uk-35471624**).

So how about that? Getting older isn't all bad. In fact, reaching retirement age suggests that there's everything to play for. Retirement for most of us is essentially a new beginning, a new chapter in life, and one that should be fulfilling. Pensioners today have power, the luxury of choice, the likelihood that we will live longer than the previous generation, be healthier and better off financially than our parents. Being secure financially, happy with who we are, with no career anxieties and fewer parental and filial burdens, no wonder new retirees are delighted, feeling free to enjoy the finer things of life. If that isn't good news, then what is?

Key points in this chapter

- *Understand the life you wish to lead in retirement.* Food and drink, your home, the car and transport, holidays, hobbies and a potentially endless list of items that come at a cost. Do you shop in Waitrose or Aldi, or do you not care? Is it a car or public transport, or again do you not care? Do you want one holiday or two or three a year?
- *Use our simple approach to doing the sums.* The word 'budget' can send most sane folk running to the hills. But let's face facts from the start of this book. The life you wish to lead in retirement will come at a cost, and the simple fact is (come on, put your hands up here!) many folk just have no grasp of the cost of the lifestyle they aspire to and what funds they will actually have in retirement (or could have). We set out an approach, and if you really want more we provide a few extra signposts to further help.

So, happy New Year! Have you made your New Year resolutions yet? Or are you instead considering compiling your 'bucket list' as retirement approaches? Maybe you've had a glance at some of the anniversaries that will be celebrated during the year. In the first few months of 2017:

- Music lovers will be celebrating the 450th anniversary of the birth of the composer Claudio Monteverdi.
- History enthusiasts will remember it's the 90th anniversary of the first transatlantic telephone service established from New York City to London.
- Radio devotees will know that it is the 75th anniversary of the first broadcast of *Desert Island Discs* presented by Roy Plomley (Vic Oliver being the first castaway).

- Sports fans will be aware of the 90th anniversary of the first live radio commentary of a football match anywhere in the world, between Arsenal FC and Sheffield United at Highbury.
- Aviation buffs will mark the 80th anniversary of Sir Frank Whittle ground testing the first jet engine designed to power an aircraft.
- And Kogan Page has published the 31st edition of *The Good Retirement Guide*. Well done for purchasing your copy.

Whatever you feel about reaching retirement, it is well worth taking time to think seriously about how you would like to spend the rest of your life. This book is designed to help you do just that. Many people make promises about getting fitter and losing weight, but although this is laudable it's not very exciting and some of these resolutions fail within a few weeks. It might be better to work on the mantra of 'having more fun' in retirement instead. Laughing and having good times is great for reducing stress, so maybe this is the resolution to keep for the year ahead.

Starting a new phase in life gives us time to reflect on things past, be thankful for what we have achieved and consider how we might improve things in future. At any age it is sensible to refocus on what is important and work out ways to keep our stress levels as low as possible and get maximum enjoyment out of everything we do. A number of pensioners, when asked what their New Year resolutions were, said their top five wishes were:

- to be around next year to make another resolution;
- to socialize more and spend quality time with family and friends;
- to celebrate all the little things in life and be thankful;
- to volunteer – helping others in need made them feel useful;
- to smile – be kinder, more understanding and patient.

Your resolutions may echo these, or be much more wide ranging. But they should represent a fresh, new beginning for you. Don't forget, it is important to keep resolutions realistic. In retirement, for example, one of the great luxuries is being able to make time for yourself. You've spent decades caring for others, building a successful career, so now you can give yourself permission to think about you, and take some time out. Thinking of yourself, your personal needs, and how your retirement resolutions could improve your life, health and well-being is not selfish; it is essential to ensure your future is well ordered. This simple act should reduce the stress in your life and make for a happier you.

As members of the Baby Boomer generation, those of us in our early 60s are often reported as 'never having had it so good'. Most of us are financially secure, we are definitely more careful with money, have paid off our mortgages having bought property when it was more affordable, and now enjoy a degree of flexibility and choice. According to the TV documentary *Tonight: Old and Wealthy – End of the Golden Years*, today's wealthy pensioners appreciate how fortunate they are (ITV, 10 March 2016). They are aware that tomorrow's pensioners (those now in their 40s) will be worse off when reaching their 60s, with many having to work until they are 75 to achieve a comfortable retirement.

Pre-retirement planning

The important thing to remember is that it's well worth taking time now to do some pre-retirement planning. Things to consider include: what standard of living you want; how much money you will need to achieve it; and what sort of social life you wish to enjoy. *The Good Retirement Guide* covers all these matters: pensions, tax, investment, starting your own business, your home, leisure and holidays, paid work and volunteering, how to avoid being scammed, health, looking after elderly parents and wills. Buying the book is an excellent first step. While planning for retirement can be complex, *The Good Retirement Guide* is designed to make it easier and enjoyable.

A pre-retirement course should be helpful – does your employer offer some kind of course or guidance? If not, ask friends who have already retired for their advice – what did they do? They may come up with useful recommendations or have information that their employer provided – some retirement courses are extensive, informative and provide invaluable assistance. Can you access or borrow some of the help they received?

Typically, the information will cover finances, health, housing, leisure and the implications and adjustments needing to be made before or when you retire. Your research may also unearth residential courses on retirement planning where discussions will take place with your partner and others in similar situations, designed to stimulate your planning efforts around these areas:

- reviewing your current and future expenditure;
- making a list of all your financial assets;
- whether or not to consider deferring retirement;
- whether you should buy an annuity and what other options there are;

- making sufficient provision for living longer;
- and helping you to assess whether your plans are practical.

The following websites provide some information about planning for retirement.

- www.activeageplanning.co.uk;
- www.laterlife.com;
- www.res-ltd.net;
- www.retirement-courses.co.uk;
- www.retirementreinvented.com;
- www.the-retirement-site.co.uk.

The power of the 'grey pound'

In the UK the expression 'grey pound' refers to the economic power of the over 50s. According to Saga's latest report, the over 50s control a staggering £6.2 trillion of wealth, and a report by the Centre for Economics and Business Research found that the over 50s in the UK hold over two-thirds of all household wealth. Now that's impressive, but let's do the sums to make sure we put it to good use and, potentially, lead the life we aspire to.

Doing the sums

You will have to accept that once you retire there will inevitably be changes in your financial affairs. Your income will certainly change but so, too, will your pattern of expenditure. Many people worry about this, but the good news is that provided you have made some sensible pension arrangements and are prepared to do a little planning then practical experience suggests that normally everything will work out fine.

It will, however, be helpful, not least for your peace of mind, if you spend just a little time putting together an annual budget. If you are someone who has always had a personal budget when you were working then things should be pretty straightforward and you simply need to take a hard look at your changed income and expenditure once you retire and slot in the revised figures on the basis of the suggestions in the following paragraphs. However, some people operate on a sort of auto budget during their working life. They get used to an income level and then in the light of experience know more or less what they can afford to do on that budget without thinking about it a great deal. But even they must understand that things will change on retirement.

If you are not used to personal budgeting it may at first glance seem somewhat daunting. But that is really not the case: unless your financial affairs are extremely complex budgeting is no more than simple addition and subtraction. You simply add together all your likely actual income and subtract from that all your estimated expenditure, and if the two balance then you can rest easy. It may take a little time when you first do it but you will find it time well spent. It becomes much easier once you have the basic figures in place for the first time.

Estimating income

Let's start with your income calculations, which should be relatively straightforward. You first need to get an estimate of any pension entitlements, as described in Chapter 2. Those entitlements might come from your previous employment or from any private pension provision you might have made. Such pensions are, however, taxable. In your calculations you would need to make an allowance for any tax due on them, less tax allowances (such as the Personal Allowance; again, more in Chapter 2). If you are of pensionable age you then include any State Pension due to you, as per Chapter 2. State pensions are not taxable at source. However, the tax authorities will adjust your Personal Allowance to take account of what you receive and you will need to allow for this. All of this should eventually be dealt with in your tax code.

An additional point about a State Pension is that some people retire before pensionable age. In those circumstances they may have to use any capital savings they may have to balance the books until such time as they become eligible for their State Pension. One positive thing about this is that when the State Pension does eventually arrive they may well feel significantly better off.

You then need to add any income you expect from investments or savings – again taking account of any tax which may be due, albeit there are beneficial new tax breaks that you should familiarize yourself with (see Chapter 2). Finally, you may have prospects of some paid work (employed or from your own new small business) or perhaps you may plan to serve as a non-executive director on some advisory body or quango (see Chapter 8).

Any income from such sources should be included – again allowing for income tax. It is probably safer not to include such items until your position has been formally confirmed – and when that happens it will be seen as a bit of a bonus!

Estimating expenditure

Estimating expenditure, while perhaps slightly more complex and somewhat less precise than income, is also relatively straightforward. The first thing is to identify those areas of expenditure for which you are responsible; this can vary between individuals and within families. If expenditure on certain areas is shared with others you need to check that their circumstances are unchanged – if that is not the case you need to take account of this in your planning.

Broadly speaking, expenditure is likely to fall within the following areas:

- food and drink;
- household and property;
- travel (including cars);
- leisure (especially holidays);
- sundry expenditure.

Food and drink

This is a top priority. What is purchased and what it costs can vary greatly from family to family. Your eating and drinking habits are not likely to change dramatically on retirement – apart from the possibility that you may have more meals at home. You probably will therefore need to keep a careful check of everything you spend on food and drink over, say, a two-month period and use that figure in your estimates – adjusting it upwards if you do think you will have more meals at home. If you have not done this before the total will surprise you, so don't put this task off.

Household and property

The obvious items are rent, council and water rates insurance and any outstanding mortgage – although many may well have planned to end mortgage payments around the time they are due to retire, so that might represent a major saving in retirement. There are other major items such as telephone – and don't overlook the cost of mobiles – energy and TV payments. You also need an amount to cover upkeep – eg things such as window cleaning and decorating. Don't forget that if you are a keen gardener costs here can mount up – and indeed as you get older you may need some part-time help with the heavier gardening tasks. Repair and maintenance household costs tend to trip up any budget. Rather than making no provision, you'd be best advised to set something aside when doing the sums.

Travel

If your employment involved extensive travelling this is another area where you might find there are savings. But in all probability you will still retain one or more cars. If you were provided with a company car while working then this could involve quite significant additional expenditure. So you need to include fuel, tax, insurance, servicing, replacement parts (eg tyres) and any subscriptions to motoring organizations. Also, don't forget that cars don't keep going forever, so you may need to think about setting something aside for an eventual replacement. The good news is that many new cars come with exceptionally good three-, five- or even seven-year warranty provision so do shop around and look for value here – even if you do have to give up that cherished 'brand' that you have always bought.

Leisure

The whole idea of retirement is that you should have more time to enjoy yourself. While some of the most enjoyable things in life are free, others do require some expenditure. If you are a golfer you will still have to pay your club fees and any other social clubs with which you may be involved, and you may wish to broaden your horizons in this respect. But probably the main item of expenditure could be holidays and other shorter trips – you will almost certainly have more time to do so. This is a difficult area to estimate but you should not ignore it and should make your best guess. If you are overly ambitious you can cut back, and conversely if you are overly careful you may find you can afford to do more than you anticipated. Don't forget holiday insurance and the fact that premiums tend to increase as you get older. It would be impossible to list all leisure pursuits – each person needs to look at what interests them and make an appropriate allowance.

Sundry expenditure

You will need to set aside something to cover sundry expenditure. These are relatively small amounts that, taken individually, you may scarcely notice but which can mount up. For example, if you buy a newspaper every day of the week this could well amount to something in the region of £500 over the whole year. Similar comments apply to the odd morning coffee and eating out generally. You will also need to allow for entertaining at home, nights out and other entertainment. You will probably want to update your wardrobe from time to time and you will need to purchase a range of small items regularly – such as toiletries. If you have a pet their food and insurance can be increasingly expensive. There is also the occasional gift. The list could go on and on as, by their nature, sundries are virtually impossible to define. You need to look at your own lifestyle and set aside a reasonable amount each month to cover this type of expenditure. This could be one area where there is an element of trial and error, and it may just take a little time to get the full measure of what you might need. But it would be unwise to ignore it, as it will mount up over the year.

Balancing the books

Having set everything out the next step is to see if it balances. If at the first count income balances with expenditure you are either very lucky or are a financial genius. If income exceeds expenditure you have no problems, and after checking that there are no errors in your figures you can go and book an extra holiday! The likelihood is, however, that you will find that expenditure exceeds income.

In these circumstances, now that you are retired, you might find it more difficult to increase your income. You should, however, check that you have included everything in the income column – for example have you missed a pension entitlement or an investment? You might also look at the possibility of paid work but, as suggested earlier, it is better not to include this until you are quite certain of the position. Or, if radical rebalancing is required, you may need to look at releasing capital in your home by downsizing, relocating, selling off part of your garden for a house to be built on (if you are lucky enough to have a big garden with access), or via some form of equity release (see Chapter 2).

If you have a low income there are a number of state benefits and allowances available to help. It is estimated that every year huge amounts of such benefits go unclaimed. Age UK has produced a helpful book entitled *More money in your pocket*, which is a guide to claiming benefits for people of pensionable age. This is available on the Age UK website (**www.ageuk.org.uk/moneymatters**).

It will probably be necessary to review your expenditure. There are certain areas where you can't do much – you will still need to eat, most household and property related expenditure cannot be avoided and if you keep the car the running costs will be largely unchanged – although if you are a two-car family you may need to review this now that you are retired. The likelihood is that you will need to look at your leisure/holiday expectations and cut back a bit – at least until you see how things pan out after a year. You may also need to look at your sundry expenditure and ensure you are not overly indulgent.

How to go about it

You can't keep all of this in your head: as a minimum you need a yearly budget set out on paper. Table 1.1 gives an outline of how you might do this. Just look at the general headings and ignore the months at this stage. It must be stressed that the headings are not set in stone – people have differing patterns of income and expenditure and you need to tailor it to your own personal needs and circumstances. The intention of the table is to give you a broad framework within which you might operate.

While you may be able to get by with a yearly budget, it is probably well worthwhile to take just a little more time and set everything out on a monthly basis along the lines of Table 1.1. Many payments, and probably some income, do not occur on a regular monthly basis – eg many bills come in quarterly, insurance policies are often paid annually and holidays and other breaks tend to be irregular. It is therefore much easier to keep track of things if you operate on a monthly basis. This also has the advantage that you can see if things are not quite working out as you go along, rather than being surprised at the end of the year. In this respect it is very unlikely that in practice everything will work out as you plan. There can be unforeseen expenditure, some things may cost more than you have estimated, and you may even find your income increases. All of this is easier to deal with if you can adjust things on a monthly basis to compensate for what will probably be inevitable changes.

One final suggestion is to put it all on a spreadsheet. If you have been used to dealing with spreadsheets in your working life this will not be difficult – indeed it would probably come naturally to do so. If you are not familiar with them, the sort of very simple spreadsheet suggested in Table 1.1 is very easy to set up and run. If you are stuck, any younger member of your family circle should be able to help you. It would certainly be worthwhile as it enables you to update things virtually automatically, and an additional advantage is that when it comes to the next year all you need do is slot in updated figures and the spreadsheet does the sums automatically.

A final word on doing the sums

Don't be put off by all of this – you do not need to follow the suggestions slavishly. The intention has been to start you thinking about the way your financial affairs might change when you retire. Everyone has different circumstances and you need to just pause and think about your own situation. If you follow the suggestions in this section, adjusted as necessary to your own personal needs, then you should have better control over your affairs. But don't forget that personal budgeting is not a precise science: you have to be flexible and be prepared to make adjustments as you go along.

Independent Age provides a range of advice guides, fact sheets and leaflets (most of which are downloadable in pdf format). See **www.independentage.org** and search 'advice guides'.

Other possible ways of increasing your retirement income

There is one other possibility that might yield results if you have not already tried it – tracking down lost insurance policies, pensions or shareholdings, which can be done quite easily via Experian's Unclaimed Assets Register (**www.uar.co.uk**). There is a £25 charge to run a search but it trawls 4.5 million records from about 80 different companies, saving you the trouble of calling firms directly. Alternatively, try the Government's pension tracing service, which will trace any missing work pensions for you free of charge (**www.gov.uk/find-lost-pension**). For lost or dormant bank accounts, try **www.mylostaccount.org.uk**.

The co-editors would like to thank Stanley Smith for his assistance with this chapter and the example budget on the following page.

Table 1.1 Example budget for the year

	January	February	Repeat monthly (March–December)	Annual total
INCOME				
Private/work pension received (after tax)				
State pension				
Any other pension (after tax)				
Interest on savings (after tax)				
Dividends from investments (after tax)				
Paid work (after tax)				
Boards, trusts, etc				
Any other sundry income				
Total income (A)	January (A)	February (A)		(A) total for year
EXPENDITURE				
Food and drink				
Food and drink (eating in)				
Meals out				
Household/property				
Mortgage				
Rent				
Council tax				
Water rates				
Insurance				
Electricity				
Gas				
Oil				
Telephone				
Mobile				
General upkeep				
Garden				
Repairs and maintenance				
Any other				
Total household				
Transport/car				
Petrol				
Tax				
Insurance				
Service				
Motoring organizations				
Replacement tyres, etc				
Any other regular transport costs				
Total travel/transport				
Leisure				
Subscriptions to clubs, etc				
Short trips				
Major holidays				
Anything else				
Total leisure				
Sundries				
Overall monthly estimate of incidental expenditure				
Total expenditure (B)	January total (B)	February total (B)		(B) total for year
Surplus/deficit to carry forward each month (A–B)				(A–B) total for year

Chapter Two
Pensions, savings and financing your retirement
The 'treacle' chapter

'The question isn't what age I want to retire. It's at what income.'
GEORGE FOREMAN

This chapter could be like wading through treacle but dip in and it may leave a sweet taste. The treacle factor comes from the simple fact that the biggest financial decision you will make, even bigger than a mortgage, gets little attention, is poorly understood and is surrounded in baffling 'pensions speak'. For that reason pensions are put on the back burner and too many people get a nasty shock when the reality strikes about how they have financed their retirement. By then it may just be too late to do anything meaningful to make any significant impact. Some of the options to work around the harsh reality of a modest pension and higher living aspirations could be to work longer, start your own small business or raid your savings. Best of all, however, could be to wade through the treacle and get a head start on pensions, savings and investment. This chapter will not have all the answers but you really can start to remove the complications and misunderstandings and get some pension knowledge and then, if there is time, get some planning in place.

Having started on a relatively negative note, one big cause for optimism is that from April 2015, the Chancellor radically altered the way 'defined contribution' pensions are operated and taxed and this has made sweeping changes to how people can finance their retirement. When combined with new tax-free incentives on income from dividends and interest this chapter may see a sweet taste emerging from the treacle.

If you can answer 'no' to any of the following two questions you really should read on:

1. Will your financial situation allow you to lead the lifestyle you aspire to in retirement?
2. Are you sure you know the income you will receive in retirement and how it will be taxed?

Importantly, this chapter is only a guide and it is neither legal nor financial advice, and is no substitute for taking professional advice from an independent financial adviser or other professional adviser (see Chapter 4). Any potential tax advantages may be subject to change and will depend upon your individual circumstances, and individual professional advice should be obtained.

Key points in this chapter

- *Information to help you understand your State Pension entitlement and any company and private pension entitlement.* You should get a State Pension forecast and ask your current and former employers for pension forecast and also if they are providing access to any financial advice on pensions – some may do this.
- *Pointers to free guidance offered by the government's impartial service about your defined contribution pension options.* Provides clarity on your pension pot and how much money you'll have in retirement. Book an appointment via **www.pensionwise.gov.uk**.
- *Reminders about the importance of getting proper financial advice if you remain unsure.* If the sums involved are significant, the benefits should outweigh fees that you may have to pay. Ask friends and work colleagues if they can recommend a financial adviser or check **www.unbiased.co.uk** but, as a wealth warning, always ensure your adviser is on the Financial Conduct Authority register at **www.the-fca.org.uk**.
- *An alert to beware of the 'pensions predators'.* There are unauthorized advisers out there trying to help you get your hands on part of your pension before the age of 55. Beware – you will probably get stung.

And never deal with an adviser who is not on the FCA register, irrespective of how impressive they may seem (crooks in suits are clever!).

- *An action point to remember to split your savings up* so that no more than £75,000 is held per bank or building society and check the institution is covered by the Financial Services Compensation Scheme. Cover after certain life events (selling a house) may get you £1 million coverage for a short period of time.
- *Tips around combining your pensions planning with your savings plan to finance your retirement.* But keep half an eye on the tax implications (which can change) of both, as therein lies both opportunities and pitfalls.

The importance of pensions and investment planning

The Prudential estimate that the average income for those retiring in 2016 is expected to be about £17,700 including the State Pension. Could this be your income and how would that impact your retirement goals? As a rough rule of thumb a reasonable retirement goal is to expect an income in retirement of between 50 and 75 per cent of your employed earnings. Say, for instance, you were a high earner with your own business bringing in around £75,000 per annum (from salary and dividend income) your retirement goal may be, for example, an income in retirement of £43,000. To fund the gap between the average £17,700 of pension income (from State Pension and, say, an old employer pension) you would have needed to build up a pension pot of around £450,000 to pay further pension income of around £25,000 to reach your goal. Against this back drop Martin Gorvett, a Chartered Financial Planner, provides his top five pension tips to assist the context and actions that may flow from reading this chapter:

1 *Keeping track of retirement goals*. Retirement is not uniform. Everyone has different expectations. Start by understanding your expenditure patterns splitting expenses into three categories:
   - *must*-have: food, heating, etc;
   - *like*-to-have: a holiday twice a year;
   - *nice*-to-have: a new car, a new kitchen or a legacy for the children.

Consider how these categories interact during the three stages of retirement: active (up to 75), transitional (75–83) and passive retirement (83+). Then you can start to consider the income you need to meet your personal retirement goals.

2 *Don't rely on the state.* The State Pension is certainly no substitute for private pension provision and other savings but it does provide a secure guaranteed baseline income on which to build. Ensure you understand what you will be entitled to and when on the State Pension.

3 *Retirement isn't just a pension.* You may need professional help to think differently about your goals for later life and how you want to finance them. The traditional view is that your pension provides income, and other investments are viewed as 'rainy day' funds.

Retirement income doesn't have to come from the pension alone. Having a variety of different savings and investments can achieve the optimum tax efficient income. Do take professional advice – the benefits arising usually justify any cost.

4 *Understand just how long retirement could last and the effect of inflation.* A 65-year-old can now typically expect to live for another 20 years, and in all likelihood may well live a lot longer. Any income that will finance your retirement that is not inflation proofed will reduce in value over time so getting the investment strategy right is integral to achieving sustainability along with selecting funds to provide the desired investment returns while limiting volatility.

5 *Pensions are still the most tax-privileged savings.* Pensions still offer the best tax breaks for mainstream savings. Where else can you get tax relief on contributions, tax-free investment returns and take 25 per cent out tax-free? Treat the pension annual allowance of £40,000 like your ISA allowance of £15,240 and save, save, save.

Understand your State Pension entitlement

The State Pension is regular, weekly income. Funded by national insurance contributions it is based on the amount you have contributed. Because people are living longer the state cannot afford to fund this benefit and therefore the funding solution was met by the State Pension being equalized for men and women and waiting longer to receive it. The State Pension will be paid at age 66 for both sexes by 2020, then to 67 by 2027 and, currently, age 68 by 2044. The **www.gov.uk** website and a search for 'State Pension *calculator*' will give the age at which you will receive it.

The State Pension and related additional elements to it have changed over the years and this has led to further potential confusion in addition to the confusion caused by shifting the entitlement age. The latest change was from April 2016 when a new flat rate pension structure was brought in for those retiring after 6 April 2016. Those retiring before then remain on their old scheme.

To qualify for the old State Pension scheme and receive a full basic State Pension you required 30 years' full National Insurance (NI) contributions. For 2016/17 the full single-person basic state retirement pension rose by £3.35 per week (from £115.95 to £119.30 – or £6,203 per year). If you're married and both you and your partner have built up State Pension, you'll get double this amount.

Some people also receive an additional State Pension (also called the State Second Pension or, before 2002, it was called SERPS), which is the government's earnings-related additional pension. How much additional State Pension you get is complicated and depends on your National Insurance contributions and whether or not you 'contracted out'. You will have been contracted out if you opted for National Insurance contributions to be diverted to a work or personal pension. Just so you are aware, a range of further options include: deferring your pension (by deferring it you can have a bigger pension when it starts); adult dependency increases (for a husband, wife or someone who is looking after your children); Pension Credit (an income-related benefit); payments to an overseas address; provisions for married women and widows; divorce, death and disputes; and the Christmas bonus. More detailed information can be found at **www.gov.uk** and at **www.pensionsadvisoryservice.org.uk**, whose help is always free.

Then we have the new 'simpler' regime where for those retiring after 6 April 2016 the old two-tier system as described above is being replaced by a single-tier system from 6 April 2016 paying £155.65. To qualify for the new State Pension you will need at least 10 qualifying years on your National Insurance record and will need 35 years to get the full new State Pension. You will receive a proportionate amount of the full new State Pension if you have between 10 and 34 qualifying years and you may receive more if you have accrued SERPs or State Second Pension. Whatever figure you are due to receive, no one will receive an amount under the new scheme which is less than they would have done under the old scheme.

State pension top up

From 12 October 2015 to 5 April 2017 a scheme was introduced to allow pensioners to top up their additional State Pension (also known as SERPS or State Second Pension – 'S2P') which is paid along with the basic pension called 'State Pension top up'.

It will be available to all pensioners who reach State Pension age before the introduction of the new State Pension on 6 April 2016. The scheme will be open until 5 April 2017.

The State Pension top up will give pensioners an option to boost their pension by up to £25 a week, an index-linked return and offer protection to a surviving spouse or civil partner. In particular, it could help some women and those self-employed with low earnings in the past. (More at **www.gov.uk** – search for 'State Pension top up' or call 0345 600 4270.)

Early retirement and your State Pension

Because some people retire early, they can mistakenly assume it is possible to get an early pension. While the information is correct as regards many employers' occupational pension schemes, as well as for personal pensions (albeit there may be a trade off resulting in a smaller annualized pension) it does not apply to the basic State Pension.

Next steps – getting that State Pension forecast

You can request a pension statement estimating your new State Pension based on your current National Insurance record. The statement offers an estimated amount, not a guaranteed amount, as it is based on an individual's current National Insurance record and doesn't take into account future National Insurance contribution years you may build.

You can apply online at **www.gov.uk/check-state-pension**
By telephone on 0345 3000 168 or text phone 0345 3000 169
Or by post to:
Newcastle Pension Centre, Futures Group
The Pension Service 9
Mail Handling Site A
Wolverhampton
WV98 1LU

Sources of further free help or advice on the State Pension

The Pension Service provides information to current and future pensioners so that making informed decisions about pension arrangements is straightforward: **www.pensionsadvisoryservice.org.uk**.

The Service Personnel and Veterans Agency: **www.gov.uk/government/organisations/veterans-uk**.

Citizens Advice: **www.citizensadvice.org.uk**.

Defined contribution pensions

Defined contribution pension schemes are a pension 'pot' from which future pension income payable to you will depend on the investment growth of your contributions (and those of your employer if it is a workplace scheme). These contrast with defined benefit schemes, which are often known as final salary pension schemes and were the norm until the mid-1980s. Much reduced, these can still be found in the public sector. Defined benefit schemes will pay an income linked to your number of years' service with an organization and your final salary earned at the point of retirement (some schemes have changed to an 'average' rather than final salary).

The 2014 Budget brought in 'pensions liberation' in April 2015. In the 'old world' most people bought an annuity with their pension pot on retirement. The annuity paid a fixed income for life. The 'old world' system attracted criticism as it was perceived as representing poor value apart from the 25 per cent tax-free payment available at the start and before investing the remainder in an annuity. Once bought, the annuity could not be changed and the pre-determined rate of income paid was subject to Income Tax. Some annuities were mis-sold to those in ill health, or resulted in no financial protection for dependants.

The 'new world' of pensions liberalization resulted in a dramatic change and since April 2015 everyone now has a right to access their defined pension pots from age 55; no one is forced to buy an annuity, withdrawals beyond the 25 per cent tax-free cash can be made (in theory) as and when you wish but are subject to Income Tax. You can take as little or as much as you need and therefore income levels can be varied to take advantage of other income you may be earning (perhaps from a new part-time job, or having started a small business or whilst waiting for the State Pension to kick in) to make your tax affairs more efficient. Importantly, the new regime ensures you can now pass on your pension on death to a loved one (perhaps a concern to pensions savings in the old world to those in poor or deteriorating health) with less tax to pay. This is because pensions are not counted as someone's estate for Inheritance Tax purposes. Under previous rules there used to be a 55 per cent Pensions Death Tax. Now, if you die before 75 there is no tax to pay on funds passing from defined contribution schemes. If you die after your 75th birthday any payments will be subject to the beneficiaries' marginal rate of Income Tax. (Note the new rules do not apply to your State Pension, which cannot be passed to someone else, and these options are not available under final salary schemes, albeit there may be separate pension entitlements for a spouse and dependent children in these.)

Most pension experts agree that pensions liberation is a good thing but also add a note of caution. Martin Gorvett, a Chartered Financial Planner, says:

> The rules changes have helped enormously in making my clients' retirement strategies more efficient. But the new freedom brings temptation and a lot of new responsibility. There's a danger that some pension savers will draw their pension savings and fritter it all away without any constraints to hold them back.

You can save as much as you like (defined contributions, ie towards your pension) but there is a limit on the amount of tax relief you can get and for that reason linking savings together with pensions is essential for your retirement planning. The lifetime allowance is the maximum amount of pension savings you can build up over your life. If you build up pension savings worth more than the lifetime allowance you will pay a tax charge on the excess. The rules on how much you can contribute have been tightened over recent years. The amount that can be saved into a pension each year (known as the annual allowance) and still receive tax relief is currently £40,000 per year. There are provisions to use three previous years' unused allowance and if this becomes a potential issue the sums involved would justify specific professional advice. A new 'tapered reduction' reduces the amount of tax relief that can be obtained on pension contributions for taxpayers with 'adjusted income' in excess of £150,000. Where an individual is subject to the taper, their annual allowance will be reduced by £1 for every £2 by which their income exceeds £150,000, subject to a maximum reduction of £30,000. The annual allowance of £10,000 will, therefore, apply to taxpayers with adjusted income of £210,000 or more. The carry forward of unused annual allowance will continue to be available, but the amount available will be based on the unused tapered annual allowance.

The other big issue that impacts on the tax relief on pension contributions is the 'lifetime allowance'. The lifetime allowance is the maximum amount that can be paid into pensions savings over a lifetime and was reduced from £1.25 million to £1 million from 6 April 2016. Transitional protection for pension rights already over £1 million was introduced alongside this reduction to ensure the change is not retrospective. The lifetime allowance will be indexed annually in line with the Consumer Prices Index (CPI) from 6 April 2018. It is important to bear in mind that tax rules and tax reliefs can and do change and their exact value depends on each individual's circumstances, however, pension savings are still one of the most tax-effective investments. This is because you receive Income Tax relief on contributions at your highest tax rate and the growth in your pension fund is currently totally exempt from Income Tax and Capital Gains Tax.

Company pension schemes

Types of company pension schemes

The pension that your employer offers may be 'contributory' (you and your employer pay into it) or 'non-contributory', which means that only your employer does. As set out below, there are four main types of company pension: final salary, career average, money purchase and group/personal pension.

Final salary

These are known as a type of defined benefit scheme. You build up a pension at a certain rate – one-sixtieth is quite common – so for each year you've been a scheme member, you receive one-sixtieth of your final salary. The pension benefit keeps paying for as long as you live and, therefore, the cost and risk of funding the pension sits with the employer. This is, potentially, a very big win for employees with extending life expectancy rates and the main reason why many private sector employers have exited this sort of arrangement. More public sector workers (such as teachers, police, NHS and local government workers) pay into a final salary scheme. The biggest winners of all are those employees who secure big salary increases towards the end of their employment. If you work for one of the few remaining employers with a final salary scheme, you would need a compelling reason not to join it, or to ever shift the benefits if you have one from a previous employer. Martin Gorvett advises:

> Final salary pension schemes are usually the 'golden goose' of the pensions world as these schemes just keep paying, which will be a nice win if you live to over 100. Only in the rarest of exceptions would there ever be a need to shift

out of a final salary pension scheme – **if you are unmarried or fear decreased mortality due to health concerns you may wish to seek advice on this topic.** Also there is only modest risk, as if a salary-related occupational scheme or the sponsoring employer gets into financial trouble, the Pension Protection Fund can provide some protection. You can normally get a pension of up to 90 per cent of your expected pension, subject to a cap. (See the Pension Protection Fund website for more information: **www.pensionprotectionfund.org.uk**.)

Career average

This is another type of defined benefit scheme, because the benefit (your pension) is worked out using your salary and the length of time you have been a member of the pension scheme and based on an average of your earnings in the time that you're a member of the scheme, rather than the final salary.

As it is an 'average', you should have a fair idea of how much your pension will be before retirement.

Money purchase

These are also known as defined contribution schemes, as described earlier. The money paid in by you and your employer is invested and builds up a fund that buys you an income when you retire and, significantly, the funding risk sits with the employee (in contrast to the defined benefit alternatives summarized above), ie if life expectancy increases, the amount you need to fund your retirement income beyond your initial prediction and then the contributions you have made may not be enough to fund your retirement expectations.

The fund is invested, usually in stocks and shares and other investments, with the aim of growing it over the years before you retire. You can usually choose from a range of funds to invest in. The Pensions Advisory Service (TPAS) has an online investment choices planner to help you decide how to invest your contributions (see **www.pensionsadvisoryservice.org.uk/about-pensions/saving-into-a-pension/choosing-investment-funds**).

Group personal pension

These are also money-purchase schemes, so the funding risk sits with the employee; ie the pension you get is not linked to your salary. Your employer offers access to a personal pension plan, which you own, and can take with you if you get a new job. Your employer will choose the scheme provider, deduct the contributions you make from your salary and pay these to the provider, along with employer contributions.

Auto-enrolment

In 2012 the government introduced 'pensions auto-enrolment'. This was introduced because people in the UK were living longer but were not saving enough to finance their increasing retirement. Before the introduction of auto-enrolment only 47 per cent of UK employees were enrolled in a qualifying workplace pension scheme. Auto-enrolment was designed to help shift the responsibility away from the state and towards the individual and their employer. Automatic enrolment began in October 2012 and is being phased in so that by 2018 auto-enrolment will cover all employers.

To be eligible an individual must live in the UK and be between 22 and State Pensionable age and earn more than £10,000 a year. Each individual will pay 0.8 per cent of their qualifying earnings, rising to 4 per cent by 2018. Their employers will pay a minimum of 1 per cent rising to 3 per cent by 2018. The government makes a contribution through tax relief.

Many employers use the National Employment Savings Trust (NEST) as their pension scheme for auto-enrolment purposes, which is a national defined contribution workplace pension scheme established by the government to support auto-enrolment. It is transportable between employers and has relatively low charges. More at **www.nestpensions.org.uk**. Other auto-enrolment schemes are available.

Questions on your company pension scheme

If you have a query or if you are concerned in some way about your company pension, you should approach whoever is responsible for the scheme in your organization or their delegated representative. They should be able to assist with any of the sample questions below, which may assist your understanding and planning.

- Could you have a refund of contributions if you were to leave shortly after joining?
- Should you want to move the transfer value to another scheme, how long would you have to wait from the date of your request?
- What happens if you become ill or die before pension age?
- What are the arrangements if you want to retire early? Most schemes allow you to do this if you are within about 10 years of normal retirement age, but your pension may be reduced accordingly. Many schemes operate a sliding scale of benefits, with more generous terms offered to those who retire later rather than earlier.

- What will your pension be on your present salary? And what would it be assuming your salary increases by, say, 2 or 5 per cent before you eventually retire?
- What spouse's pension will be paid? Can a pension be paid to other dependants?
- Similarly, can a pension be paid to a partner, male or female?
- What happens if you continue working with the organization after retirement age?
- What are the arrangements if you retire from the organization as a salaried employee but become a retained consultant or contractor?
- Are any changes envisaged to the scheme? For example, if it is a final salary scheme, is there any chance that it might be wound up and a money-purchase scheme offered instead?
- If there were a new money-purchase scheme, would the company be making the same contributions as before or would these be lower in future?
- Is there any risk that benefits – either members' own or those for dependants – could be reduced?
- Is there a possibility that members might be required to pay higher contributions than at present?
- Are there any benefits to transferring old pensions into one new scheme?

Self-invested personal pensions (SIPPs)

If you want to use a pension to save for your retirement, you don't have to give your money to a fund manager. You can manage your own retirement fund with a self-invested personal pension (SIPP). You can pay a lump sum to a pension provider and/or drip feed in monthly amounts. The latter can be made via a scheme into which both you and your employer pay. But instead of your employer directing where your money goes, you get free rein over where it's invested. You can buy a range of asset classes, from stocks to bonds to gold bullion (though you can't buy fine wines). Monthly contributions can be as low as £50. You can pay in amounts equal to 100 per cent of your annual salary up to a current ceiling of £40,000 per year. You can access your SIPP from age 55, when you can draw down as much as you want. These were designed for people who wanted to play a more active part in their investment strategy. The investments that can be held in the SIPP are quite wide and can even include commercial property, and for this reason some owners of small businesses may look at holding their commercial property within their SIPP to good end effect. A specialist pension adviser should be able to assist further. Martin Gorvett advises that 'specialist pension products, SIPPs, are becoming a lot more mainstream. If you are venturing away from the more traditional investment routes, especially buying commercial property, it is important to ensure that a "pure" SIPP is used where you are a co-trustee of the SIPP and hence a co-landlord of the property'.

As SIPPs are fee-based arrangements, the smaller the fund the more expensive they are. If you are someone who finds the idea of investing your own money daunting, a SIPP may not be for you.

Lifetime Individual Savings Account (LISA)

A new lifetime ISA will be available from April 2017 for adults aged under 40. There will be an annual contribution limit of £4,000 and savers will receive a 25 per cent government bonus.

The LISA seems attractive, and at the moment (summer 2016) remains under consultation and could be subject to change. The intention seems to be to encourage individuals to save towards one of two important life events. The first is for first-time buyers to use it to pay towards a residential property, which can be done at any time providing the LISA has been held for 12 months. The second is to use it in retirement once aged 60. With both there is no tax to pay when you take the money out. It could be an early step in a new approach to pension funding where taxed money goes in and is tax-free on the way out (with the 25 per cent government bonus being a welcome addition). This switches the traditional pensions world on its head, whereby we are used to receiving tax relief on contributions being paid into pensions and then being taxed on the income then received in retirement. The difficulty for many imminent retirees is that this new ground-breaking product will only be available to the under 40s according to current draft legislation.

If you have a small pension pot

If the value of your pension rights is below a certain level, it may be possible to give up those rights in exchange for a cash sum. If all your pension savings in all the pension schemes you belong to are worth no more than £30,000 you may be able to take all your pension pots as a lump sum. You can do this even if one or more of your pension pots is worth more than £10,000 or if you've already started to take one of your pensions.

Minimum retirement age

The minimum age at which you are allowed to take early retirement and draw your pension has been 55 since 6 April 2010 and this is likely to rise in line with State Pension age, maintaining a 10-year gap. It may be possible to draw retirement benefits earlier if you are in poor health and unable to work.

Beware of predators stalking your pension

Beware of anyone claiming that they can help to cash in a pension early and before you are 55. Whilst initially attractive, the sting in the tail is that you could face a tax bill of more than half your pension savings. The Pensions Advisory Service warns that this activity is known as 'pensions liberation fraud' and it is on the increase in the UK. The main warning signs are unsolicited text messages and phone calls, a transfer overseas and seeking to access a pension fund before the age of 55 (access to your pension before the age of 55 can only be achieved in rare circumstances) – and the scammers' usual ploy (see Chapter 4 for much more on this) of urgency so that you have no time to think, pause and check it out.

To counter this, always check that any financial adviser is registered with the Financial Conduct Authority (see Chapter 4), obtain a statement about any tax charges and never be rushed into agreeing to a pension transfer. The benefit of dealing with a financial adviser who is registered with the Financial Conduct Authority is that there is a safety net when things go wrong – in the form of the Financial Ombudsman Service – and, if the firm fails and is insolvent the UK safety net, the Financial Services Compensation Scheme, pays up to £50,000 per person per firm (and up to £75,000 per person per institution on savings and deposits).

Other help and advice

Previous schemes

In addition to understanding your current pension scheme, you may also need to chase up any previous schemes of which you were a member. For free help tracking down a pension, contact the Pension Tracing Service, which assists individuals who need help in tracing their pension rights:

www.gov.uk – choose the link 'Working, jobs and pensions' then 'Workplace and personal pensions'.

If you have any queries or problems to do with your pension, there are three main sources of help available to you. These are the trustees of your pension scheme, the Pensions Advisory Service and the Pensions Ombudsman.

Trustees or managers

These are the first people to contact if you do not properly understand your benefit entitlements or if you are unhappy about some point to do with your pension. Pension managers (or other people responsible for pensions) should give you their names and tell you how they can be reached.

The Pensions Advisory Service

The Pensions Advisory Service provides members of the public with general information and guidance on pension matters and assists individuals with disputes with personal, company and stakeholder pensions. More information can be found at: **pensionsadvisoryservice.org.uk**.

Pensions Ombudsman

You would normally approach the ombudsman *only* if neither the pension scheme manager (or trustees) nor the Pensions Advisory Service is able to solve your problem. The ombudsman can investigate: 1) complaints of maladministration by the trustees, managers or administrators of a pension scheme or by an employer; 2) disputes of fact or law with the trustees, managers or an employer. The ombudsman does not, however, investigate complaints about mis-selling of pension schemes, a complaint that is already subject to court proceedings, those that are about a state social security benefit, or disputes that are more appropriate for investigation by another regulatory body. There is also a time limit for lodging complaints, which is normally within three years of the act, or failure to act, about which you are complaining.

There is no charge for the ombudsman's service. The Pensions Ombudsman has now also taken on the role of Pension Protection Fund Ombudsman and will be dealing with complaints about, and appeals from, the Pension Protection Fund. It will also be dealing with appeals from the Financial Assistance Scheme (see overleaf). More information at: **www.pensions-ombudsman.org.uk**.

Some aspects of complaints about pensions can be investigated by the Financial Ombudsman Service (FOS) where the maximum award that the Financial Ombudsman can give is £150,000. A typical example of the type of pension case the FOS investigates is where a consumer complains about the suitability of advice to start a personal pension arrangement (perhaps they would have been better off being advised to join, remain or top-up their employer's company pension scheme). More information is at **www.financial-ombudsman.org.uk** and also see Chapter 4 for the FOS's top tips. The interaction between the FOS and the Pensions Ombudsman can seem confusing but don't worry too much as they have good arrangements to point you in the right direction if you end up with the wrong ombudsman.

Protection for pension scheme members

The Pension Protection Fund (PPF) helps final-salary pension scheme members who are at risk of losing their pension benefits owing to their employer's insolvency. Members below the scheme's normal retirement age will receive 90 per cent of the Pension Protection Fund level of compensation plus annual increases, subject to a cap and the standard fund rules. See website: **www.pensionprotectionfund.org.uk**.

There is more help too for members who lost pension savings in a company scheme before the introduction of the Pension Protection Fund. The Financial Assistance Scheme (FAS) offers help to some people who have lost out on their pension. It makes payments to top up scheme benefits to eligible members of schemes that are winding up or have wound up. Assistance is also payable to the survivor of a pension scheme member. It is payable from normal retirement age, subject to a lower age limit of 60 and an upper age limit of 65 (see **www.pensionprotectionfund.org.uk**).

Another organization that could help is the National Federation of Occupational Pensioners (NFOP). This is an independent organization that exists to help and support those in receipt of a company pension. For more information see the website: **www.nfop.org.uk**.

Other sources of help in retirement – benefits

According to leading charities Age UK and Elizabeth Finn Care, an estimated 1.5 million people could claim benefits, but the means test puts some people off claiming the top-ups they are entitled to. Every year as much as £5.5 billion of benefits that older people are entitled to go unclaimed, despite many people struggling to make ends meet. Much needs to be done in terms of raising awareness of welfare benefits available and reducing some of the negative perceptions against claiming when times are tough. Don't be afraid to ask and then, if appropriate, make a claim.

For help relating to benefits, Turn2Us (**www.turn2us.org.uk**) is a charity set up specifically to identify potential sources of funding for those facing financial difficulty. Individuals can log on to this website for free and in confidence. Also, look at Age UK's website, Britain's leading charity for older people: **www.ageuk.co.uk**.

Community care grants, budgeting loans and crisis loans can all help with exceptional expenses if you are facing financial difficulties. These are all dealt with through the government website. See **www.gov.uk** – Jobseeker's Allowance and low-income benefits, for the widest range of online government information for the public, covering benefits, financial support, rights, employment, independent living and much more. For information for disabled people, see **www.gov.uk** – disability benefits.

Pension Credit is an income-related benefit. It's an extra payment that guarantees most people over 62 a minimum income, and many people fail to claim it. For single pensioners with weekly income (including pension) below £155.60, Pension Credit will top you up to £155.60. If you have a partner and your joint weekly income is below £237.55, it'll top you up to £237.55. When you apply, the Government looks at all of your income. This includes both your basic and additional State Pension, any income from other pensions, income from any jobs you have and any savings above £10,000. For more information contact the Pension Credit claim line on 0800 99 1234.

Equity release (selling off part of your home)

Funding the gap between the retirement lifestyle you desire and the actual reality of your pension income (above) and your investment income (below) can be achieved by two main alternatives. The first is earning more (see Chapters 7 and 8). The second is using the equity stored in property to borrow money to help provide additional income. This can work well if you are asset rich and cash poor and don't want to downsize. The process works by taking out a mortgage on your property whilst continuing to live there and then receiving a lump sum or drawing down funds against that mortgage. Interest then rolls up on the mortgage debt, which will be repaid when you do come to sell the house and downsize or move into alternative accommodation. The interest on the mortgage may be slightly more than on other commercial mortgages. The industry was subject to significant mis-selling in the late 1980s and early 1990s when rogue financial advisers persuaded elderly home-owners to re-mortgage their houses and then gamble on the stock market to try and achieve returns to beat the interest. It went spectacularly wrong for many and has left even more people wary of the concept. However, if arranged properly equity release mortgages can provide a solution, but you should ensure your adviser is a member of the Equity Release Council (**www.equityreleasecouncil.com**). Think carefully about whether you need all of the funds in one go or if you can draw it down in tranches (the latter is usually cheaper on interest costs as you don't draw the money until you need it – maybe for four big cruises over the next 10 years).

Savings as part of your retirement planning

While the nation has been attempting to extricate itself from the banking crisis and the recession, many pensioners and savers have been left out in the cold. Money in savings and deposit accounts at banks has been earning virtually no interest and the value of capital sums has been eroded by inflation. This has caused real pain to many who have led thrifty lives and saved for old age.

Savings play a critical role in the way that the whole economy works. The more encouragement people have to save, the better it is for new investment, future growth, greater productivity and higher living standards. The £15,240 overall annual investment limit (2016/17) will be increased to £20,000 from 6 April 2017 in the Individual Savings Account (ISA). This is most welcome news and allows savers to protect part of their wealth from Income Tax and Capital Gains Tax. Between a couple and over several years that can equate to a powerful tax-free fund that can help in retirement. From April 2016 the first £1,000 (£500 for higher rate taxpayers) of interest and the first £5,000 in dividends will not be subject to Income Tax on your self-assessment return – another useful tax planning tool.

The 'fun' of investing up to £50,000 per person in premium bonds provides a tax-free 'average' return that beats many routine savings accounts (but you can do better in ISAs and if you shop around); you can get a return of the capital within days (so it is easy access, if need be) and you may even win a million pounds – but the odds are 17 billion to one!

Successful investing has never been easy but for those who are interested in saving for retirement, and for the long term, the principles remain the same: keep the costs down; shelter as much money from the tax office as you can; buy assets when they are cheap and sell when they are expensive (albeit that few people have the financial knowledge or crystal ball to really make a success of this but the motto, generally, is worth remembering). To be a successful investor you have to be disciplined. You need to decide on a strategy, allocate your money to your investment accordingly, then stick with that through the ups and downs that the markets will inevitably bring.

But there's a big difference between 'saving' and 'investing'. Investing is for the long term. It is money you can put away for your retirement, and in the long run it should grow more rapidly than in a savings account. If you are saving for a shorter-term goal, perhaps in less than five years, then you're looking to get the most interest paid on your money. Here are some more tips from Martin Gorvett that you may find useful:

1. *Buy what is right for you and don't believe everything you read or hear.* Just because an investment works well for someone else doesn't necessarily mean it will be right for you. Social media promotions can be misleading. Ensure that the investment provider is regulated by the FCA, you don't have to wander off the beaten track just to avoid the herd.
2. *Diversify and don't put all your eggs in one basket.* Consider spreading your risk by diversifying across a mixture of asset classes, industry sectors and geographical areas. When the value of one asset is falling, another might be rising so could help to compensate.
3. *Invest for the long term.* Adopt a strategy and stick with it. Investing isn't a matter of 'timing the market', it is about 'time in the market'. Similarly, try not to get emotionally attached to your investments. Review and re-balance your portfolio regularly to ensure you haven't strayed from the original strategy.
4. *Take professional advice.* Investing is not free. Every avenue to market has a cost. Professional advisers will have a tried-and-tested process, often accessing institutional prices, rather than retail classes available to direct investors.
5. Lastly, *don't risk investing money that you can't afford to lose.* Investments carry a huge caveat – you may get out less than you put in. So don't over stretch, stick within your means and know when to walk away.

Thanks to the internet, investors have unprecedented opportunity to access information and advice and price comparisons on savings and investment products. These websites are worth saving as a 'favourite':

- The Motley Fool: **www.fool.co.uk**;
- Money Advice Service: **www.moneyadviceservice.org.uk**;
- Money Facts: **www.moneyfacts.co.uk**;
- Money Supermarket: **www.moneysupermarket.com**;
- Money Saving Expert: **www.moneysavingexpert.com**;
- This is Money: **www.thisismoney.co.uk**;
- Which?: **www.which.co.uk**.

Since everyone has different financial aims, there is no 'one-size-fits-all' approach to investing. In very simple terms, there are four different types of investment you could consider:

1. *Cash investments*. Made into a bank account or cash ISA. These are generally short-term and offer easy access to your money and lower risk, so the potential returns are much less than other types of investment. Your money is secure up to £75,000 (covered under the Financial Services Compensation Scheme limits) but it could lose value due to tax and inflation.
2. *Bonds and gilts*. Effectively, an IOU from the government or big companies. When you buy one you are lending money that earns an agreed fixed rate of interest. Government bonds (called gilts) are backed by the state and hopefully are as good as guaranteed. Corporate bonds carry greater risk in the event that the issuing company goes bust or cannot afford to repay you but because of this element of risk they offer the possibility of improved returns.
3. *Investing in property*. Directly as a buy-to-let investor or indirectly through certain investment funds carry more risk. Property prices go down as well as up, and it can take time to sell property and get your cash back. Be sure to seek advice beforehand and, even better, don't do anything without reading *Successful Property Letting: How to Make Money in Buy-to-Let*, by David Lawrenson (2015, website: **www.littlebrown.co.uk**).
4. *Shares*. Sometimes referred to as 'equities', this basically means putting money on the stock market. You can do this by buying shares in individual companies or by investing through a professionally managed investment fund, such as a unit trust.

As a rule of thumb, some investors keep an emergency fund equal to at least three months' living costs. Once you work out what you need to have put away for a rainy day and once you have this sum set aside you could consider investing for higher potential returns.

Sources of investable funds

If you are looking at investment options from your resources, possible sources of quite significant capital include:

- *Commuted lump sum from your pension*: One-quarter of your pension can be taken as a tax-free lump sum. The remainder can be taken as cash, subject to the ordinary rates of Income Tax.
- *Insurance policies*: Designed to mature on or near your date of retirement. These are normally tax-free.
- *Profits on your home*: If you sell it and move to smaller, less expensive accommodation. Provided this is your main home, there is no Capital Gains Tax to pay.
- *Redundancy money, golden handshake or other farewell gift from your employer*: Currently you are allowed £30,000 redundancy money free of tax.
- *Sale of SAYE and other share option schemes*: The tax rules vary according to the type of scheme and the rules are liable to change with each Budget statement.

General investment strategy

Investments differ in their aims, their tax treatment and the amount of risk involved. If you are taking the idea of investing seriously, the aim for most people is to acquire a balanced portfolio. This could comprise a mix of investments variously designed to provide some income to supplement your pension and also some capital appreciation to maintain your standard of living in the long term. Except for annuities and National Savings and Investments, which have sections to themselves, the different types of investment are listed by groups, as follows: variable interest accounts, fixed interest securities, equities and long-term lock-ups.

Annuities

Since April 2015 it is no longer necessary to buy an annuity to fund your pension, giving the individual power to manage their own pension and how it finances their retirement.

The option of purchasing an annuity still remains. When you buy an annuity you hand over a lump sum (usually your pension fund, although you can first withdraw up to 25 per cent of it as a tax-free lump sum) to an insurance company in return for a regular, guaranteed income for the rest of your life. Under the current rules the earliest age you can do this is 55. This income is taxable if it exceeds your personal allowance. If you are retiring today, low annuity rates probably make you wince. That doesn't mean you should necessarily ignore them. Once you have bought your annuity, the income you receive is effectively free of investment risk. That has been transferred to your provider. There is little danger of running out of money, as your provider has to pay you for as long as you live.

When you approach retirement your pension company will contact you about purchasing an annuity and will outline the recently announced changes and options available to you. They will provide you with a quotation, which will tell you the amount of money you have in your 'pension pot', the amount of tax-free lump sum you are entitled to take, and the level of income you will receive each month (should you convert your pension fund to an annuity with them). Check you are getting the correct allowance and that you have the right tax code. This tells the pension company how much tax to deduct, but there is no guarantee that it will be right. Specialist help for older people is available from **www.taxvol.org.uk**.

You only get one chance to purchase an annuity, and once you have done so there is no going back. The benefit of shopping around is that you could very well receive more money by doing so. Each annuity provider will have different rates dependent on its own underwriting criteria and your own position. Research shows that by shopping around you may be able to increase the amount of income you receive by up to 20 per cent. Choosing an annuity is a decision that should not be taken without the help of a specialist financial adviser who has experience in this field.

Types of annuities

There are several different kinds of annuities. The most basic is a *level annuity*. This pays you a fixed income for the rest of your life. If you die, the income usually stops. And – crucially – it will not change if prices rise. So in an inflationary world, your purchasing power will fall every year. For example, if inflation averages 4 per cent per year, the purchasing power of your annuity income will halve in 18 years.

To avoid this you could buy an *increasing annuity*. Here, the amount of income you receive will rise in line with inflation each year, or by a set percentage. And if you are worried about your insurance company keeping a large chunk of your pension fund should you die after only a few years of retirement, you could buy a *guaranteed annuity*. So if you bought a five-year guarantee, and you died after two years, your nominated beneficiary (your spouse perhaps) would receive annuity income for another three years.

Another option is a *joint-life annuity* where your partner can receive some or all of your pension income if you die before them. If you want to take a bit more of a risk, you could choose an *investment-linked annuity*. Here you start with an initial level of income while your fund is invested in an insurance company's with-profits fund. If the fund makes a profit, your income goes up. If it loses money, however, your income goes down.

Your health can also have a significant impact. If you are a smoker or have an illness, you may be eligible for an *enhanced annuity* or *impaired life annuity*. These pay a higher annual income than a standard annuity. In short, the annuity provider is betting that you won't live as long, so it can afford to pay you more.

Other options

If you don't want to buy an annuity because of low rates, there are a number of strategies you can use. One is known as *phased retirement*. This is where you set up a series of annuities and drawdowns with 25 per cent tax-free lump sums. You will get a lower starting income but if you think annuity rates are going to rise it might be worth considering.

Another possible option is *fixed term annuities*. Here you set up an annuity for a fixed period (say 5 or 10 years). You get paid an income for the fixed term but at the end of the period you have a guaranteed pot of money to reinvest again. As with phased retirement, your income will be lower than from a standard annuity.

How to obtain an annuity

The annuity market is large and there is a vast choice of products. A helpful free booklet is Martin Lewis's *Guide to Taking Your Pension*. It is available from Martin Lewis's website **www.moneysavingexpert.com** and contains a useful section on annuities.

Other useful websites include:

- Hargreaves Lansdown: **www.h-l.co.uk/pensions**;
- Origen Annuities: **www.origenfsannuities.co.uk**;
- William Burrows: **www.williamburrows.com**.

You can also buy an annuity direct from an insurance company or via an intermediary, such as an independent financial adviser (IFA) – see Chapter 4. You can also consult these professional advice websites: **www.unbiased.co.uk**; and the Institute of Financial Planning: **www.financialplanning.org.uk**.

National Savings and Investments (NS&I)

NS&I Savings Certificates, of which there are two types (fixed interest and index linked), are free of tax. They do not pay much interest but any tax-free investment is worth considering. For non-taxpayers who invest in NS&I products there is no need to complete an HM Revenue and Customs (HMRC) form to receive money in full, as this is automatic. (See the website: **www.nsandi.com**.)

The main NS&I investments are:

- *Easy-access savings accounts*: This is an easy way to build up your savings, with instant access to your money and the option to save regularly by standing order.
- *Income Bonds*: A safe and simple way of earning additional income every month. They pay fairly attractive, variable, tiered rates of interest, increasing with larger investments. Interest is taxable, but paid in full without deduction of tax at source. There is no set term for the investment.
- *Fixed Interest Savings Certificates*: Lump-sum investments that earn guaranteed rates of interest over set terms. There are two terms: two years and five years. For maximum benefit, you must hold the certificates for five years.
- *Index-Linked Savings Certificates*: Inflation-beating tax-free returns guarantee that your investment will grow in spending power each year, whatever happens to the cost of living. Certificates must be retained for either three or five years. Interest is tax-free.

- *Children's Bonds*: These allow you to invest for a child's future in their own name – and there's no tax to pay on the interest or bonuses. Interest rates are fixed for five years at a time, plus a guaranteed bonus. These are tax-free for parents and children and need not be declared to HMRC.
- *Pensioner Bonds*: These became available in 2015 and were quickly snapped up as supply is limited. Pensioners were allowed to save a maximum of £10,000 in each bond, offering a total of £20,000. Interest on the bonds will be taxed in line with all other savings income at the individual's personal tax rate. Watch out for any news on a further release of these attractive investments.
- *Premium Bonds*: One of Britain's most popular savings products with about £60 billion invested. The maximum amount that can be saved into Premium Bonds is £50,000 and the number of £1 million prizes handed out every month doubled from one to two in August 2014. Prizes range from £25 per month (odds of winning are about 26,000 to 1 to £1 million (odds are 30 billion to 1). Over 21 million people hold Premium Bonds and prizes are paid out tax-free every month.

Variable interest accounts

You can save in a wide range of savings accounts with banks, building societies, credit unions and National Savings and Investments (NS&I) – already mentioned. With around 54 million current accounts in the UK, banks and building societies frequently introduce new accounts with introductory bonuses, to attract new customers. Although keeping track may be time-consuming, all advertisements for savings products must now quote the annual equivalent rate (AER). AER provides a true comparison, taking into account the frequency of interest payments and whether or not interest is compounded.

Other than the interest-bearing current accounts described above, these are all 'deposit'-based savings accounts of one form or another, arranged with banks, building societies, the National Savings and Investments Bank, and some financial institutions that operate such accounts jointly with banks. The accounts include instant access accounts, high interest accounts and fixed term savings accounts. Some institutions pay interest annually; others – on some or all of their accounts – will pay it monthly. Although you may get a poor return on your money your savings will nearly always be safe.

Should the bank or building society get into serious financial difficulty, up to £75,000 (double that if in joint names) of your money will be 100 per cent protected under the Financial Services Compensation Scheme and the cover can increase for a short period to £1 million to cover certain life events (for instance moving home). More at **www.fscs.org.uk**. As an action point, should you seriously consider splitting your savings across different banks. You can check that you are covered by listing your banks and building societies at the FSCS website where there is a handy 'check your savings are protected' section.

From April 2016, the first £1,000 of interest earned is tax-free, reducing to £500 for higher rate taxpayers and £0 for additional rate taxpayers. If you largely rely on your savings income and believe you are or have been paying excess tax you can reclaim this from HMRC.

Choosing a savings account

There are two main areas of choice: the type of savings account and where to invest your money.

Instant access savings account

This attracts a relatively low rate of interest, but it is both easy to set up and very flexible, as you can add small or large savings when you like and can usually withdraw your money without any notice.

High interest savings account

Your money earns a higher rate of interest than it would in an ordinary savings account. You will need to deposit a minimum sum, which could be £500 to £1,000. Terms vary between providers. Usually interest is only paid yearly but you will be able to identify some providers that pay monthly interest if this is a need.

Fixed term savings account

You deposit your money for an agreed period of time, which can vary from a few months to over a year. In return for this commitment, you will normally be paid a superior rate of interest. The minimum investment is usually around £1,000 to £10,000. If you need to withdraw your money before the end of the agreed term, there are usually penalties and terms can be long, perhaps as much as five years.

Fixed interest securities

Gilt-edged securities

Gilts, or gilt-edged securities, are bonds issued by the UK government that offer the investor a fixed interest rate for a predetermined, set time, rather than one that goes up or down with inflation. You can either retain them until their maturity date, in which case the government will return the capital in full, or sell them on the London Stock Exchange at market value. Index linked gilts are government-issued bonds – glorified IOUs – that you can buy to obtain a guaranteed rate of return over inflation. If you are less worried about preserving your capital and require inflation-linked income then these can still be useful in a balanced portfolio.

Gilt interest is paid gross, which means that you must allow for any tax due before spending the money. A particular attraction of gilts is that no Capital Gains Tax is charged on any profit you may have made, but equally no relief is allowed for any loss.

Permanent interest-bearing shares (PIBS)

These are a form of investment offered by some building societies to financial institutions and private investors as a means of raising share capital. They have several features in common with gilts including a fixed rate of interest that is set at the date of issue. The interest is usually paid twice yearly; there is no stamp duty to pay or Capital Gains Tax on profits. Despite the fact that PIBS are issued by building societies, they are very different from normal building society investments. In the event of any losses PIBS are not covered by the Financial Services Compensation Scheme.

Equities and some other investments

These are all stocks and shares, purchased in different ways and involving varying degrees of risk. They can achieve capital appreciation as well as give you some regular income. Those traded on recognized stock exchanges can allow you to get your money out within a week. Millions of people in the United Kingdom invest in shares. Equity securities usually provide steady income as dividends but they fluctuate with the ups and downs in the economic cycle. Investing has never been easier with the growing number of internet-based trading facilities. Equities include ordinary shares, unit trusts, open-ended investment companies (OEICs), investment trusts and real estate investment trusts (REITs).

Unit trusts and OEICs

Unit trusts and OEICs, a modern equivalent of unit trusts, are forms of shared investments, or funds, which allow you to pool your money with thousands of other people and invest in world stock markets. The advantages are that they are simple to understand, you get professional management and there are no day-to-day decisions to make. Additionally, every fund is required by law to have a trustee (called a 'depository' in the case of OEICs) to protect investors' interests.

Unit trusts have proved incredibly popular because your money is invested in a broad spread of shares and your risk is reduced, but they are rapidly being replaced by the OEIC (pronounced 'oik'). The minimum investment in some of the more popular funds can be as little as £25 per month or a £500 lump sum. Investors' contributions to the fund are divided into units (shares in OEICs) in proportion to the amount they have invested. Unit trusts and OEICs are both open-ended investments. As with ordinary shares, you can sell all or some of your investment by telling the fund manager that you wish to do so. The value of the shares you own in an OEIC, or units in a unit trust, always reflects the value of the fund's assets. The key differences between the two are:

- *Pricing*: When investing in unit trusts, you buy units at the offer price and sell at the lower bid price. The difference in the two prices is known as the spread. To make a return, the bid price must rise above the offer before you sell the units. An OEIC fund contrastingly has a single price, directly linked to the value of the fund's underlying investments. All shares are bought and sold at this single price. An OEIC is sometimes described as a 'what you see is what you get' product.
- *Flexibility*: An OEIC fund offers different types of share or sub-fund to suit different types of investor. The expertise of different fund management teams can be combined to benefit both large and small investors. There is less paperwork as each OEIC will produce one report and accounts for all sub-funds.
- *Complexity*: Unit trusts are, legally, much more complex, which is one of the reasons for their rapid conversion to OEICs. Unit trusts allow an investor to participate in the assets of the trust without actually owning any. Investors in an OEIC buy shares in that investment company.

- *Management*: With unit trusts, the fund's assets are protected by an independent trustee and managed by a fund manager. OEICs are protected by an independent depository and managed by an authorized corporate director.
- *Charges*: Unit trusts and OEICs usually have an upfront buying charge, typically 3–5 per cent, and an annual management fee of between 0.5 and 1.5 per cent. It is possible to reduce these charges by investing through a discount broker or fund supermarket, but this means acting without financial advice. Charges on OEICs are relatively transparent, shown as a separate item on your transaction statement.

Investment trusts

One of the biggest benefits that investment trusts offer is to income investors. While open-ended funds must pay out all the income they receive, investment trusts can hold some back in reserve. This allows them to offer a smoother and more certain return. There are four major advantages that an investment trust has over a unit trust:

1. *Cost*. The initial charges on unit trusts typically range from 4 to 6 per cent but there is also the annual fee costing in the region of 1.5 to 2 per cent. An investment trust also levies annual fees, but on average they are lower because most investment trusts don't pay commission to financial advisers.
2. *Gearing*. Like other companies, investment trusts are fairly free to borrow for investment purposes. Unit trusts, however, are usually restricted by regulation. But when markets are rising and the trust is run well, gearing will deliver superior returns.
3. *Size*. Investment trusts tend to be smaller than unit trusts on average, and so are less unwieldy and more focused on their investment objectives. To grow beyond their initial remit, they need permission from shareholders. Many also have a fixed life expectancy. Conversely, unit trusts are called 'open ended' because they can expand and contract to meet demand – 'big' is not always beautiful.
4. *Discounts*. Because their shares are listed and traded freely (unlike a unit trust), investment trusts can end up with a market capitalization that is greater than (at a 'premium'), or lower than (at a 'discount') its assets under management (the 'net asset value', or NAV). If the discount narrows after you buy, you'll make a small gain on top of any increase in the trust's NAV.

Ordinary shares listed on the London Stock Exchange

Public companies issue shares as a way of raising money. When you buy shares and become a shareholder in a company, you own a small part of the business and are entitled to participate in its profits through a dividend, which is normally paid every six months. It is possible that in a bad year no dividends at all will be paid. However, in good years, dividends can increase very substantially. The money you invest is unsecured. This means that, quite apart from any dividends, your capital could be reduced in value – or if the company goes bankrupt you could lose the lot. The value of a company's shares is decided by the stock market. The price of a share can fluctuate daily, and this will affect both how much you have to pay if you want to buy and how much you will make (or lose) if you want to sell.

See the London Stock Exchange website, **www.londonstockexchange.com**, to find a list of brokers in your area that would be willing to deal for you. The securities department of your bank or one of the authorized share shops will place the order for you, or you can do it online. Whichever method you use, you will be charged both commission and stamp duty (the latter is currently 0.5 per cent). Unless you use a nominee account (see below), you will be issued with a share certificate that you or your financial adviser must keep, as you will have to produce it when you wish to sell all or part of your holding. It is likely, when approaching a stockbroker or other share-dealing service, that you will be asked to deposit money for your investment up front or advised that you should use a nominee account to speed up and streamline the share-dealing process.

Prior to April 2016 all UK shares paid dividends net of 10 per cent corporation tax (the 1/9 tax credit as it is sometimes called) and basic rate and non-taxpayers have no further liability to Income Tax. Higher rate 40 per cent taxpayers must pay further Income Tax that works out at 25 per cent of the net dividend received and for additional rate taxpayers (earning over £150,000) the amount of tax works out at 30.5 per cent of the dividend received. After April 2016 the situation changes significantly as follows:

- There is a new annual dividend allowance of £5,000 that is tax-free.
- The 1/9 tax credit will disappear.

The new rates of tax on dividend will then be 7.5 per cent if the dividend falls in the basic rate tax band, 32.5 per cent if it falls in the higher rate tax band (£42,785 to £150,000) and 38.1 per cent if it falls in the additional rate tax band (£150,000 plus).

An important wealth warning on shares – the financial pages of the Sunday newspapers carry regular stories about investors who have been scammed into buying worthless shares traded on some obscure stock exchange. Don't be caught out by the scammers – read Chapter 4.

Individual Savings Account (ISA)

ISAs prove popular because of the tax breaks as you do not pay any tax on the interest or the profits you make and there is no Capital Gains Tax. Shop around for the best rates and take full advantage of your annual allowance. You can currently (2016/17) put up to £15,240 into an ISA and from 6 April 2017 this increases to £20,000.

Lifetime Individual Savings Account (LISA)

A new Lifetime ISA will be available from April 2017 for adults aged under 40. There will be an annual contribution limit of £4,000 and savers will receive a 25 per cent government bonus. As this is a new product and, potentially, quite important to those under 40 and planning their retirement now the following paragraph is repeated from an earlier section in this chapter.

The LISA seems attractive, and at the moment (summer 2016) remains under consultation and could be subject to change. The intention seems to be to encourage individuals to save towards one of two important life events. The first is for first-time buyers to use it to pay towards a residential property, which can be done at any time providing the LISA has been held for 12 months. The second is to use it in retirement once aged 60. With both there is no tax to pay when you take the money out. It could be an early step in a new approach to pension funding where taxed money goes in and is tax-free on the way out (with the 25 per cent government bonus being a welcome addition). This switches the traditional pensions world on its head, whereby we are used to receiving tax relief on contributions being paid into pensions and then being taxed on the income then received in retirement.

Enterprise Investment Scheme and Seed Enterprise Investment Scheme

Unquoted companies (ie those whose shares are not traded on a recognized stock exchange) can face problems when trying to raise finance. The Enterprise Investment Scheme and Seed Enterprise Investment Scheme offer tax relief at 30 per cent and 50 per cent and for amounts up to £1,000,000 and £100,000 respectively if the shares are held for three years. The risk level of such investments is high and specialist advice and recommendations should be secured before venturing down this path, albeit the tax breaks prove enticing to some with the appropriate risk attitude and, perhaps, with specialist knowledge of the business concerned (perhaps through family or other connections). Another variant is **Venture Capital Trusts** where tax relief can be secured at 30 per cent on new shares up to £200,000 in any tax year providing the shares are held for five years. Further tax breaks have also become available under Entrepreneurs Relief which enables a low 10 per cent Capital Gains Tax rate on selling shares in, for instance, a family company. These were previously only available to employees and officers of a company who held more than 5 per cent of shares for more than three years before selling them for a gain. The relief has now been extended to include external investors.

Other tax incentives for interest and dividends

There will be winners and losers as a result of the change to dividend tax outlined above. The higher rate taxpayer with dividends of £9,000 a year (net amount) will pay around £950 less tax in 2016/17 compared to 2015/16 and thus dividend income may start to be more actively considered as part of financing your retirement. The counter-balance is that shares carry more risk than interest as noted elsewhere in this chapter – both in terms of income variability and credit risk (and without the fallback of FSCS protection if a bank/building society should fail).

The separate £1,000 allowance for basic rate taxpayers (£500 for higher rate taxpayers) upon which no tax would be payable from April 2016 is welcome 'tax-free income' for many. It also may take away the headache of scrambling around to count up small levels of interest to ensure they are disclosed in your self-assessment.

Investing for your grandchild

Children's savings account

All you need to set this up is the child's birth certificate. The interest on money deposited by grandparents isn't subject to tax, and interest rates are currently as high as 4 to 6 per cent if you shop around.

Junior ISA (JISA)

You can't open a Junior ISA for your grandchild – that's one for the parents – but you can make contributions up to the JISA's annual limit. You can currently save up to £4,080 a year into a JISA. Junior ISAs are available to all children born on or after 3 January 2011, or born before September 2002, or are under 18 and do not have a child trust fund. The fund is locked until the child is 18 when they get control of the money.

Help-to-Buy ISA

These new accounts are available from banks and building societies (for four years from the autumn of 2015) and can be opened by individuals who are at least 16 years old. Help-to-Buy ISAs are available to prospective first time buyers purchasing properties in the United Kingdom and are only paid when purchasing the first home (on purchases up to £250,000 outside London and £450,000 in London). Deposits can then be made of up to £1,000 when the account is opened followed by deposits up to £200 each month. The government will then boost the young person's savings by 25 per cent, ie £50 for every £200 saved. The maximum bonus is £3,000 on £12,000 of savings. Once the new LISAs come through in April 2017 you can transfer from the Help-to-Buy ISA to the LISA providing you meet the LISA conditions (aged 18 to 40).

Child Trust Funds (CTF)

All babies born between September 2002 and 2 January 2011 got £500 or more free from the Government to save in a CTF. Children born after December 2010 are not eligible for a child trust fund. However, accounts set up for eligible children will continue to benefit from tax-free investment growth and you can still add £4,080 a year tax-free. Withdrawals will not be possible until the child reaches 18. These are now a defunct product and with less competition the interest rates tend not to be as good as a JISA. You are allowed to transfer these accounts to a new JISA; **www.moneysavingexpert.com** has a good article entitled 'Should you switch to a Junior ISA?', which may help your children/grandchildren.

Children's Bonds

Unlike the lottery of Premium Bonds – which require a minimum investment of £100 – Children's Bonds offered by National Savings and Investments

(NS&I) offer a guaranteed rate of return, with only a £25 minimum investment; the best five-year deal currently pays 2.5 per cent.

Pension

For really long-term saving, pay into a pension. Your grandchild takes control at 18, but can only access the money aged 55. Tax relief currently applies so the government will top up a payment of £2,880 to the limit of £3,600.

Useful reading

How the Stock Market Works, by Michael Becket of the *Daily Telegraph*, published by Kogan Page; see website: **www.koganpage.com**.

Long-term lock-ups

Certain types of investment, mostly offered by insurance companies, provide fairly high guaranteed growth in exchange for your undertaking to leave a lump sum with them or to pay regular premiums for a fixed period, usually five years or longer. The list includes life assurance policies, investment bonds and some types of National Savings Certificates.

Life assurance policies

Definition

Life assurance can provide you with one of two main benefits: it can either provide your successors with money when you die or it can be used as a savings plan to provide you with a lump sum (or income) on a fixed date. There are three basic types of life assurance: whole-life policies, term policies and endowment policies.

1. *Whole-life policies* are designed to pay out on your death. You pay a premium every year and, when you die, your beneficiaries receive the money. The insurance holds good only if you continue the payments. If one year you did not pay and were to die, the policy could be void and your successors would receive nothing.
2. *Term policies* involve a definite commitment. As opposed to paying premiums every year, you elect to make regular payments for an agreed

period, for example until such time as your children have completed their education, say eight years. If you die during this period, your family will be paid the agreed sum in full. If you die after the end of the term (when you have stopped making payments), your family will normally receive nothing.

3 *Endowment policies* are essentially savings plans. You sign a contract to pay regular premiums over a number of years and in exchange receive a lump sum on a specific date; this could be from 10 to 25 years. Once you have committed yourself, you have to go on paying every year (as with term assurance).

An important feature of endowment policies is that they are linked to death cover. If you die before the policy matures, the remaining payments are excused and your successors will be paid a lump sum on your death. The amount of money you stand to receive, however, can vary hugely, depending on the charges and how generous a bonus the insurance company feels it can afford on the policy's maturity. Over the last decade payouts have been considerably lower than their earlier projections might have suggested.

Both whole-life policies and endowment policies offer two basic options: with profits or without profits:

- *Without profits*: Sometimes known as 'guaranteed sum assured'. The insurance company guarantees you a specific fixed sum, you know the amount in advance and this is the sum you – or your successors – will be paid.
- *With profits*: You are paid a guaranteed fixed sum plus an addition, based on the profits that the insurance company has made by investing your annual or monthly payments. The basic premiums are higher and the profits element is not known in advance.
- *Unit linked*: A refinement of the 'with profits' policy, in that the investment element of the policy is linked in with a unit trust.

Premiums can normally be paid monthly or annually, as you prefer. The size of premium varies enormously, depending on the type of policy you choose, the amount of cover you want and any health underwriting that may be required – you may be required to have a medical check if large sums are involved. More usually, you fill in and sign a declaration of health. If you make a claim on your policy and it is subsequently discovered that you gave misleading information, your policy could be declared void and the insurance company could refuse to pay.

Under current legislation, the proceeds of a qualifying policy – whether taken as a lump sum or in regular income payments – are free of all tax. If, as applies to many people, you have a life insurance policy written into a trust, there is a possibility that it could be hit by Inheritance Tax rules affecting trusts if the sum it is expected to pay out is above the £325,000 IHT threshold. Check matters with an IFA or solicitor.

Policies are usually available through banks, insurance companies, independent financial advisers (IFA) and building societies. Be careful with the small print: terms and conditions that sound very similar may obscure important differences that could affect your benefit. To be sure of choosing the policy best suited to your requirements, consult an IFA. For more information about IFAs and help when things go wrong see Chapter 4.

Alternatives to surrendering a policy

If you wish to terminate an endowment policy before the date of the agreement, and avoid the punitive costs, you could sell the policy for a sum that is higher than its surrender value. See the Association of Policy Market Makers website: **www.apmm.org**. For those looking for investment possibilities, second-hand policies could be worth investigating. Known as traded endowment policies (TEPs), they offer the combination of a low-risk investment with a good potential return. A full list of appropriate financial institutions and authorized dealers that buy and sell mid-term policies is obtainable from the Association of Policy Market Makers. It can also arrange for suitable policies to be valued by member firms, free of charge.

Bonds

The London Stock Exchange operates a retail bond platform designed to make trading corporate bonds as easy as trading listed shares. Since March 2011 nearly £1.7 billion has been raised by companies in the market. Bonds generally offer less opportunity for capital growth; they tend to be lower risk as they are less exposed to stock market volatility; but they have the advantage of producing a regular guaranteed income. The three main types of bonds are:

- *Gilts*: These are government bonds, and were explained earlier in this chapter. They are the least risky. They are secured by the government, which guarantees both the interest payable and the return of your capital in full if you hold the stocks until their maturity.

- *Corporate bonds*: These are fairly similar to gilts except that you are lending to a large company, rather than owning a piece of it, as you do with an equity. The company has to repay the loan at some point, known as the bond's redemption date. It will pay out the 'face value' of the bond and the company also has to pay interest on the loan, known as the 'coupon'. After they are issued, bonds trade in the secondary market, just like shares. Bond prices are driven by two main factors: interest rates and credit risk. Most bonds have a fixed income; the longer the time to maturity, the more sensitive the bond is to changes in interest rates.

One reason to hold bonds is for income. Should corporate profits stall, companies might have to cut dividends. But unlike dividends, bond coupons can't be suspended, so your income is more predictable. The main risks to bonds are rising interest rates and credit risk.

Investment bonds

Not to be confused with debt-based investments, they are tax wrappers, rather than specific investment instruments. They are a method of investing a lump sum with an insurance company over the long term.

Available in both onshore and offshore variants, both offer life assurance cover as part of the deal, although this is usually only 101 per cent of the fund value at time of death.

The underlying investment of any type of investment bond will be retail unit trusts and OEICs – similar to those available under ISA or SIPP wrappers. The manager/adviser will be able to tailor the investment strategy to meet your risk/reward requirements. They are generally used to produce long-term capital growth and can generate regular (tax deferred) income.

The tax position of an investment bond depends on whether it is onshore or offshore. Whilst both types can offer the investor withdrawals of up to 5 per cent of the initial investment each year without creating a liability to tax, the amount drawn does remain restricted to the value of the original investment and can therefore be deemed to reduce in line with inflation each year.

Onshore investment bonds are subject to a special rate of corporation tax (roughly 18.4 per cent) on any growth or income within the bond so basic rate taxpayers are deemed to have no further liability on surrender or encashment (known as a chargeable event).

Any further tax liability for higher and top rate taxpayers is calculated using complicated 'top slicing' rules – where, in short, the overall growth is annualized and then assessed alongside the recipient's other income for the tax year in question. If this pushes the recipient into the higher rate threshold or top rate of tax threshold, further tax will be due.

Offshore investment bonds, on the other hand, are only subject to a nominal withholding tax, so all investors will be subject to tax at their marginal rate on any growth achieved on repatriation of the funds to the United Kingdom – including the value of the permitted 5 per cent withdrawals drawn, which are added back in.

Any gain on an investment bond is subject to Income Tax, therefore your personal allowance can be used to reduce any tax payable but your capital gains allowance cannot be used to offset tax.

There has been much interest in offshore bonds from high earners looking for an alternative to pensions for their retirement savings. These can provide significant tax savings because of the 5 per cent withdrawals, with no immediate tax to pay.

Ongoing charges for offshore bonds are high: typically an extra 0.4 per cent per annum in addition to usual investment costs. Professional adviser charges on top means that bonds are generally best for investments greater than £100,000.

It should also be noted that any ongoing professional adviser charges deducted from the bond will either create a chargeable event each year, or reduce your 5 per cent withdrawals. So a bond with a 1 per cent annual fee will only provide net 4 per cent withdrawals.

Structured products

A structured product is a fixed term investment where the payout depends on the performance of something else, typically a stock market index (eg FTSE 100 or S&P 500). They are complex and can carry hidden risk because they can appear on the surface to be an alternative to cash.

There are two main types of structured product – structured deposit and structured investments.

1. *Structured deposits* are savings accounts but they are certainly not cash-based. The rate of interest (or rate of annual return) provided depends on how the underlying stock market index performs. So if the stock market index rises you receive a predetermined rate of interest; if it falls you will get nothing.
2. *Structured investments* offer either an annual rate of return, or a return over a fixed term. They are typically comprised of two underlying investments, one designed to protect your capital and another to provide

the bonus/'kicker'. The return you get will be stated at outset and depend on how the underlying stock market index performs. If it performs badly, or the counterparty (the company providing the stated return) fails, you may lose some or all of your original investment.

Be careful to peel back the label on these investments. The use of the word 'guaranteed' in the literature does not mean what you may first think! It means you are 'guaranteed' to get the returns stated *only* if the stock market index performs as required in the product's terms and conditions – noting that fees and charges may ultimately mean you get back less than you put in. Professional advice would be recommended for anyone seeking to make this type of investment.

Investor protection

As we say in Chapter 4, most financial transactions involving banks, investments, pensions and insurance take place without any problems but sometimes things go wrong. This is where the UK's regulatory regime steps in. As it is vitally important to your protection, part of that chapter is repeated here.

The **Financial Conduct Authority (FCA)** is accountable to the Treasury and aims to make sure the UK financial markets work well so that consumers get a fair deal. It registers individuals and companies that are suitable to work in the industry and checks that they are doing their job properly and fines them if they do a bad job. The FCA has a range of helpful guides and factsheets to help consumers understand the UK financial markets and the role of the FCA. More at **www.the-fca.org.uk**.

The Financial Ombudsman Service (FOS) is a free service set up by law with the power to sort out problems between consumers and registered financial businesses. It is an impartial service and will investigate your complaint if you have been unable to resolve matters with the registered individual or company (ie registered with the Financial Conduct Authority as above). If the ombudsman considers the complaint justified it can award compensation. More at **www.financial-ombudsman.org.uk**.

The **Financial Services Compensation Scheme (FSCS)** is the body that can pay you compensation if your financial services provider goes bust. The FSCS is independent and free to access. The financial services industry funds the FSCS and the compensation it pays. There are limits on how much compensation it pays and these are different for different types of financial products. To be eligible for compensation the person or company must have been registered by the FCA. More at **www.fscs.org.uk**.

In addition, and for your protection when dealing with company and certain other pensions, the protection may come from a different route. Although this may appear complicated, the relevant ombudsman is very good at pointing you in the right direction if you end up in the wrong place. For further help on pensions:

Information and assistance from the Pensions Advisory Service (more at **www.pensionsadvisoryservice.org.uk**).

Protection comes from the Pensions Ombudsman (more at **www.pensions-ombudsman.org.uk**) and the Pension Protection Fund (more at **www.pensionprotectionfund.org.uk**).

Finally, possibly the biggest change and issue for many are the decisions to be taken about defined pension schemes and the new regime of pensions liberation. Use the free and impartial government service for guidance on what you can do with your pension pot, how to shop around and what to look out for on taxes and fees, and how to avoid pension scams. The service is at **www.pensionwise.gov.uk** and it can help you make sure your money lasts as long as you do.

Chapter Three
Tax

'I like to pay taxes. With them I buy civilization.'
OLIVER WENDELL HOLMES JR

Tax in the UK is unnecessarily complicated and we can't promise to cut through it all in one chapter. We will, however, highlight some key aspects for retirement planning. Most importantly, we again plead that the government finally and properly delivers on the majority of UK taxpayers' one wish – to massively reduce red tape on taxation. The tax rulebook is now – wait for it – an astonishing and unfathomable four-foot-high stack of pages. It really should be burnt and the process started afresh again. In 2009, an article in the *Daily Telegraph* (Jonathan Russell, 6 September 2009) drew our attention to an announcement by LexisNexis, publishers of *Tolley's Tax Guide*, that:

> The UK now has the longest tax code in the world... the handbook of tax legislation now runs to 11,520 pages, a 10 per cent increase on last year and more than double the number of pages from 12 years ago.

Fast forward six years and for a sense of balance we turn to *The Guardian* newspaper's Marina Hyde (13 February 2015), who was also scratching her head over the well-posed question: 'Why does the UK have the longest tax code in the world?' Hyde observed:

> The Hong Kong tax code, widely held by tax lawyers to be the most admirably efficient in the world, is 276 pages long. The British tax code, rapidly beginning to look like the most disingenuous in the world, is currently in excess of 17,000 pages. It has more than trebled in size since 1977.

Taxes are necessary. Few would disagree with the view of Oliver Wendell Holmes Jr (one of the most widely cited United States Supreme Court Justices and quoted at the beginning of this chapter) and seek to disown the schooling, roads, health service, security and rescue services that our taxes pay for (in one way or another). But with taxes can't we do more to 'keep it simple stupid' (or KISS – to use another quote from the United Sates, this time from the 1960s US Navy)?

Maybe we can then strive to earn more in retirement and not engage expensive lawyers and accountants to weave around the 17,000 pages to either (a) just make sure we are doing things correctly or (b) spot gaps, holes and t's that are not crossed if that happens to be your thing. Time will tell but the trend line on the page count in the big tax book does not look promising. So our target remains: no more than 1,000 pages in the big tax book by the time the 2018/19 *Good Retirement Guide* is published.

In our current low-interest rate environment financing your retirement from savings has been difficult ground to find crumbs of comfort. However, there has been some good news for savers and imminent or new pensioners in recent Budgets. Tax restrictions on interest and dividends have been improved for most people; the tax-free limit on ISAs increases from £15,240 to £20,000 per annum from 6 April 2017 and there is the new Lifetime ISA that will come in in April 2017 for adults aged under 40. These are anticipated (as at summer 2016) to have an annual contribution limit of £4,000 and savers will receive a 25 per cent government bonus (more in Chapter 2). Then there is the introduction of significant new access arrangements on defined contribution pension schemes which.

With these changes and the longest tax book in the world, tax knowledge and planning remains essential and saves you money. This is not 'dodgy' – it is simply knowing the rules and applying them. The problem is not in this planning activity, it is the long and complicated rule book. It is not the effect; it is the cause that is the real problem.

On the other hand, there is tax evasion, which you can always remember because E is for evasion and E-legal. This shorthand might help reinforce that it is illegal. That is the work of the tradesperson who takes cash and does not declare it to the taxman. And it is the individual who forgets that the reason they had a few flights to some offshore tax jurisdiction was to hide money offshore to try and evade tax on the interest they were earning. HMRC's own definition of tax evasion is 'when people or businesses deliberately do not pay the taxes that they owe' (source: **www.gov.uk**).

HMRC's own definition of tax avoidance:

> Bending the rules of the tax system to gain a tax advantage that Parliament never intended. It often involves contrived, artificial transactions that serve little or no purpose other than to produce tax advantage. It involves operating within the letter – but not the spirit – of the law.

It is also the crook in a suit who resides in the UK and takes an income and routes it round the world, writes it off through loans and puts it in and out of trusts and ends up spending the same money in the UK and, hey presto, there is a rich lifestyle and no tax paid. But then again in this latter 'category' there is probably a barrister's opinion that is produced showing that 'technically' the scheme has navigated the 17,000 pages, and the route to tax-free money is not E-legal. The individual concerned would probably dismiss Oliver Wendell Holmes Jr's quote at the head of this chapter while still enjoying the free benefits their society provides. HMRC are targeting just this sort of person with increased resources and commitment (and powers) – more later.

Importantly, this chapter is only a guide and it is neither legal nor taxation advice and is no substitute for taking advice from a professional adviser (see Chapter 4). Any potential tax advantages may be subject to change and will depend upon your individual circumstances, and individual professional advice should be obtained. The information outlined in this chapter may, however, assist you in understanding some of the issues you may face and the terminology used, and assist you in planning for and achieving a more financially rewarding retirement.

Key points in this chapter

- If you are a higher rate taxpayer because of a pension and other employed or business income, take professional advice. Consider using your pension allowance to contribute to a defined benefit pension, receive extra Income Tax relief and then manage your defined benefit pension fund withdrawals to keep within a lower tax rate band.
- If you do not use your £15,240 ISA allowance by 5 April 2017 the tax shelter for that amount will be lost forever. If you have a spouse or civil partner the amount doubles if they also have not used their allowance. Then open up and start funding your 2017/18 ISA or new LISA, if eligible, and you can start saving more tax from 6 April 2017.
- Use up gains of £11,100 by 5 April 2017 without paying tax if you hold shares outside a tax wrapper (like an ISA or SIPP) which have gained by less than £11,100. Consider selling them and using the proceeds to fund an ISA, LISA, if eligible, or SIPP.
- Reduce your Inheritance Tax liability by gifting using the reliefs set out in this chapter. Larger gifts are normally tax-free if the giver survives a further seven years. New Inheritance Tax rules could result in

unmarried couples with children and a house worth more than £650,000 walking down the aisle after April 2017.

- Remember the new reliefs introduced in 2016 allow you £5,000 of dividend Income Tax-free and £1,000 of interest tax-free (for basic rate taxpayers and for higher rate taxpayers the amount reduces to £500). If married or in a civil partnership you should consider how best to structure who holds investments and bank deposits.
- If you are both basic rate taxpayers you may be able to transfer part of your Personal Allowance to make you jointly more 'tax efficient' if you are a married couple or in a civil partnership.
- Review and update your will and power of attorney.

But it's all so complicated – and what about Betty down the road?

The Good Retirement Guide 2017 will try and help but remember you are not alone; here's our pick of free further help (which could be all that Betty down the road needs after she lost her husband and has no relatives close by, so don't keep these tips to yourself):

- *Tax Help for Older People* (TOP) is a charity that provides independent, free tax-advice for vulnerable and unrepresented people on low incomes – **www.taxvol.org.uk**.
- *Tax Aid* is a charity that advises only those people on low incomes whose problems cannot be resolved by HMRC – **www.taxaid.org.uk**.
- *Citizens Advice* has a very useful website to help you understand tax and how it is collected and what to do if you have a tax problem. They can also provide face-to-face and telephone support – **www.citizensadvice.org.uk**.

Self-assessment

Self-assessment is the system HM Revenue & Customs (HMRC) uses to collect Income Tax. Income Tax is usually deducted automatically from wages, pensions (but not the State Pension) and savings but people with other income must report it in a tax return. The tax you have to pay depends on allowances you have, the Income Tax band you're in and also there are different rates for Capital Gains Tax (CGT) and Inheritance Tax. Self-assessment notices to complete the form are sent out in April. The details you need to enter on the form you receive in April 2017 are those relating to the 2016/17 tax year, ie 6 April 2016 to 5 April 2017. Not everyone has to complete a self-assessment form but one is required for a number of specified circumstances which include: the self-employed; being a company director; having income from savings and investments of £10,000 or more; having employment income on PAYE above £100,000; and having CGT to pay. If you don't receive a self-assessment request but owe tax to HMRC you are required to notify HMRC. Do this initially by writing to HMRC at HM Revenue & Customs Self-Assessment, PO Box 4000, Cardiff CF14 8HR. All taxpayers have an obligation to keep records of all their different sources of income and capital gains. These include:

- details of earnings plus any bonus, expenses and benefits in kind received;
- bank and building society interest;
- dividend vouchers and/or other documentation showing gains from investments;
- pension payments, eg both state and occupational or private pensions;
- income and costs of any trading or other business activity;
- rental income from letting a property and associated costs;
- taxable social security benefits (for instance Jobseeker's Allowance and Carers' Allowance);
- gains or losses made on selling investments or a second home;
- payments against which tax relief can be claimed (eg charitable donations or contributions to a personal pension).

If you don't voluntarily disclose the fact that you may owe tax and HMRC finds out about untaxed income and launches an inquiry (or investigation) into your tax affairs you could face stiff penalties as well as paying any tax due and interest (more on this later).

Income Tax

This is calculated on all (or nearly all) of your income, after deduction of your tax allowances. The reason for saying 'nearly all' is that some income you may receive is tax-free; types of income on which you do not have to pay tax are listed a little further on in this chapter.

The tax year runs from 6 April to the following 5 April, so the amount of tax you pay in any one year is calculated on the income you receive (or are deemed to have received) between these two dates. Points to note – with effect from 6 April 2017 and the new tax year 2017/18:

- The point at which most people start paying Income Tax will be the Personal Allowance of £11,500 (this will increase from £11,000 on 6 April 2017). The target of the current government is to increase this to £12,500 by the end of the current parliament. Once the Personal Allowance has reached £12,500, legislation will apply so that it increases automatically in line with the equivalent of 30 hours a week at the national minimum wage for employees aged over 21.
- The 20 per cent basic rate of tax is payable on further income beyond the Personal Allowance up to £33,500 (this will increase from £32,000 on 6 April 2017).
- The combined effect of the above measures is that the 40 per cent Income Tax threshold rises from £43,000 in 2016/17 to £45,000 in 2017/18. The target of the current government is to increase this to £50,000 by the end of the current parliament.
- The top rate of 45 per cent is levied on incomes in excess of £150,000.

The current government has pledged a lock on these 20 per cent, 40 per cent and 45 per cent rates of Income Tax and will not raise them in the current parliament. This lock will also apply to the standard (20 per cent) and reduced (5 per cent) rates of VAT and employer (13.8 per cent) and employee (12 per cent) class 1 national insurance rates. This is good news but there remains scope to increase other taxes, for instance, as happened in the summer 2015 with Budget increases in insurance premium tax from 6 per cent to 9.5 per cent. We could expect an increase to the current self-employed National Insurance rate of 9 per cent (given it was not 'locked' and the disparity with employed National Insurance levels).

Tax allowances

Personal allowance

Your Personal Allowance stated above is the amount of money you are allowed to retain before Income Tax becomes applicable. For big earners and since 2010 the Personal Allowance is reduced by £1 for every £2 of income over £100,000. The Personal Allowance will therefore disappear if your income in 2016/17 is above £123,000.

Tax tip

For 2016/17 'big earners' you may still be able to preserve part or all of your Personal Allowance if your income is between £100,000 and £123,000 by making pension contributions, but due to other potential restrictions professional advice should be sought. See also Chapter 2 for further information and possible opportunities around pensions and financing your retirement.

Other tax allowances to which you may be entitled include:

- Married Couple's Allowance of £8,355 (2016/17) is available to people born before 6 April 1935. Tax relief for this allowance is restricted to 10 per cent. This is reduced by £1 for every £2 over £27,700.
- A widowed partner, where the couple at the time of death were entitled to Married Couple's Allowance, can claim any unused portion of the allowance in the year he or she became widowed.
- Registered blind people can claim an allowance (the Blind Person's Allowance) of £2,290 per year (2016/17). If both husband and wife are registered as blind, they can each claim the allowance.

Tax tip

Transferable tax allowances between married couples and civil partnership came into effect on 6 April 2015 and this could reduce your tax in 2016/17. For 2016/17 a spouse or civil partner who is not liable to Income Tax above the basic rate can transfer £1,100 of their Personal Allowance to their spouse/civil partner, provided that the recipient of the transfer is not liable to Income Tax above the basic rate.

Same-sex partners

Same-sex couples in a civil partnership are treated the same as married couples for tax purposes.

Tax relief

Separate from any Personal Allowances, you can obtain tax relief on the following:

- A covenant for the benefit of a charity, or a donation under the Gift Aid scheme.
- Contributions to occupational pensions, self-employed pension plans and other personal pensions (more later).
- £1,000 of interest (£500 for a higher rate taxpayer) and £5,000 of dividends (more later).
- Rental income of up to £7,500 per year from letting out a room in your home.
- Mortgage interest relief in respect of loans secured on an older person's home to purchase a life annuity. However, to qualify, the loan must have been taken out (or at least processed and confirmed in writing) by 9 March 1999. Borrowers in this situation can continue to benefit from the relief for the duration of their loan. As before, the relief remains at 10 per cent on the first £30,000 of the loan.
- Some maintenance payments on arrangements set up prior to 5 April 2000. Individuals in receipt of maintenance payments are not affected and will continue to receive their money free of Income Tax. Those who had to pay tax under the pre-March 1988 rules now also receive their payments free of tax. Most individuals paying maintenance no longer get any relief at all. An exception has been made in cases where one (or both) of the divorced or separated spouses was aged 65 or over at 5 April 2000, where those paying maintenance are still able to claim tax relief – but only at 10 per cent.

Tax-free income

Not all income is taxable and the following list indicates some of the more common sources of income that are free of tax:

- Attendance Allowance;
- Child Benefit (NB: Child Benefit cuts introduced in 2013 result in a partial tax clawback if one parent earns more than £50,000 and child

benefit was received and results in all child benefit being repayable via a tax assessment for those on £60,000 or more);

- Child Tax Credit;
- Disability Living Allowance and Personal Independence Payment;
- Housing Benefit;
- Industrial Injuries Disablement Pension;
- Income-related Employment and Support Allowance;
- Income Support (in some circumstances, such as when the recipient is also getting Jobseeker's Allowance, Income Support will be taxable);
- pensions paid to war widows (plus any additions for children);
- certain disablement pensions from the armed forces, police, fire brigade and merchant navy;
- the Winter Fuel Payment (paid to pensioners);
- Working Tax Credit;
- National Savings Premium Bond prizes;
- winnings on the National Lottery and other forms of betting;
- income received from certain insurance policies (mortgage payment protection, permanent health insurance, creditor insurance for loans and utility bills, various approved long-term care policies) if the recipient is sick, disabled or unemployed at the time the benefits become payable;
- income and dividends received from savings in an Individual Savings Account (ISA);
- dividend income from investments in venture capital trusts (VCTs);
- virtually all gifts (in certain circumstances you could have to pay tax if the gift is above £3,000 or if, as may occasionally be the case, the money from the donor has not been previously taxed);
- a redundancy payment up to the value of £30,000;
- a lump sum commuted from a pension;
- a matured endowment policy.

If in doubt take professional advice on any 'unusual' income that you have received or further information is available at the Citizens Advice website: **www.citizensadvice.org.uk** – taxable and non-taxable income.

Income tax on savings and investments

Savings

From April 2016 most people can earn some interest from their savings without paying tax as there is a new tax-free savings interest £1,000 allowance for basic rate taxpayers (£500 for higher rate taxpayers). There is no allowance for additional (45 per cent) rate taxpayers. This will provide a welcome additional £200 tax break for many. In addition, time could be saved for those who remember when they had to scramble around to count up small levels of interest to ensure they were disclosed in their self-assessment. For 2016/17 there is a £5,000 tax-free (0 per cent) savings income band on top of the Personal Allowance (see Chapter 2 and the section 'Other tax incentives for interest and dividends').

Tax tip

These changes will increase the number of savers who are not required to pay tax on savings income. It may also represent a good tax-planning opportunity for a husband and wife (or partners in a civil partnership) on different tax rates.

Investments

From April 2016 there was a significant change to the way dividends are taxed in your self-assessment. The £5,000 dividend allowance allows dividends up to this value to be taken 'tax-free'. Higher dividend taxes would then be levied on amounts above £5,000. More information on this is set out in Chapter 2 in the section 'Other tax incentives for interest and dividends'.

Tax tip

Again this may also represent another good tax-planning opportunity for a husband and wife (or partners in a civil partnership) on different tax rates.

Tax tip

If you are a few years from retirement and currently employed, think about investing in your employer. Shares acquired under share incentive plans or sharesave schemes usually provide price discounts and tax breaks for taking part. Think about and plan your annual contribution limits so that there could be a steady flow of share sales in the future so you can maximize your CGT exemption (see below).

Income received gross

Exceptionally, there are some investments where the income is paid to you gross – without the basic rate tax deducted. These include NS&I income bonds, capital bonds, the NS&I Investment Account and all gilt interest (albeit people who prefer to receive gilt interest net can opt to do so). This can lead to a surprise tax liability for the unwary.

This is similar to higher and additional rate taxpayers who have to play 'catch-up' every 31 January on the difference between the tax they have paid on their interest at source (charged at 20 per cent basic rate tax and deducted at source) and the tax due at the higher rate (40 per cent) and/or additional rate (45 per cent). If appropriate, you will need to save sufficient money to pay the additional tax due by 31 January after the end of the tax year.

Reclaiming tax on savings income

You can reclaim tax paid on savings interest within four years of the end of the relevant tax year by filling in form R40 and sending it to HMRC. It normally takes about six weeks to get the tax back.

Tax tip

If you have a joint account with a husband, wife or civil partner you declare half of the income respectively. If this could result in a tax liability as one is a higher or additional tax payer and one is a nil or basic rate tax payer the accounts may be better from a tax perspective if held by the nil or basic rate tax payer rather than in joint names.

Mis-sold PPI compensation 'interest'

Millions of consumers have been receiving refunds after being mis-sold payment protection insurance (PPI) with credit cards and personal loans. Successful claimants are also being paid interest on the refunds to compensate for being without their money all that time. *But*, while there is no tax to pay on the refund element, which simply returns your own money to you, you may have to pay tax on the interest, just as you do on earned interest in a savings account. If you have received a compensation payment check what the lender advises and whether they have deducted basic tax at 20 per cent already (which non-taxpayers can reclaim and higher rate payers report to HMRC on their self-assessment).

Mistakes by HMRC

HMRC does sometimes make mistakes. Normally, if it has charged you insufficient tax and later discovers the error, it will send you a supplementary demand requesting the balance owing. However, a provision previously known as the 'Official Error Concession' and now labelled 'Extra Statutory Concession A19' provides that, if the mistake was due to HMRC's failure 'to make proper and timely use' of information it received, it is possible that you may be excused the arrears.

Undercharging is not the only type of error. It is equally possible that you may have been overcharged and either do not owe as much as has been stated or, not having spotted the mistake, have paid more than you needed to previously. If you think there has been a mistake, write to your tax office explaining why you think the amount is too high. If a large sum is involved it could well be worth asking an accountant to help you. If HMRC has acted incorrectly you may also be able to claim repayment of some or all of the accountant's fees (your accountant will be able to advise you on this).

As part of the Citizen's Charter, HMRC has appointed an independent adjudicator to examine taxpayers' complaints about their dealings with HMRC and, if considered valid, to determine what action would be fair. Complaints appropriate to the adjudicator are mainly limited to the way that HMRC has handled someone's tax affairs (perhaps undue delays, errors and discourtesy). Before approaching the adjudicator, taxpayers are expected to have tried to resolve the matter with their tax office.

Important dates to remember

The deadline for filing paper self-assessment forms for the 2016/17 tax year is 31 October 2017. Those filing online will have until 31 January 2018.

The penalty for breaching these deadlines is £100. If your return is more than three months late an automatic penalty of £10 per day commences up to a maximum of £900 in addition to the initial £100 penalty. If your return is still outstanding after a year another penalty arises based on the greater of £300 or 5 per cent of the tax due. In serious cases of delay a higher penalty of up to 100 per cent of the tax due can be imposed.

One final key date – you can amend your self-assessment at any time in the 12-month period after the latest 31 January deadline.

Tax tip

Submit a 'best efforts' self-assessment tax return rather than a late one. Indicate the figures that are provisional and in the additional notes section apologise and explain that you will rectify matters as a priority (and do so!).

Tax rebates

When you retire, you may be due a tax rebate because tax has been collected using PAYE assuming you will earn your salary for a whole year. Rebates usually arise for summer or autumn leavers. The tax overpayment would normally be resolved automatically, especially if you are getting a pension from your last employer or move into part-time employment. The P45 (tax form for leavers) should be used by the pension payer or new employer and, normally, the tax sorts itself out. If not and the potential reclaim is for a previous tax year HMRC may be ahead of you as they may spot it (usually by the end of July following the tax year) and send you a P800 tax calculation if they know you have paid too much tax. You will then get your refund automatically within 14 days of the P800.

If you have not received a P800 or can't wait to the end of the tax year you may make a claim to HMRC for any of the four previous tax years. You will need to know your National Insurance number, your P45 if you have one and details of the jobs or state benefits you were getting at the time. HMRC will process the payment or explain what further information they need. Use this address for all Income Tax correspondence with HMRC: Pay As You Earn and Self-Assessment, HM Revenue & Customs, Direct, BX5 5BD.

Capital Gains Tax

You may have to pay CGT if you make a profit (or, to use the proper term, 'gain') on the sale of a capital asset. CGT applies only to the actual gain you make. There is an exemption limit of currently £11,100 per year. This means that in 2016/17 a married couple or a couple in a civil partnership can make gains of £22,200 that are free of CGT. However, it is not possible to use the losses of one spouse to cover the gains of the other. Transfers between husband and wife or civil partners usually remain tax-free, although any income arising from such a gift will be taxed in due course in the hands of the recipient.

Any gains you make are taxed at 10 per cent for basic rate taxpayers and 18 per cent for higher rate and additional rate taxpayers; however, sales of a second interest in a residential property (mainly aimed at the buy to let market) remain at older rates of 18 per cent for basic rate taxpayers and 28 per cent for higher rate and additional rate taxpayers

Company owners benefit from further tax breaks, including 'entrepreneurs' relief', which can get relief limits on disposals of shares in certain companies (usually family companies) on CGT down to 10 per cent (professional advice should be sought on this).

The following assets are not subject to CGT and do not count towards the gains you are allowed to make:

- your main home (but see the section opposite);
- your car;
- personal belongings up to the value of £6,000 each, such as jewellery, paintings or antiques;
- proceeds of a life assurance policy (in most circumstances);
- profits on UK government loan stock issued by HM Treasury;
- National Savings certificates;
- gains from assets held in an Individual Savings Account (ISA and older PEPs);
- Premium Bond winnings (maximum holding was increased to £50,000 in 2015/16);
- betting and lottery winnings and life insurance policies if you are the original owner;
- gifts to registered charities;

- usually small part-disposals of land (limited to 5 per cent of the total holding, with a maximum value of £20,000);
- gains on the disposal of qualifying shares in a venture capital trust (VCT) or within the Enterprise Investment Scheme (EIS) and Seed Enterprise Investment Scheme provided these have been held for the necessary holding period. These are complex and tax-efficient investment schemes and carry risk but are outside the scope of this book. Further information can be gained from **www.gov.uk/government/organisations/hm-revenue-customs**, and professional advice should be sought.

Your home

Your main home is usually exempt from CGT. However, if you convert part of your home into an office or into self-contained accommodation on which you charge rent, the part of your home that is deemed to be a 'business' may be separately assessed and CGT may be payable when you come to sell it (CGT would not usually apply if you simply take in a lodger who is treated as family, in the sense of sharing your kitchen or bathroom).

If you leave your home to someone else who later decides to sell it, then he or she may be liable for CGT when the property is sold (although only on the gain since the date of death). There may also be Inheritance Tax implications, so you are strongly advised to consult a solicitor or a chartered accountant. If you own two homes, only one of them is exempt from CGT, namely the one you designate as your 'main residence', although there may be some overlap opportunities and, providing a dwelling home has been your only or main home for a period, the final period of ownership that qualifies for relief can be useful. The final period of ownership of a private residence that potentially could qualify for relief is 18 months. HMRC's helpsheet 283, 'Private residence relief', available from **www.gov.uk** provides more information.

Tax tip

If you have two homes and have lived in both consider taking professional advice on whether to make a main residence election for your second home if it is standing at a large gain or you are thinking of selling it first. One of the tests used by HMRC when considering the availability of such reliefs is the actual period of residence and the quality rather than quantity of that residence.

Selling a family business

CGT is payable if you are selling a family business, and is 18 per cent for higher rate and additional rate taxpayers, but the reduced level of 10 per cent for basic rate taxpayers. There are a number of CGT reduction opportunities or deferral reliefs allowable including the potential to attain entrepreneurs' relief, which could produce a tax rate of 10 per cent. This, however, is a complex area and timing could be vital, so well before either retiring or selling shares you should seek professional advice.

Inheritance Tax and wills

No one knows precisely when our clock is going to stop and we also can never truly tell what is round the corner. We all know of enough life experiences from friends and family to tell us, deep down, that this rather morbid tax needs to be talked about sooner rather than later to help manage, wherever possible, Inheritance Tax (IHT) paid on your 'estate'. Side issues abound and are interlinked on this rather dark issue but, frankly, the planning issues are significant. Above all else there is the straightforward wish of not wanting ambiguity about what should happen after you die. So time for a deep breath and read on and then promise to talk to those that matter to you about this one or put a large circle around these words and pass this book to them.

The tax threshold (the level at which you'll need to pay tax) is set at £325,000 and frozen at this rate until 2020/21. The threshold amount for married couples and civil partners is £650,000. The value of estates over and above this sum is taxed at 40 per cent. So the starting point is for you and your partner to sit down and make a list of your assets and then deduct all outstanding liabilities.

Tax tip

Many people underestimate how much they are worth and forget other assets – that is why this is a two person job as it is easy to overlook assets acquired over a long time.

Some people mistakenly think that giving away your wealth gets around IHT. This is where the clouds of confusion sometimes arise from 'pub talk'. Yes there are some detailed points where this can be true such as gifts for the national benefit. There are also other exemptions that have been brought into the debate such as servicemen dying on active service being exempt from IHT. There are then grey areas such as war service hastening a veteran's death, which found, upon challenge, that the estate could be exempt from IHT.

However, the root of the confusion referred to above usually arises from the fact there is no immediate tax on lifetime gifts between individuals – it is only deferred. The gifts can then become wholly exempt if the donor survives for seven years. So when the donor dies, any gifts made within the previous seven years become chargeable to some extent as their 'tapered down' value is added to the estate. For this reason, in the seven-year period they are known as 'potentially exempt transfers' or PETs for short. For instance, the 40 per cent tax is reduced to 32 per cent if there are between three and four years between the gift and death and then 24 per cent for between four and five years. Gifts with strings attached are treated as if they did not happen.

The £325,000 threshold allows married couples or civil partners to transfer the unused element of their IHT-free allowance to their spouse or civil partner when they die, giving an attractive effective threshold of £650,000. IHT will, however, still be levied at 40 per cent above £325,000 on the estate of anyone who is single or divorced when they die.

One of the biggest fanfares in the summer 2015 Budget was for the 'main residence nil rate band' which will be an extra relief planned to commence from April 2017. It will be an extra relief available where the value of the estate is above the IHT threshold and contains a main residence that is being passed on to 'lineal descendants'. It will raise the IHT free allowance to £500,000 per person by 2020/21 and means that where married couples jointly own a family home and want to leave this to their children, the total IHT exemption will be £1 million.

The key aspects (at summer 2016) are:

- The relief will be introduced in April 2017, for deaths on or after that date.
- It will be phased in, starting at £100,000 in 2017/18, rising to £125,000 in 2018/19, £150,000 in 2019/20 and £175,000 in 2020/21. For a couple, the £175,000 plus the existing £325,000, each, makes the £1 million maximum relief quoted by the government.
- The relief will then increase in line with CPI from 2021/22 onwards.
- The relief applies only on death, not on lifetime transfers.
- The amount available will be the lower of the net value of the property and the maximum amount of the main residence nil rate band. The net value of the property is after deducting liabilities such as a mortgage.

- The property will qualify if it has been the deceased's residence at some point.
- The property must be left to lineal descendants: children, grandchildren, great-grandchildren, etc. Children include step-children and adopted children.
- The relief is transferable, so the estate of the second spouse to die can benefit from the main residence nil-rate band of their deceased spouse, regardless of when that spouse died.
- The relief will be tapered away for estates with a net value over £2 million, at the rate of £1 for every £2 over that limit, so will be reduced to zero on an estate of £2.35 million.

Tax tip

Could these new IHT rules result in unmarried couples with children and a house worth more than £650,000 walking down the aisle after April 2017?

Other encouragement includes the charitable donations exemption with a reduced rate of IHT payable on estates that give at least 10 per cent of the value of their estate above the nil rate band (£325,000) to charity. The remainder is taxed at 36 per cent against the usual 40 per cent IHT rate.

Gifts or money up to the value of £3,000 can be given annually free of tax. If you didn't use last year's allowance you can carry it forward and use it this year to give £6,000 away to your children, for example. The allowance is per donor, not per child.

Additionally, it is possible to make small gifts to any number of individuals free of tax, provided the amount to each does not exceed £250. You cannot combine this with the £3,000 allowance.

Another opportunity for gifting in a way that does not see the money caught by the IHT trap is gifts to mark a wedding or civil partnership. The limits for these gifts are up to £5,000 given to a child, £2,500 given to a grandchild or great grandchild or £1,000 given to anyone else.

Tax tip

Planning and longevity go hand-in-hand, as most lifetime gifts to individuals who are not covered by one of the exemptions mentioned do not trigger IHT if you survive for seven years.

Recent Budgets also created new and welcome provisions to enable the tax and other advantages of ISAs and pensions to be passed onto the deceased's spouse (for instance in the case of ISAs that funds could remain in the ISA tax-effective wrapper). Could it be tax-efficient to ensure that your spouse inherits your ISA under your will rather than the investments passing to other family members?

Remember that the government can change the tax rules without notice and exemptions can be withdrawn or reduced.

Finally, as we draw this morbid but important section to a close please remember the importance of a will and how it ties into IHT. Without a will in place it will be the intestacy laws that decide how your estate is distributed, not you. Having a will allows you to state precisely who your beneficiaries are and what they receive and allows you to appoint administrators who will administer the estate after your death. So make a will either through an online or postal service or, if your affairs are more complicated, with a face-to-face Professional Adviser, and consider a power of attorney. Keep them up to date so that they are effective and efficient from both a legal and a tax perspective. For further information, see 'Wills', in Chapter 11.

More at **www.gov.uk** (search 'probate and inheritance tax').

Tax treatment of trusts

There may be IHT to pay when assets – such as money, land or buildings – are transferred into or out of trusts when they reach a 10-year anniversary. There are complex rules that determine whether a trust needs to pay IHT in such situations and professional advice is highly recommended. Further information is available on the website: **www.hmrc.gov.uk** – 'Inheritance tax and trusts'.

Help in dealing with a tax investigation

HMRC is increasing its investigation capability, arming itself with more staff and more power. If HMRC believes your errors were deliberate they can go back 20 years. Add in interest on any late tax and further additional penalties of up to 100 per cent of the tax shortfall and you could be facing an eye-watering tax assessment.

HMRC will listen carefully to facts that may mitigate any penalty due – and if you are looking at serious amounts of tax due then early discussion with a professional adviser will assist you in dealing with the unwelcome situation you may find yourself in. You should also check whether any insurance or professional association memberships that you have could provide free tax investigation cover. This is a very useful piece of cover.

Abbey Tax has one of the leading tax consultancy teams in the UK, which is headed by Guy Smith, a former HMRC tax inspector. Indeed, all of Guy's team are ex-tax inspectors and cumulatively have spent over 125 years working for HMRC.

We asked Guy for his views on the compliance landscape and how HMRC has been performing:

> In many ways, the transformation of HMRC over the five years of the coalition government was remarkable. Against a backdrop of falling staff numbers and the closure of tax offices, HMRC consistently produced higher compliance yields year after year, as processes were streamlined and digital systems developed.
>
> Since the Conservative government was elected, a further £1.3 billion of investment in HMRC has been approved by the Chancellor, with the objective of raising an additional £5 billion a year on top of that already being achieved. £300 million of that pot of money is to allow HMRC to pursue small- and medium-sized enterprises (SMEs), as well as wealthy individuals.
>
> You may well be wondering why there is such a focus on the sole trader, partnership or professional person. According to HMRC's calculations the current tax gap is some £34 billion with 44 per cent of this down to SMEs and 12 per cent down to individuals failing to declare and pay the right amount of tax.
>
> HMRC has responded by transferring more staff into enforcement and compliance work.
>
> Many people 'in the know' are now aware of HMRC's award-winning 'Connect' technology which helps identify risks across a wide variety of sources including tax returns, third-party data, tax evasion reports made by the public, social media activity and information reported by other government agencies, including the Land Registry.
>
> HMRC is now exploiting this data even further. It is moving all of its information into a single storage space called the 'enterprise data hub', where tax staff will see everything they need to know about an individual in one place. HMRC intends to make this information available to all operational teams who need it, from contact centres to debt management staff.
>
> The new hub will give HMRC the capacity to store 960 terabytes of data – ten times more than the current capacity and 20 times more what the Hubble Space Telescope has collected in the last 20 years.

In addition, HMRC has obtained extensions of its data gathering powers including powers to collect data from merchant acquirers – businesses that process credit and debit card transactions.

The landscape has therefore changed significantly and HMRC not only has the intention to narrow the 'tax gap' but the targeted resources and a much more focused capability. Apart from deploying extra staff and closing tax loopholes, we sought Guy's views on what we should be looking out for in the year ahead:

With all the background information HMRC now holds on SMEs and individuals, it is uncommon for a tax investigation to begin as a 'fishing trip'. The tax inspector will usually have been provided with a package of information that HMRC has collated and risk-assessed, which identifies potential issues either with the business accounts which have been declared and filed, where there is believed to be 'hidden wealth', online trading or even undisclosed rental income.

Examples

Potential issues with the business accounts declared and filed: We see a lot of tax enquiries launched when business losses are declared year after year. HMRC will often ask for proof that the business is being run as a commercial venture and ask for sight of business and marketing plans. The tax inspector will also ask how the losses are being sustained, which will usually be followed by a request to see personal bank statements to judge how the individual's lifestyle is being funded, whilst business losses are being incurred.

Hidden wealth: HMRC operates a series of taskforces every year, where a specific risk is identified in a designated geographical area. One of the taskforces which has been running recently involves HMRC staff calling upon individuals it believes have hidden wealth. HMRC may have information of an offshore bank account held, or an expensive asset like a yacht or aeroplane or luxury car, or aerial photos from Google Earth showing extensive external improvements to the residential property. Put simply, after looking at the tax returns filed by those individuals, HMRC may be unable to ascertain how the assets were acquired or home improvements have been funded, or where the money has come from to be deposited in the offshore account.

Online trading: This is a typical paragraph from a letter from HMRC: 'eBay records show that you became a business seller on 1 June 2010 and you have sold at least 19,251 items since that date. When submitting your business accounts, please also provide copies of your PayPal accounts to substantiate the figures shown.' We anticipate this will continue to be a tactic used by HMRC to dispute the turnover declared by businesses with a significant online presence.

Rental income: HMRC receives information from the Land Registry outlining when properties have been bought and sold, can access the voters list records to check for multiple occupancy properties and can also analyse housing benefit payments made. This data enables HMRC to check the accuracy of rental income being declared by known landlords, but also helps HMRC identify 'ghost' landlords who have not registered to pay tax. HMRC has been running the Let Property Campaign to encourage landlords who may have understated their rental income to come forward, to settle on favourable terms.

If HMRC discovers an error during an investigation, it can re-open other closed years as well. For example, if a careless error is discovered, HMRC can include up to six years within any settlement negotiations. If a deliberate error is uncovered, HMRC can include up to 20 years in the most serious cases. In addition to settling any tax owed you will have to pay interest on that tax and a penalty, which can be up to 100 per cent of the tax owed. Needless to say, tax investigations can prove to be extremely stressful and very expensive. So we turned to Guy for his concluding hints and tips:

1. *Engage an accountant.* Make sure the accountant is a chartered accountant and a member of one of the tax professional bodies. In other words, get an accountant who has passed their exams and has qualifications.
2. *Keep good records.* Although there is an obligation to keep business records, it is always sensible to keep personal records as well. Dividend vouchers and interest certificates will always need to be retained for completing the self-assessment tax return, but it is wise to keep records relating to house moves and monies received from third parties, whether from an inheritance or savings maturity.
3. *Talk to your accountant.* It is always surprising how many people simply give their business records to their accountant and then sign their tax return when it is presented, without asking any questions. The danger is that the accountant may have to make assumptions when preparing the accounts and introduce estimates to get the accounts to balance. If a tax inspector finds estimated or other balancing figures during a tax investigation, it calls into question the accuracy of the business records and this can lead to all sorts of problems.

4 *Get tax investigation insurance cover.* Many accountants will offer this type of insurance; specialist providers such as Abbey Tax do too, as well as trade membership bodies such as the Federation of Small Businesses. It is always worth comparing prices and benefits before taking out fee protection insurance, as it is often called.

5 *Be discreet.* HMRC views social media websites so, for example, if your business has had a bad year and made low profits, don't start posting pictures of an expensive foreign holiday on Facebook or a luxury car on Instagram.

Retiring abroad

A vital question is the taxation effects of living overseas. There are many examples of people who retired abroad in the expectation of being able to afford a higher standard of living and who returned home a few years later, thoroughly disillusioned. If you are thinking of retiring abroad, do thoroughly investigate the potential effects this will have on your finances in order to avoid unpleasant surprises.

Tax rates vary from one country to another: a prime example is VAT, which varies considerably in Europe. Additionally, many countries levy taxes that don't apply in the UK. Wealth tax exists in quite a few parts of the world. Estate duty on property left by one spouse to another is also fairly widespread. There are all sorts of property taxes, different from those in the UK, which – however described – are variously assessable as income or capital. Sometimes a special tax is imposed on foreign residents.

Apart from the essential of getting first-class legal advice when buying property overseas, if you are thinking of retiring abroad the golden rule must be to investigate the situation thoroughly before you take an irrevocable step, such as selling your home in the United Kingdom.

Many intending emigrants cheerfully imagine that, once they have settled themselves in a dream villa overseas, they are safely out of the clutches of the HMRC. This is not so. You first have to acquire non-resident status. If you have severed all your ties, including selling your home, to take up a permanent job overseas, this is normally granted fairly quickly. But for most retirees, acquiring unconditional non-resident status can take up to three years. The purpose is to check that you are not just having a prolonged holiday but are actually living as a resident abroad. During the check period, HMRC may allow you conditional non-resident status and, if it is satisfied, full status may be granted retrospectively.

At a very high level and start point is HMRC's Statutory Residence Test, which states that you are likely to be treated as a UK resident if you spend more than 183 days in the UK in any one tax year, or have a home in the UK and don't have a home overseas, or work full time in the UK over a period of 365 days. An online tool, the 'Tax residence indicator', can provide more guidance and is available by searching **www.gov.uk**.

Even if you are not resident in the UK, some of your income may still be liable for UK taxation, so, as with previous suggestions above, professional advice should be sought. In the meantime, more information can be found via **www.gov.uk** – search for 'Guidance note: residence, domicile and the remittance basis'.

Double tax agreement

A person who is a resident of a country with which the UK has a double taxation agreement may be entitled to exemption or partial relief from UK Income Tax on certain kinds of income from UK sources, and may also be exempt from UK tax on the disposal of assets. The conditions of exemption or relief vary from agreement to agreement. It may be a condition of the relief that the income is subject to tax in the other country.

Further information

- HMRC has closed all of its enquiry centres that provided face-to-face help to people with tax queries. This service has been replaced by an enhanced information service via **www.gov.uk** and a telephone support service. The most frequently used telephone line is the self-assessment: general enquiries number 0300 200 3310.
- Use this address for all Income Tax correspondence with HMRC: Pay As You Earn and Self-Assessment, HM Revenue & Customs, BX9 1AS.
- Contact the Adjudicator's Office for information about referring a complaint about HMRC: **www.adjudicatorsoffice.gov.uk**.
- The TaxPayers' Alliance campaigns towards achieving a low-tax society: **www.taxpayersalliance.com**.
- Tax Help for Older People (TOP) is a charity that is an independent, free tax-advice service for vulnerable and unrepresented people on low incomes: **www.taxvol.org.uk**.

- Tax Aid is a charity that advises only those people on low incomes whose problems cannot be resolved by HMRC: **www.taxaid.org.uk**.
- Citizens Advice has a very useful website to help you understand tax and how it is collected and what to do if you have a tax problem. They can also provide face-to-face and telephone support: **www.citizensadvice.org.uk**.

Useful tax forms that can help you pay less tax:

- *R40*: If you want to claim back tax paid on savings and investments, you need to complete this form.
- *P53*: If you have recently taken a lump sum rather than buying an annuity (pension), an enormous amount of tax was deducted before you received it. To claim this back you should complete a P53.
- *P45*: You should receive one of these when you finish work with an employer. If you start a new job in the same tax year it is important that you give it to your new employer. It will ensure you are given the correct tax code and the right tax is deducted.
- *P46*: As important as the P45. If you start a new job and you do not have a P45 you must complete a P46. Your employer should prompt you to do this. If not, ask for one. This form also sorts out your tax codes.

Most forms can be obtained via the HMRC website: **www.gov.uk/government/organisations/hm-revenue-customs**.

Useful reading

The Daily Telegraph Tax Guide 2016 by David Genders, published annually by Kogan Page; see website: **www.koganpage.com**.

Chapter Four
Super Saturday, scams and complaints

'A fool and his money are soon parted.'

THOMAS TUSSER

Intelligent, honest people don't over-pay, fall victim to scammers and meekly roll over without complaint, do they? And do we know how to spot a professional reputable adviser from a 'crook in a suit'? Do we need to be a little bit un-British and get better at complaining?

Key points in this chapter

- *There is not much law around over-charging.* Whilst internet online scams present threats, the flip side should be recognized, as should the massive opportunity created in the last decade to turn information into action. This aspect and power is usually untapped and so we end up accepting the price and over-paying. Every year we sit inside on a cold and wet February weekend and often achieve little. Welcome to Super Saturday and a day that will save you, potentially, £1,000 on services you may have been over-paying for.
- *Then we turn to how we can protect ourselves from the scammers.* First of all, forget the 'it could never happen to me' line. How many times have we read a story and thought the victim should have known better? However, many of the victims are just like you and I but have encountered very professional scammers who have employed all their

tricks and, before you know it, a payment has been made. If it was a few pounds you might write it off to bad luck and experience, but what if it was a few hundred pounds, a few thousand, or even more?

- *The main solution is knowledge and awareness, and looking after each other.* Our five 'tests' and the further tips from the very best in the industry will help you. Taking professional advice and ensuring that the person really is a 'professional' will help to reduce the risk of falling victim to a scammer or a 'crook in a suit', and this chapter will guide you through some of the professionals that can help.
- *Inevitably, however, things do sometimes go wrong in life.* If you do lose out and have encountered a genuine business that is at fault there is also a section in this chapter on complaints – how to complain and how not to.

Super Saturday defeats over-charging

Let's face it, there is, in reality, little protection against over-charging, and the buck usually stops with you on what you choose to pay for utilities, insurance, phone and TV contracts, and even big transactions like estate agency fees.

Quite often, suppliers rely on lethargy, as there just never seems to be enough time to sit back and review your main financial transactions. The automatic renewal comes through and you pay up (yet again). So we looked again at the calendar and spotted Super Saturday – any Saturday in February. And it works! In February it is cold and wet and we have no money after Christmas. This year you will have the utter joy of totting up your Super Saturday savings and find a little glow to this dark month. Sometimes it will pay for another holiday. So make your diary note now. Here is how it works.

Savings

Contact your bank and ask what upgrades are available on your savings – that could be a quick win. If it all looks a little average check out a few of the money comparison websites – we like **www.moneysavingexpert.com**. Account switching is a lot easier than you would imagine, and if you have been dissatisfied with customer service in the past voting with your feet can be quite satisfying.

Insurance

This is potentially one of the biggest areas for a saving. Log your insurance renewal dates: home buildings, home contents, car, pet and other. Contact them and ask what discounts can be applied to any renewal and then check out their biggest competitor with equivalent policies. Be careful, however, about life and health insurance policies, and pet insurance, so you don't lose any existing cover for pre-existing conditions.

Utilities

Check with your supplier if you are on their best tariff and compare this to other options via Ofgem approved comparison sites such as **uswitch.com** or **theenergyshop.com**.

TV and broadband bundles

So, who is paying more than £75 a month? This is a hugely competitive market, with Sky, Virgin Media and BT all biding for your money. Compare the deals and make the switch, and remember there may also be dramatic price drops if you tell them you are leaving.

Cash back and air mile credit cards

A quick look at **moneysavingexpert.com** could find you cutting your existing card in half and shifting to someone who will reward you more. Some even come with neat little extras like a complimentary coffee and a bun each month!

The 'ooops, I forgot about that direct debit' moment

Get your bank statements and credit cards statements together and sit down with your partner and check you recognize and can account for all those direct debits. If you don't use that club or gym membership, stop paying for it.

Lost premium bonds or other National Savings and Investment

These can be traced via **mylostaccount.org.uk**.

Overpay your mortgage

Mortgages cost more than savings interest can earn. Assess whether you can start over-paying on your monthly mortgage payments and save money.

Estate agent fees

If selling your current home, use an online estate agent to slash your costs.

A helping hand

The Property Ombudsman – estate agents and letting agents
Some of the biggest financial transactions we entrust to professional advisers are around possibly the biggest asset we own – the house. Things can go wrong, and protection and industry standards have been hit-and-miss in the past. The Property Ombudsman is penetrating into this area and has the power to make awards of compensation for loss and/or aggravation, distress and inconvenience. The service is free of charge for the public. Its website at **www.tpos.co.uk** contains all the information that you need for making a complaint to an agent and then bringing that complaint to the Property Ombudsman if you remain dissatisfied. The website also lists all agents that are members. If an agent is not a member then you are not covered.

The consumer ombudsman – utilities, phone, internet and property
The consumer ombudsman, Ombudsman Services, will assist with unresolved complaints about your internet or telephone provider, a gas or electricity provider and some property matters including chartered surveyors and surveyor, agents and valuers. More at **www.ombudsman-services.org**.

Protecting yourself from the scammers

Having worked so long to build up a wealth and asset base we want to protect it and enjoy the benefits of our decades of hard work or perhaps lucky opportunities over the years. There are, however, predators out there who may want a slice of our cake. Scammers are basically clever crooks who deploy sleight of hand, fast talk and a few back-up techniques such as vanity and knowing that people never want to admit to being stupid. You may never spot what they have done, in the same way as a good magician really will leave you believing that they made someone 'float' on stage. The equivalent of smoke, mirrors and sleight of hand can make anything look possible. With the help of our friends in the know we have put together this section to serve as a common-sense approach to help you ignore the smoke and mirrors deployed by the scammers, and hopefully stay safe.

The five tests for staying safe from scammers

Trust your instincts

It's a simple common-sense approach – ignore the smoke and mirrors and sleight of hand that crooks and scammers are so capable of pulling off – anything that is used to distract you from the real issue. Does it look, feel, and 'smell' like a scam? Does it get your hackles up? If so, trust your instincts and walk away, put the letter in the bin or put down the phone. Instincts have been honed in the human species over thousands of years – if they have served you well in the past, learn to trust them.

Actions speak louder than words

Scammers, generally, are all talk (unsurprisingly, they are very good at it) and no action. Any reasonable person should be able to deliver against what they promise or apologise and explain before you have to ask 'what's going on?' If the actions don't happen, then just walk away and don't give them a second or third chance to take advantage of you if you have to keep chasing.

Too good to be true?

Scammers know that greed can get the better of many people and employ it to their purposes. If it sounds too good to be true, it is probably a scam. Walk away.

Thank you, but I'll just check with...

We have great financial institutions in the United Kingdom and this goes to the very heart of the UK economy. Our regulatory system is sound. You should therefore check precisely who you are dealing with, and more on this follows in the 'Professional advisers' section of this chapter. If it is a company and not a high-street name check out the company at Companies House (**www.gov.uk/government/organisations/companies-house**) to see how long it has been in existence and whether it has filed its accounts on time for any warning signs – the service is free. For investments and pensions you must check that the firm is regulated by the Financial Conduct Authority (**www.the-fca.org.uk**).

Also linked to the 'I'll just check with...' tip is the simple fact that crooks have one other objective in addition to taking your hard-earned cash – and that is not getting caught out. This is where nosy neighbours are brilliant – a stroll over and a few questions can be of great assistance.

Share this with Granny

If you only do one thing as a result of this chapter, do this: require any friend or relative that is over the age of 70 to learn the above tips.

Top tip

Share this chapter with Granny or an elderly friend, and remember, nosy neighbours are just what she needs, along with visits from you!

Some common scams

Advance fee fraud

This is one of the scammer's favourites and has been dressed up in a hundred different guises. The scam is remarkably simple. A payment is made by you with the promise of a bigger pay-out in return. Perhaps it is cloaked in terms of funds left to you by a mystery relative, where you pay a processing fee of £50, then maybe you are asked to pay another release fee of £150 and on it goes with a promise of £10,000 sucking you in (which, of course, you will never actually receive). Walk away.

The surprise prize-ballot win

There is usually a premium-rate telephone number to call in order to claim the prize and the ultimate actual prize is probably worthless or trivial. File anything like this under 'B' for bin. It is, however, sometimes fun to read the small print in such 'prizes' in order to spot the scam or the impossibility of winning the surprise big prize. This is how it works: there will be a token nominal prize for which there may be 10,000 or more winners and it will probably take you more than £15 in phone or other 'processing' charges to 'win' and the prize will be pretty useless at best or may even be non-existent. As a final deterrent – if you are foolish enough to reply to something you didn't enter in the first place you are likely to be put on a 'suckers list' and will be bombarded by even more junk ballots and scams.

Top tip

File mystery ballot wins under 'B' for bin and don't let your greed get in the way.

Romance scams

The new lover, or someone showing you interest or attention who shows you the attention you crave just when you may need it (maybe you are at a low point – remember, these scammers are clever crooks in suits). Maybe they tell you they need some money for a sick mother or child. Scammers know how to manipulate you to get the response they want. They usually want you to keep things 'secret' as they know that any friend you confide in will tell you to run a mile. Sadly, emotional involvement and shame prevent some people from acting rationally – and the scammers know this. Charming chat, sleight of hand and, just like a magician, your money is gone before you know it. Be brave and confide in someone you really trust.

Credit and bank card cloning or snatching

This can be the jackpot for the scammers, but how can they actually get your credit or bank card? The cloning devices that they attach to a bank's cash machine are not so far-fetched these days. But how about the scammer who calls you and pretends to be from the police, explaining that they have just arrested someone who 'apparently' was caught with a clone of your card. They arrange for a courier to call and collect your actual card as part of their investigations. Unfortunately, it is all just another scam and the supposed police officer is just another scammer. These guys really do have balls, but the bottom line is never, ever, be worried about feeling made to look silly.

Follow our five tips – and then if you spot a scam or have been scammed, report it and get help. Contact the Police Action Fraud contact centre on

0300 123 2040 or online at **www.actionfraud.police.uk**, or contact the police in your area – unless a crime is in progress or about to happen, the suspect is known or can be easily identified, or the crime involves a vulnerable victim, in which case dial 999 if it is an emergency or 101 if it isn't.

But don't just take my word for it. The Metropolitan Police are at the forefront of fighting fraud with their fraud prevention team – 'Sterling' – now part of FALCON (**F**raud **A**nd **L**inked **C**rime **On**line) Organized Crime Command. We asked them about current trends. Their spokesperson set the scene very neatly:

MP: The over-70s are a more trusting generation and therefore more likely to be taken in by fraudsters and they tend to have more money at their immediate disposal and more that can be readily accessed.

We are seeing individuals who have been arrested for burglary, robbery and drug dealing in the past being arrested in connection with fraud. Criminals follow the money. Where some have had success, others will follow.

GRG: We have set out some tests and tips earlier but this emerging scam sounds very sinister. Do have you any further tips?

MP: Your bank or the police will never ask for your PIN, your bank card or ask you to withdraw cash. Never share your PIN with anyone. Never give your bank card or any goods you have purchased as a result of a phone call to anyone who comes to your front door.

The Metropolitan Police spokesperson then returned to another of the common scams we featured earlier – the surprise prize-ballot win. Scam lotteries and fake inheritance scams are becoming a real menace and people are losing out. If you reply to just one of these letters you risk being inundated by more and the police spokesperson agreed that your name will form part of a 'suckers list'. This list is then traded amongst scam-mail fraudsters. Genuine lotteries will not ask you to pay a fee to collect your winnings. For more information, take a look at the *Little Book of Big Scams*: **www.met.police.uk/docs/little_book_scam.pdf**. The Metropolitan Police also has an audio version and a business edition on its website: **content.met.police.uk/Site/fraudalert**.

Advice about scam mail can be found at **www.thinkjessica.com**. The fraud prevention team 'Sterling' is also working with the Royal Mail to prevent scam mail entering the United Kingdom and being delivered to UK residents. You can help by reporting it – email **scam.mail@royalmail.com** or report concerns by calling 03456 113413.

Keeping safe from telephone cold calls, email scammers and online fraud

The above examples are just some of the higher-profile and potentially higher-value scams, but there are many more. Some of them you may encounter over the phone and internet on a weekly basis.

Cold callers on the telephone can be irritating at best and sometimes downright scary. They may not take 'no' for an answer. The way these calls are intruding into our life is becoming a real problem.

Top tip

Use the magic words 'I am signed up to the Telephone Preference Service and you should not be calling this number', which helps them 'go away'.

The Telephone Preference Service (TPS) is a free service. It is the official central opt-out register on which you can record your preference not to receive unsolicited sales or marketing calls. It is a legal requirement that all organizations (including charities, voluntary organizations and political parties) do not make such calls to numbers registered on the TPS unless they have your consent to do so. You can register your phone number with the telephone preference service by calling 0845 070 0707 or you can do this online at **www.tpsonline.org.uk**. If you are worried about an elderly relative, neighbour or friend who is on their own and could be vulnerable, the best thing you could do is talk to them and buy them a telephone that displays the inbound number and, even better, blocks certain numbers, including overseas numbers (other than those you want to receive).

Email scammers

The ingenuity and creativity of email scammers is reaching new heights. Someone somewhere has gathered thousands of email addresses, including yours, and mass-mails them with a piece of information – designed with only one purpose in mind. That purpose is to gain your attention and engagement. All scam emails end up the same way, which is you losing out. Maybe they offer a refund from HMRC or it is a bank indicating that the security of your account has been compromised. The email asks you to click on a link and then follow the instructions. The quality of the websites you link to is usually convincing, with lots of branding and official-looking information. Unfortunately, the reality is that they have been built by scammers and they want to steal your money – the link you are asked to click or document you are asked to open could contain a harmful virus intended to monitor the activity on your computer or cause other security problems.

Top tip

Never, never, never click on any links from strange email accounts, and if in doubt check it out with the organization directly – hover over the displayed email address to show the actual email account the scammer may be using.

Generally try to protect yourself by restricting yourself to known organizations and deal directly with their websites. If it is a UK business they must clearly show the company or business operating the website (usually in the 'contact us' or 'about us' section), which you can then check out. If it is a company and it is not a high-street name check out the company at Companies House (**www.gov.uk/government/organisations/companies-house**) to see how long it has been in existence and whether it has filed its accounts on time (these are possible warning signs) – the service is free. This will never be definitive but it is something you can check for yourself – and it can be very telling if the company involved has only been around for a year. The watchwords here are 'if in doubt... leave them out'.

Online fraud

The online world offers rich pickings for crooks as the criminal can engage with the victim without having to meet them. They can be sitting in an internet café on the other side of the world! This makes it increasingly difficult for law enforcement to trace the suspects' victims, who are frequently scammed when trying to make purchases online, including vehicles, event tickets and holiday lettings. Criminals also prey on people through dating sites, trying to win the victims' trust and engineer them to send money.

The Metropolitan Police has just investigated a case involving 3,500 victims across the United Kingdom and indeed the world, with a total combined loss of over £10 million. Victims had transferred thousands of pounds into UK bank accounts in the belief that they were buying a vehicle or some other valuable item (maybe a ticket to a prized event) that never turns up. As knowledge is the key in the fight against the scammers a Metropolitan Police spokesperson explained:

MP: Often, there is a series of emails going between the suspect and the victim when the victim believes they are building a relationship with the suspect and levels of trust are increased. The criminal uses a name they think will engender trust and a scripted cover story as to why the victim cannot see the vehicle before they buy, eg it is in storage in Scotland. Often the victim is persuaded that any money will go into an escrow/holding account and will only be released once the vehicle has been delivered. They want you to believe the money is safe in the event that anything goes wrong. In reality the bank account the victim pays into has been opened purely for the purpose of receiving fraudulent funds. The victim pays the money but the vehicle is never delivered. When the victim realizes their mistake the money is gone as it gets withdrawn from the account on the same day, and you will eventually find out it was opened with false documents using a false address.

GRG: So what can we do to protect ourselves?

MP: Read and follow the fraud prevention advice given on the auction websites themselves. Do not be tempted to stray from that advice. Pay by credit card, as that offers some degree of protection for amounts over £100. If the seller refuses to talk over the phone and/or meet with you, walk away from the deal. Two of the techniques of the scammers are rushing you (take time out and think) and wanting you to keep things secret (talk it over with a trusted friend). Never let the excitement of a bargain get in the way of applying good common sense and caution. And our most important tip – wealth can be replaced or insured but always consider your personal safety before meeting with someone you have had contact with over the internet – take a friend along or walk away.

The Metropolitan Police Service's Organized Crime Command 'Sterling' has published *The Little Book of Big Scams*. This is now in its third edition and can be viewed online. It has also been given to other forces, who are printing their own copies. The booklet can be seen and printed by visiting **www.met.police.uk/fraudalert**. The booklet provides further information on a variety of common frauds and advice on how to prevent yourself from falling victim.

Reporting fraud can be done online at **www.actionfraud.police.uk** or call the Action Fraud contact centre on 0300 123 2040. In an emergency, dial 999. Be assured that the most effective method to combat fraud is to prevent it in the first place. Awareness of common frauds and taking simple action to prevent yourself from falling victim are the most vital things you can do.

We are delighted to be able to help *The Good Retirement Guide 2017* and its ability to spread the word, so pass on your copy to an elderly friend or relative so we can all keep people that little bit safer, as knowledge is the key to protecting yourself.

Top tip

Pay by credit card, as that offers some degree of protection for amounts over £100 (the detail is in Section 75 of the Consumer Credit Act).

The worst passwords

This almost beggars belief but, according to the **lovemoney.com** website, the top 25 worst passwords in 2015 include: 123456, password, qwerty, abc123, welcome, letmein, and princess. Remember the old saying that a fool and their money are soon parted!

Your password should be, where allowed, at least 12 digits long, contain a mix of upper case and lower case letters, numbers and a character. Remember to password protect your smart phone as there is probably more information on your smart phone than can be obtained from breaking into your house. Only download apps from trusted sites such as Apple (**www.apple.com/uk**). If you sell or dispose of your phone always clean it down by restoring factory settings to blank it and remove media cards (younger relatives can show you how to do this if need be), or smash it to pieces.

Top tip

For free online security advice visit: **www.getsafeonline.org.**

The Financial Ombudsman Service's top tips to fight back against the financial predators that are stalking your wealth

David Cresswell is Director of Engagement at the Financial Ombudsman Service and is a well-known and trusted voice on radio and television. His knowledge on keeping your wealth safe is second to none. David's top tips for our readers are listed overleaf and will continue to help keep investors safe.

1 *Are they regulated?* The Financial Ombudsman Service and Financial Services Compensation Scheme are there to help, if the person or company you are dealing with is on the official Financial Conduct Authority (FCA) register and things go wrong. Because of this added protection you should always check, if you are offered investments or pension products or advice, whether the company is on the register at **www.the-fca.org.uk/firms/financial-services-register** or phone 0800 111 6768. Both organizations are unlikely to be able to help if the business you think you have been scammed by isn't regulated, but if you're not sure, call the Ombudsman to ask. Prevention is better than cure, so the tips below will help you steer a safer course.

2 *Out of the blue.* They say you have more chance of being repeatedly struck by lightning than you have of winning the lottery. And yet every day hundreds of us receive emails claiming that we've won money from a mysterious foreign country, or that we've been selected by a strange organization for a random prize.

Most of us know better than to fall for this. But in recent years, fraudsters have invested time and effort into making fake emails and letters look more convincing. They look like messages from official organizations such as your bank, HMRC or even the ombudsman, and ask you to confirm your personal details. Recently, we've even seen pleas for help that look like they've been sent to you by friends in trouble who need you to send them cash. Don't fall for them. Watch out for questionable email addresses that are either from personal accounts (Gmail, Hotmail) or other countries (check the letters after the 'dot' – as in '.ru' for Russia) and emails or letters that fail to address you by your name.

3 *Vishing and smishing.* In the last two years, the ombudsman has seen the rise of new telephone scams that can be devastatingly effective. Vishing (using the telephone) and smishing (using text messages) are scams where the fraudster pretends to be from your bank (or another official organization) and tricks you into transferring or handing over your savings by pretending your account security has been breached. These scams work in a range of different ways so it's simpler to remember this one fact – *your bank will never ask you to transfer or hand over your money because of a threat of fraud, and they won't ask you for your online or telephone banking passwords.* If someone asks you to do this, be suspicious. These scams are horrifically effective and some people have lost over £100,000.

4 *Too much information.* Phone or online banking passwords are often the source of much frustration – but they are a necessary hassle in many ways. Your bank will ask you for random letters, numbers or characters from your password. But they will not ask you to confirm your full password on the phone or ask for your PIN number. If you're asked for this information, this should be a clear warning that something is wrong. If you're struggling to remember a password, or you're worried your existing ones are too simple, try getting creative, like taking the first letter of each word in a line of your favourite song.

   Many people are concerned about 'chip-and-PIN' cards – the ombudsman gets lots of enquiries from people suggesting their card has been cloned. This is extremely unusual. In fact, the most common form of PIN fraud is the most low-tech – 'shoulder-surfing', or peering over your shoulder at an ATM or when typing in your pin at the local supermarket.

5 *Pry before you buy.* Every year, the number of things we buy online increases dramatically. Crowded shopping centres and stuffy shops mean many of us are going online and bargain hunting. But sometimes we let down our guard when surfing the web. Websites are always competing to offer you the best possible price and it's tempting to think that 'cheapest is best'.

   If you've never used a website before, before you confirm the purchase you should run a quick internet search to check out reviews and see what your fellow consumers are saying. If it seems too good to be true, be sceptical. Regardless, use a form of payment that offers you some protection, such as PayPal or MoneyGram. Alternatively, if you're making a larger payment, your credit card gives you some rights under the Consumer Credit Act if something goes wrong.

6 *Look after yourself.* The easiest way to spot something untoward with your money is to know your finances inside out. Reading your bank statements and knowing what you've got coming in and going out each month is the best way to avoid any cashflow surprises. Most importantly, trust your instincts. If something doesn't feel right, it's probably because it isn't.

Hopefully, these tips will help you keep one step ahead of the scammers. But, if something does go wrong, the most important thing is to keep calm. Contact your bank straight away and it may be able to sort things out. If you don't feel like it's being helpful, or you're not sure what it should be doing to help, call the ombudsman – they might be able to help. Financial Ombudsman Service: 0800 023 4 567; **www.financial-ombudsman.org.uk**.

Top tip

Trust your instincts. If something doesn't feel right it's probably because it isn't.

Professional advisers

Choosing an independent financial adviser (IFA)

The role of IFAs has become more important since the number of investment, mortgage, pension protection and insurance products has multiplied and financial decision-making has become increasingly complicated. An IFA is the only type of adviser who is able to select from all the investment policies and products on offer in the marketplace. It is his or her responsibility to make sure you get the right product for your individual needs. This means they have to gain a full understanding of your circumstances and requirements before helping to choose any financial products.

Common areas where you might want expert help include:

- annuities;
- financial and tax planning and structuring;
- investments;
- mortgages;
- pensions and pension transfers.

Advisers are divided into one of two types:

- *Independent financial advisers*: IFAs are unbiased and can advise on, and sell, products from any provider right across the market. They are obliged to give 'best advice'.
- *Restricted advisers*: they specialize in particular providers' products or specific areas of advice. Their 'restricted' status means they can only sell and advise on a limited range of products, or from a limited number of firms.

Since 31 December 2012, independent and restricted advisers have to charge a fee for investment and pension advice rather than accepting commission. You can pay up front for the adviser's time, rather like an accountant or solicitor, or you can agree a commission-like fee that is deducted from the money you invest in a product purchased through them. Don't worry about asking up front what the cost will be – it is vital – so just take a deep breath and ask the question so that you can compare different IFAs.

When choosing an adviser ask for and consider their qualifications, FCA registration, fee structure, how long they have been in business (and with whom) and convenience. Ask family or friends who they would recommend. Or try talking to some of an adviser's existing clients and don't be afraid to ask for references. Most reputable professionals will be delighted to assist, as it means that the relationship will be founded on a basis of greater trust and confidence.

Most importantly (and worth repeating), check whether your adviser is registered on the FCA's Central Register website, **www.the-fca.org.uk/firms/financial-services-register**, or phone 0800 111 6768.

To find an IFA near you, look at the Unbiased.co.uk website: **www.unbiased.co.uk**.

Also remember:

- *Get it in writing*: Be sure to get their recommendations in writing. Read them through carefully, and if you don't understand, ask.
- *Final checks*: The decision is yours alone. You do not have to do what they tell you. Make sure their advice is really right for you.

Top tip

You must check whether your financial adviser is registered on the FCA's Central Register website, **www.the-fca.org.uk/firms/financial-services-register**, or phone 0800 111 6768.

For your protection

Most financial transactions involving banks, investments, pensions and insurance take place without any problems but sometimes things go wrong. This is where the UK's regulatory regime steps in.

The **Financial Conduct Authority (FCA)** is accountable to the Treasury and aims to make sure the UK financial markets work well so that consumers get a fair deal. It registers individuals and companies that are suitable to work in the industry and checks that they are doing their job properly, and it fines them if they do a bad job. The FCA has a range of helpful guides and factsheets to help consumers understand the UK's financial markets and the role of the FCA. More at **www.the-fca.org.uk**.

The **Financial Ombudsman Service (FOS)** is a free service set up by law with the power to sort out problems between consumers and registered financial businesses. It is an impartial service and will investigate your complaint if you have been unable to resolve matters with the registered individual or company (ie registered with the Financial Conduct Authority, as above). If the ombudsman considers the complaint justified it can award compensation. More at **www.financial-ombudsman.org.uk**.

The **Financial Services Compensation Scheme (FSCS)** is the body that can pay you compensation if your financial services provider goes bust. The FSCS is independent and free to access. The financial services industry funds the FSCS and the compensation it pays. There are limits on how much compensation it pays and these are different for different types of financial products. To be eligible for compensation the person or company must have been registered by the Financial Conduct Authority (FCA). More at **www.fscs.org.uk**.

Other types of advisers

Accountants

Accountants are specialists in matters concerning taxation. Many accountants can also help with raising finance and offer support with the preparation of business plans. Additionally, they may be able to advise on the tax implications of your pensions and investments but are unable to advise on the products themselves unless they are registered with the FCA. When choosing an accountant, ask for and consider their qualifications, registration with one of the relevant professional bodies (see below – anyone can set themselves up as an accountant without holding any qualifications so this check can be important), fee structure and hourly rate, how long they have been in business (and with whom) and convenience. Check they hold professional indemnity insurance. If you need help in locating a suitable accountant the following will have registers of their members:

- Association of Chartered Certified Accountants (ACCA): **www.accaglobal.com**;
- Institute of Chartered Accountants in England and Wales (ICAEW): **www.icaew.co.uk**;

- Chartered Accountants Ireland (for both Northern Ireland and the Republic of Ireland): **www.charteredaccountants.ie**;
- Institute of Chartered Accountants of Scotland (ICAS): **www.icas.com**.

Anyone with a complaint against an accountancy firm should contact the company's relevant professional body (from the list above) for advice and assistance.

Solicitors

Solicitors are professional advisers on subjects to do with the law or on matters that could have legal implications. Their advice can be invaluable in vetting any important document before you sign it. Often, the best way to find a suitable solicitor (if you do not already have one) is through the recommendation of a friend or other professional adviser, such as an accountant. If you need a solicitor specifically for a business or professional matter, organizations such as your local Chambers of Commerce, small business associations, your professional institute or trade union may be able to put you in touch with someone in your area who has relevant experience.

Two organizations to contact for help are the Law Society: **www.lawsociety.org.uk**; and Solicitors for Independent Financial Advice (SIFA), which is the trade body for solicitor financial advisers: **www.sifa.co.uk**.

Unlike accountants, where literally anyone can set themselves up as an accountant (hence the importance of the check points outlined above), only solicitors regulated by the Solicitors Regulatory Authority can describe themselves as a solicitor and trade as such (others may seek to skirt around this with such terms as 'legal services' and the like). If you are unhappy about the service you have received from your solicitor, you should first try to resolve the matter with the firm through its complaints-handling partner. If you still feel aggrieved, you can approach the Solicitors Regulation Authority: **www.sra.org.uk**.

For practical assistance if you are having problems with your solicitor, you can approach the Legal Services Ombudsman. See the Legal Services Ombudsman website: **www.legalombudsman.org.uk**.

For queries of a more general nature, you should approach the Law Society: **www.lawsociety.org.uk**. For those living in Scotland or Northern Ireland, see the Law Society of Scotland; website: **www.lawscot.org.uk** or the Law Society of Northern Ireland; website: **www.lawsoc-ni.org**, respectively.

Banks

Banks can provide comprehensive services in addition to the normal account facilities. These include investment, insurance and tax-planning services, as well as how to draw up a will. Regulation and protection is via the FCA, FOS and FSCS regime outlined above.

Insurance brokers

The insurance business covers a very wide area, from straightforward policies – such as motor or household insurance – to rather more complex areas, including life assurance and pensions. Whereas IFAs specialize in advising on products and policies with some investment content, brokers primarily deal with the more straightforward type of insurance, such as motor, medical, household and holiday insurance. Some brokers are also authorized to give investment advice. A broker will help you to choose the policies best suited to you, assist with any claims, remind you when renewals are due and advise you on keeping your cover up to date.

Regulation and protection is via the FCA, FOS and FSCS regime outlined above.

Stockbrokers

A stockbroker is a regulated professional broker who buys and sells shares and other securities through market makers or agency-only firms on behalf of investors. A broker may be employed by a brokerage firm. A transaction on the stock exchange must be made between two members of the exchange.

There are three types of stockbroking service:

- *Execution only*: Which means the broker will carry out only the client's instructions to buy or sell.
- *Advisory dealing*: Where the broker advises the client on which shares to buy and sell, but leaves the financial decision to the investor.
- *Discretionary dealing*: Where the stockbroker ascertains the client's investment objectives and then makes all the dealing decisions on the client's behalf.

Roles similar to that of stockbroker include investment adviser and financial adviser. A stockbroker may or may not be an investment adviser. While some stockbrokers now charge fees in the same way as a solicitor, generally stockbrokers make their living by charging commission on every transaction. You will need to establish what the terms and conditions are before committing yourself, as these can vary quite considerably between one firm and another. Nearly all major stockbrokers now run unit trusts.

To find a stockbroker: you can approach an individual through a recommendation or visit the London Stock Exchange website: **www.londonstockexchange.com**, or the Wealth Management Association (formerly the Association of Private Client Investment Managers and Stockbrokers) website: **www.thewma.co.uk**.

Regulation and protection is via the FCA, FOS and FSCS regime outlined above.

Complaints and 'how to complain'

Things in life inevitably go wrong and sometimes you lose out when it was not your fault. It is always satisfying when you explain your complaint and an organization says: 'We are terribly sorry for the inconvenience we have caused you. Thank you for taking the time to set out your concerns. We have now fixed the issue and it will not happen again and we would like you to accept a bunch of flowers as our way of saying sorry.'

This sort of response is rare and we find it irritating the way more and more companies hide behind websites and it is almost impossible to find someone to speak to directly. Perhaps some businesses will see the benefit of reverting to two-way communications and proper customer care. Many consumers are willing to pay that little bit more for decent service and the assurance that when something goes wrong there will be someone there to do something about it. Perhaps that is one of the reasons for the success of companies such as the John Lewis Partnership.

While *The Good Retirement Guide*'s campaign for better customer service continues, our hints and tips on complaints might just help you to get a better outcome:

- When something goes wrong, contact the firm or organization responsible straight away and give them a chance to sort out the problem. It is only fair that they have a chance to look into your complaint as there are usually two sides to any story and perhaps you have simply misunderstood the situation. Clearly state your complaint. Spend time thinking about this beforehand so that you can be clear and concise about what has happened and what you expect. If you are vague and unclear when you complain then you can expect a vague and unclear reply. If you want compensation, state how much and why.

- When you complain, keep a note of who you spoke to, the date and time, and what they said will happen next and by when. Ask whether it would help if you put your complaint in writing.
- If the issue is not resolved, take steps to make it a formal complaint. Ask the organization for the name, address, telephone number and email of the person or department that deals with complaints. Write a letter and head it up 'FORMAL COMPLAINT' in capitals. Spend time getting it factually correct and attach supporting evidence. If it goes beyond two pages it sounds like you could be rambling. Don't worry – we all do this when we feel aggrieved – but it probably means you need to set it aside and come back to it. Re-read it and relegate some information to an attachment if it goes beyond two pages. Send it by recorded delivery and keep a copy, together with the post office tracking receipt.
- Take the case further if the organization rejects your complaint and you believe they have not addressed your concerns. Unfortunately some customer relations teams really don't seem to care what you say or how unfairly you have been treated and will just go through a formula approach. At best they may say 'Here are some discount vouchers to use against your next booking...' or words to that effect.
- If you remain dissatisfied, say so, and ask how you can escalate your complaint. Some organizations will try to get rid of you by sending you a 'go away' letter. This needs some explanation. They will say that they have 'fully considered' your complaint and have now exhausted all opportunities to reach a conclusion. The punchline is that they will no longer respond to any further letters or communications from you and they will close their file. At this stage it is up to you to decide whether to give up (that is what they want) or take them to court (but this could be expensive and is it really worth it?).
- But there may be another route. Some organizations have independent assessors and their service is completely free (for instance, Companies House and other quasi government agencies). Some have a free ombudsman service (banks, financial advisers and estate agents as we have signposted above). Others have regulating bodies (solicitors, surveyors and chartered accountants) that may be able to intervene on your behalf. Others have oversight organizations such as Ofcom (mobile phones) or Ofgem (utilities) and there is the consumer ombudsman now

reaching into this area. Help could also be at hand from Citizens Advice, which also has very useful template letters and advice for complainants: **www.citizensadvice.org.uk**.

- If there is no external organization, you could choose to use a complaints management service. These, however, charge a fee, so make sure you understand the costs you will have to pay. You could also consider legal proceedings, but again consider the costs you will pay including, perhaps, the other side's costs if the court decides you are wrong.

  Another useful route is to consider if mediation or arbitration is possible. The ABTA arbitration scheme, for example, deals with alleged breaches of contract and/or negligence between consumers and members of ABTA, the travel organization, and has been in operation for over 40 years. The scheme is provided so that consumers can have disputes resolved without having to go to court and without having to go to the expense of instructing solicitors. It is important to understand that arbitration is a legal process; this means that if you do go through arbitration, but are not happy with the outcome, you cannot then go to court. You have to choose one or the other when pursuing your complaint.
- The final tip is to consider whether or not your complaint is really worth the effort of pursuing. Perhaps an organization has been wrong and you have been dealt with unfairly. You should, of course, think about taking the first step as outlined above. But then do you just vote with your feet and go elsewhere – and tell your friends about it? Sadly, some complainants just go on and on (and on) making the same points that had been dealt with by the organization they are complaining against. The complainants then avail themselves of all appeal mechanisms, including involving their MPs. Perhaps they just didn't fully understand the issues or maybe they had too much time on their hands and they just dig themselves into a rut. Obviously, this is to be avoided but then again some organizations create so much havoc with their 'customer don't care' attitude, side stepping any difficult questions, ignoring or mishandling your requests to focus on the evidence you have supplied and try to fob you off with vague 'standard paragraphs'. These organizations deserve being held to account and when the evidence mounts up against them regulators and oversight organizations may levy heavy fines. And don't worry if you do feel a little bit un-British!

We hope this section tunes up your ability to complain more effectively or helps you just to drop the matter and move on.

Further reading

Our top recommendations for further help, guidance and support on saving yourself money, scams and complaints are:

- Martin Lewis's website, **www.moneysavingexpert.com**, which helps you weigh up the best deals on phone, gas, banking products, travel, motoring and shopping.
- *The Little Book of Big Scams*, published by the Metropolitan Police Service, PSNI and other forces. You can download the booklet at **www.met.police.uk/docs/little_book_scam.pdf**.
- BBC's *Rip Off Britain* – go to **www.bbc.co.uk** then search for 'Rip Off Britain' and then their section on consumer advice.
- For free online security advice visit **www.getsafeonline.org**.
- Citizens Advice: **www.citizensadvice.org.uk**.
- The Financial Ombudsman Service website and their 'How to complain' section to help you tackle financial organizations that cause you loss, inconvenience and distress: **www.financial-ombudsman.org.uk/consumer/complaints.htm**.
- The Property Ombudsman Service and their consumer guide, which sets out what estate agents and letting agents should do and what you can do if they cause you loss, inconvenience and distress: **www.tpos.co.uk** and search for their consumer guide.
- Ombudsman Services, the 'consumer ombudsman', for guidance on unresolved complaints about your internet or telephone provider, a gas or electricity provider and some property matters including chartered surveyors and surveyor, agents and valuers: **www.ombudsman-services.org**.

Chapter Five
Your home

'We shape our dwellings, and afterwards our dwellings shape us.'
WINSTON CHURCHILL

It's a well-known fact that our home becomes increasingly important to us as we age, and there are a number of old familiar sayings that emphasize this: 'An Englishman's home is his castle', 'Home is where the heart is', 'Home sweet home', and 'There's no place like home'.

There is much further evidence to confirm this. The Stiglitz report (*The Stiglitz Report: Reforming the International Monetary and Financial Systems in the Wake of the Global Crisis*), which has influenced the well-being agenda in the United Kingdom, made a direct link between housing and well-being; the New Economics Foundation, the UK's leading think tank promoting social, economic and environmental justice, suggests that there are strong links between good housing and happiness (**www.neweconomics.org**); and a recent report from the BBC (**www.bbc.co.uk/news/uk-england-35855783**) states that where we live, and the wider neighbourhood, directly impacts on our happiness. The BBC report concluded that Winchester in Hampshire is 'the best place to live in Britain'. This historic cathedral city was called 'practically perfect' by the *The Sunday Times* Best Places to Live guide. But we can't all move there, otherwise it would be hopelessly overcrowded, so the 'Best places to live in Britain' have announced regional winners in their new guide. These include: North East – Harrogate, North Yorkshire; Northern Ireland – Ballycastle, Co Antrim; North West – Whalley, Lancashire; Scotland – Stockbridge, Edinburgh; Wales – Penarth, Vale of Glamorgan; London – Fitzrovia; South West – Falmouth, Cornwall. If you are interested, go to **www.bbc.co.uk/guides/z3g487h** and take the test 'Where in Britain would you be happiest?' You may live in or near one of these areas, but wherever your home is it is probably very dear to you for a number of good reasons.

There is no doubt, the three most important issues for those reaching retirement are money, health and property. Rising life expectancy and the transition into retirement of the post-war Baby Boomer generation are resulting in growing numbers of older people in both numerical terms and as a proportion of the population. The number of people aged over 65 will grow from 10 million to nearly 17 million by 2035. Currently there are 6.5 million people over 65 living in owner-occupied homes just in England, and there have been recent reports of a number of mortgage lenders extending repayment age limits for existing customers. Over a quarter of all property wealth in the UK is now owned by the over 60s, amounting to a value of around £993 billion. That figure, you will probably agree, is a not insignificant amount and brings us back neatly to the already mentioned saying 'there is no place like home'.

Key points in this chapter

As a quick guide, this chapter covers in detail a number of aspects of home and property that you might want to consider. If you feel that entering retirement is the beginning of the rest of your life, this could be the most important chapter in the book. If nothing else, look at the following points, which are vital to consider before reading the whole chapter.

1. *Future proofing your home is important.* In essence this means taking an in-depth look at where you currently live and deciding if it will work for you in your retirement.
2. *If your current home is where you wish to remain, what to do to make the best of staying put.* Suggestions and help provided.
3. *Say you are keen on moving to a new home.* There is a helpful list of the pros and cons of taking this course of action.
4. *You may decide that living in leasehold is right for you.* If so, you can find out all about it and other options in this chapter.
5. *There is much publicity about energy companies and how to keep your bills in check.* You'll find lots of help, information and practical suggestions for reducing energy bills here.
6. *What if your home requires repairs and improvements?* There's a section on this and home safety, which could save you time, trouble and money.

7 *It's never been more important to be up to date on home security and insurance matters.* You will find help and advice to steer you through these complex areas.

8 *Should it be necessary or helpful to use your home to earn money,* there are some great ideas on how you can do this.

9 *Finally, it is well worthwhile being informed on available benefits and the issues of taxes.* This section is important should any of the information be applicable to your circumstances.

Future proofing your home

Research carried out by the Joseph Rowntree Foundation states that specialist retirement housing makes up only 5–6 per cent of all older people's housing. The report also found that around 80 per cent of older home-owners wish to stay where they are currently living.

So future proofing your home is quite important. This is essentially deciding on a plan for the next ten or more years. With life expectancy rising in the UK on average to 78.7 years for men and 82.6 years for women, today's retirees are living longer and staying fitter than previous generations. Most are aware of the need to keep fit and are looking for opportunities to maintain an active and healthy lifestyle. Rather than assuming that retirement means you should contemplate 'downsizing', perhaps it would be more appropriate to suggest 'rightsizing'. The way we consider our living environment as we get older is changing. It is important the property you live in is right for you for the next phase of your life. The following questions should be taken into account:

- Can you get around your current home safely and manage its upkeep?
- Do you have good support networks in the area – family, friends and neighbours?
- Can you get to the places you need and want to go easily – by car, on foot, or by public transport?
- Are you reasonably confident that this will still be the case in 10 or 15 years, or if your health and other circumstances change?

If the answer is 'no' to some of these questions, it might be sensible to investigate other options. Even if you don't want to move now, thinking about the possibility will make things easier, if and when your circumstances change.

What to do if staying put

Recent Office for National Statistics figures show that the over-60s are no longer removing to idyllic seaside towns that seemed a decade or so ago to be their ultimate dream. Instead there are powerful reasons why they are choosing to stay put in the same area where they have lived for years. These reasons include being close to where they used to work, or near their families for whom they provide 'grandsitting' support (enabling their adult children to work), staying within reach of friends, and where their social networks are. Also, you are known to your local medical practice (which could prove a blessing in later life when more support may be needed).

Have you thought about what suits you in terms of where you live now? Is staying put a wise idea?

Things you could do to improve your property and maximize its potential include:

- *Extending your property*: If you're considering doing building works, make sure you apply for planning permission if you are adding an extension, and make it as big as permitted. Smaller extensions to the rear or side of a property can often be built without having to make a planning application, provided that the design complies with the rules for permitted development (see **www.planningportal.gov.uk**). Obtain quotes from at least three different contractors and check with friends for recommendations before going ahead with any works. Keep things in proportion – extra bedrooms aren't an advantage unless there are sufficient bathrooms or shower rooms. Many older people prefer the convenience of en-suite facilities. Remember, any new work must comply with building regulations and it is wise to check with your local authority first.
- *Buying the property next door*: If your budget allows, becoming your own neighbour is a great way to increase your property's value. Knocking through allows more space than an extension, without incurring moving costs or leaving the neighbourhood. This option is neither cheap nor simple and professional advice from an architect is essential. Even if you live in a flat you might be able to buy the adjoining unit or the one above or below, then knock through or install a staircase to achieve double living space. Any construction work being undertaken must, of course, adhere strictly to planning and building regulations and you must ensure the project is completed properly. If you can continue to live at the property while work is progressing, this often makes for a smoother and swifter conclusion to the project.

- *Garage conversion*: This is another popular way to increase space in your home and is reasonably simple. If you propose to add a room above your garage, any scheme would be subject to appropriate planning permission being granted. This is needed because of the extra height and alteration to the roof line. Whether your garage is single size or double, attached or detached, this type of extension is one of the quickest 'wins' because you are working with what you've got and you are spared the necessity of digging new foundations. Rooms above a detached garage make an ideal guest suite, office, study, granny annexe or somewhere to carry on a noisy hobby.

Moving to a new home

Pros and cons

Many people, when in the emotional excitement of moving, don't always consider the reasons why they are doing so. Instead they are swayed by seeing a lovely property without thinking how usefully it is situated. You have probably bought and sold properties several times in the past, but when buying possibly your last home it is essential to get things right. There is no *typical* last-time buyer. Some people wish to upgrade because they can afford it and want more space now they are retired, to be able to put up friends, family and grandchildren. Others prefer to downsize to release equity and help fund retirement, or pass on much needed capital to adult children. Many people are simply motivated by lower running costs. If there are mobility issues, bungalows become attractive, as do retirement apartments in buildings with lifts.

- *Don't overstretch yourself* on your last purchase because if things go wrong and you have to sell your property in a hurry there's no guarantee you will get the price you want for it.
- *Consider downsizing* if your home really is too big for you or you are, for example, finding the garden challenging. The easier it is for you to get around your property and maintain it, the longer you will be able to stay in it, should you get ill or your mobility becomes impaired. It makes sense to consider a property that will last you beyond the next few years.
- *Location, location location*: It's important to consider access to public transport as you get older. Remember the old saying: 'when you've got one foot in the grave make sure the other is on a bus route'. A property within a thriving community gives you access to other people, shops, libraries, doctors and local amenities.

- *Get advice*: When it comes to your last-time property purchase it's crucial to seek professional financial, legal and tax advice. There is more about this in Chapters 3 and 4. If you are considering equity release, this is covered in Chapter 2.
- *Do your research carefully*: Should you decide that a move to a new location is for you, even if you think you know an area well, check it out properly before coming to a final decision. If possible, take a self-catering let for a couple of months, preferably out of season when rents are low and the weather is bad. For more information on the area you are interested in look at the Office for National Statistics neighbourhood statistics website: **www.neighbourhood.statistics.gov.uk**. Another good website to check for potential properties is Rightmove: **www.rightmove.co.uk**.

Moving abroad

If you're planning to retire abroad, you should seriously consider the financial implications. Pensions, tax, buying property in another jurisdiction in a foreign language can be fraught with difficulty. However taken you may be by a location, a great place for a holiday is not always a good place to live permanently.

Some ways of protecting yourself when buying property abroad include:

- Get all documents translated.
- If you are given something to sign, make sure you have a 14-day cooling-off period.
- Take the documents home to the United Kingdom and speak to a lawyer and financial adviser over here rather than in the country overseas.
- Make sure the lawyer you use is independent and not involved in the sale in any way.
- Do not use a lawyer recommended by the seller.
- If you are buying a repossessed property, find out what happened.
- If you are borrowing money, go to a reputable bank. The bank manager will want to be sure that the deal is sound – this adds another layer of checks and protection.

There are many websites offering advice and information on retiring abroad. Have a browse through the following:

- **www.gov.uk** – Britons preparing to move or retire abroad.
- **www.propertyinretirement.co.uk** – section on retiring abroad.

- **www.buyassociation.co.uk** – section on advice on retiring abroad and homes abroad.
- **www.retirementexpert.co.uk** – section on retiring abroad and popular locations.
- **www.shelteroffshore.com** – information on living abroad.
- **www.expatfocus.com** – provides essential information and advice for a successful move abroad.

For more information on the financial implications of living overseas, see the section 'Retiring abroad' in Chapter 3.

Counting the cost

It is estimated that the cost of moving is between 5 and 10 per cent of the value of a new home, once you have added in search fees, removal charges, insurance, stamp duty, VAT, legal fees and estate agents' commission. HM Revenue & Customs website: **www.gov.uk/government/organisations/hm-revenue-customs** gives information on Stamp Duty Land Tax (SDLT). When buying a new home, especially an older property, a full building (structural) survey is essential before committing yourself. This costs upwards of £500 depending on the type and size of property, but it will provide you with a comeback in law should things go wrong. Also helpful to home buyers, the Land Registry allows members of the public to seek information directly about the 23 million or so properties held on its register via the Land Registry website: **www.gov.uk/government/organisations/land-registry**.

For your protection

The Property Ombudsman scheme provides an independent review service for buyers or sellers of UK residential property in the event of a complaint. It also covers lettings agents and residential leasehold management. As with most ombudsman schemes, action can be taken only against firms that are actually members of the scheme. See The Property Ombudsman website: **www.tpos.co.uk**.

Removals

Professional help is essential for anyone contemplating a house move. A reputable firm of removers and shippers will eliminate many of the headaches.

A full packing service can save much anxiety and a lot of your time. Costs vary depending on the type and size of furniture, the distance over which it is being moved and other factors, including insurance and seasonal troughs and peaks. The British Association of Removers (BAR) promotes excellence in the removals industry; for approved member firms all of whom work to a rigorous code of practice, see the website: **www.bar.co.uk**.

Living in leasehold

An ever-increasing number of people move into a flat in retirement. If acquiring a leasehold flat, the freeholder of the building may be an investment company, a private investor, or ideally the leaseholders themselves in the form of a management company. With the advent of 'right to manage', leaseholders do not need to own the freehold but will be able to manage the building as if they were the freeholder.

Leaseholders should be aware of their responsibilities, such as keeping the inside of their flat in good order, paying their share of the cost of maintaining and running the building, behaving in a neighbourly manner and not contravening things as set out in the lease, such as subletting their flat without the freeholder's prior consent, or keeping a pet when the lease clearly states this is not permitted.

The leaseholder has the right to expect the freeholder to maintain the building and common parts for which the leaseholder will be required to pay a 'service charge' to the freeholder (or their managing agent) to maintain, repair and insure the building as well as to provide other services, such as lifts, central heating or cleaners. These charges must at all times be 'reasonable'. Leaseholders have a right to challenge the service charge if they feel it is 'unreasonable' via the Leasehold Valuation Tribunal (LVT). For further information see Leasehold Advisory Service (LAS), **www.lease-advice.org**, and Association of Retirement Housing Managers (ARHM), **www.arhm.org**.

Other options

Caravans or mobile homes

If you want to live in a caravan on land you own, or other private land, you should contact your local authority for information about any planning permission or site licensing requirements that may apply. If you want to keep it on an established site, there is a varied choice. Check carefully, whichever you choose, that the site owner has all the necessary permissions. All disputes since 30 April 2011 are, under the Mobile Homes Act 1983, being dealt with by residential property tribunals in place of the county court.

Park mobile homes

These are modern, bungalow-style residential properties, usually sited on private estates. Impartial advice can be obtained from the NCC, the trade body that represents the UK tourer, motor home, holiday home and park home industries: **www.thencc.org.uk**. Before entering into a commitment to purchase a park home, it's well worth visiting an exhibition dedicated to park homes to gain useful information, of which there are several held annually. For further information see websites: **www.parkhomemagazine.co.uk** or **www.parkhome-living.co.uk**.

Retirement housing and sheltered accommodation

The terms 'retirement housing' and 'sheltered accommodation' cover a wide variety of housing but are designed primarily to bridge the gap between the family home and residential care. There are many well-designed, high-quality private developments of 'retirement homes' now on the market, for sale or rent, at prices to suit most pockets. As a general rule, you have to be over 55 when you buy property of this kind. For full details see Chapter 10.

Practical suggestions for reducing your energy bills

According to the Department of Energy and Climate Change, about 11 million households could save £200 or more by simply switching supplier (*The Sunday Times*, 3 January 2016, **www.thesundaytimes.co.uk/sto/business/money/investments/article1651267.ece**). Comparison sites are quick and easy to use to find cheaper offers. Look at **www.moneysavingexpert.com/cheapenergyclub**. Simply doing a few hours' research could save you hundreds of pounds.

Something else to watch out for, according to Paul Lewis, is the advent of 'smart' electric or gas meters, which send readings digitally to your supplier to tell them (and you) how much electricity and gas you have used each day. The national roll out of 50 million smart meters was expected by the end of 2016. Three big advantages to having smart meters is that consumers will have no more estimated bills; by having an 'in-home display' (IHD) they can monitor their consumption daily and hopefully reduce their energy use; and energy suppliers will be able to charge tariffs that reflect demand. The smart meter programme covers England, Scotland and Wales but not at present Northern Ireland.

Don't forget that many energy suppliers offer free annual gas-safety checks for the over-60s.

Another very useful site from *Which* magazine, to check for saving money on energy bills, is **switch.which.co.uk/energy-advice/understanding yourenergybill.**

Another site to look at which has devoted a whole section to how to cut energy bills is the This is Money website: **www.thisismoney.co.uk/money/bills.**

In summary:

- Switching suppliers really does pay. Loyalty to a longtime supplier no longer has any advantage.
- Don't forget that just a simple thing like turning down your thermostat can save you money. It is cheaper to wear an extra jumper! According to Age UK, 21 degrees centigrade is the magic number to keep your living room warm, the ideal bedroom temperature is 18 degrees centigrade. For more information see the Age UK website, **www.ageuk.org.uk** and search for 'keeping warm'.
- Turning off the lights when you go out of a room and replacing light bulbs with energy saving ones really can save you money.

The following tips can also help:

- Close curtains to cut draughts. Check on windows, doors and chimneys and get draught blockers in place.
- Find out about the Green Deal and other government schemes. See: **www.gov.uk/green-deal-energy-saving-measures.**
- If you have to replace any appliances, make sure you choose the most energy-efficient models.
- Replacing an old gas boiler may be expensive, but it could save you money if it is uneconomical to repair it.

- If you are over 61, you are eligible to claim the Winter Fuel Payment. This is an annual, tax-free benefit and is non-means tested. A separate benefit, the Cold Weather Payment, is paid in the event of exceptionally cold weather.

For further research on saving energy, see Energy Saving Trust: **www.energysavingtrust.org.uk**.

Other organizations that could help:

- Age UK: **www.ageuk.org.uk/health-wellbeing/keeping-your-body-healthy/winter-wrapped-up/keeping-warm**.
- British Standards Institution: **www.bsigroup.com/en-GB**.
- Cavity Insulation Guarantee Agency (CIGA): **www.ciga.co.uk**.
- Draught Proofing Advisory Association: **www.dpaa-association.org.uk**.
- Glass and Glazing Federation: **www.ggf.org.uk**.
- National Insulation Association: **www.nia-uk.org**.

But the ultimate energy saving solution is perhaps to purchase your own eco-home. These can be considerably cheaper to run, but they come at a price (according to Kate Palmer in the *Daily Telegraph*) – around £35,000 more than the average home. But at a cost of just £1 a day to run, packed with energy-saving gadgets, latest-technology solar panels and intelligent temperature controls, it could prove an attractive proposition to some. To find out more read this interesting article: '"Extreme green" homes where energy costs £1 per day' (*Daily Telegraph*, 6 January 2016, **www.telegraph.co.uk/finance/personalfinance/household-bills/12061471/Extreme-green-homes-where-energy-costs-1-per-day.html**).

Structural repairs and improvements

Having home improvement work done in your home can be a stressful, costly business. Whether the work you are contemplating is complex or simple, here are some top tips to help get the work done safely, efficiently and cost-effectively and avoid some of the common pitfalls.

- *If your house needs structural repairs*: The Royal Institution of Chartered Surveyors can help you find a reputable chartered surveyor. See website: **www.rics.org**.
- *Before work starts*: Don't forget to contact your local authority planning and building control departments to check if there are any restrictions on what changes can be made.

- *Budgeting, quotes and specifications*: Make a detailed list of everything you would like to have included; compare quotes and check whether VAT is included in the final cost. Include costs for labour and parts in your overall budget and agree with contractors who will purchase items and have responsibility for their delivery.
- *Finding a trader*: Check your local authority trading standards website for details of approved trader schemes. Be clear about whether you need building regulations certificates for any of the work you are doing. *Never* use anyone who comes to your door cold calling.
- *Contractual information*: Written quotations are essential, they should be broken down to itemize price of work and materials. List work you wish to have done and agree who is responsible if there are delays and who pays. Agree a timetable for the work and how payments will be made.
- *During work*: Agree a single point of contact for the project, and raise issues as they arise. If your local authority building control department has to sign off key stages of the work, check they have done so.
- *Finishing work*: Agreement must be clear as to when the project is completed, and when the final payment is required and what it covers. Some money is usually withheld to cover snagging.

With regard to structural work, here are some other useful websites:

- The Association of Plumbing and Heating Contractors holds a national register of licensed members. See website: **www.aphc.co.uk**.
- The Chartered Association of Building Engineers can supply names of qualified building engineers/surveyors. See website: **www.cbuilde.com**.
- Building Centre can give guidance on building problems. See website: **www.buildingcentre.co.uk**.
- Federation of Master Builders lists of members are available from regional offices. See website: **www.fmb.org.uk**.
- Guild of Master Craftsmen supplies names of all types of specialist craftspeople. See website: **www.guildmc.com**.
- Chartered Institute of Plumbing and Heating Engineering lists professional plumbers. See website: **www.ciphe.org.uk**.
- Royal Institute of British Architects will recommend up to three suitable architects. See website: **www.architecture.com**.
- Scottish and Northern Ireland Plumbing Employers' Federation is the national trade association for plumbing and domestic heating contractors in Scotland and Northern Ireland. See website: **www.snipef.org**.

- Trustmark Scheme, which finds reliable, trustworthy tradespeople. See website: **www.trustmark.org.uk**.
- Trading Standards, where you can search for trusted traders in your area. See website: **www.tradingstandards.uk**.

Safety in the home

According to the Royal Society for the Prevention of Accidents (ROSPA), every year in the UK more than 6,000 people die in accidents in the home. Did you know that a staggering 2.7 million people turn up at accident and emergency departments seeking treatment from accidents sustained in the home?

Accident prevention is easy, relatively inexpensive to deliver and can make a high impact – especially for the most vulnerable members of society. So it makes sense to spend some time checking that your home is as safe as possible.

Excellent advice on general safety in the home can be found at: **www.royalvoluntaryservice.org.uk** and **www.rospa.com/home-safety/advice/general**.

There is a government publication on fire safety in the home: **www.gov.uk/government/publications/fire-safety-in-the-home**.

Information on electrical safety in the home can be found at: **www.electricalsafetyfirst.org.uk/guides-and-advice/around-the-home**.

Just to recap, some sensible safety tips from ROSPA:

- *Fire*: This can damage you, your home and possessions. Better to prevent them from starting. Many fires start in the kitchen. Never leave a pan unattended. Having approved smoke detectors is vital. If a fire starts, ROSPA advises: 'Get out, stay out and call the fire brigade out.'
- *Electricity*: Wiring should be checked at least every five years by an approved contractor. If an appliance appears to be faulty, stop using it. When buying electrical equipment look for the CE mark. Never overload sockets.
- *Heating and cooking*: Air vents or airbricks should be kept clean and clear. Did you know that a gas flame normally burns blue? If it burns orange, this indicates a build-up of carbon monoxide. Appliances should be regularly checked.

Be aware of signs of CO poisoning, such as drowsiness and flu like symptoms. If purchasing gas appliances look for the BS safety mark. Should you suspect a gas leak, open windows, turn off supply and call your gas supplier.

If you smell gas or suspect a carbon monoxide leak, call the National Grid 24-hour emergency line: 0800 111 999.

Safety with medicines and cleaners

Medicines and chemicals should be kept in a safe, locked container or cupboard, where children can neither see nor reach them. Leftover medicines should be returned to the pharmacist.

DIY and garden safety

Enthusiasm and inexperience can be fatal. Use appropriate protective gear (eg when barbecuing) or sturdy shoes (eg when mowing the grass). All electrical appliances and tools should be disconnected before working on them. Barbecues should be at a safe distance from trees, buildings and fences. *Never* pour petrol on a barbecue. Remember that some plants and berries are poisonous or can cause an allergic reaction.

The ROSPA Home Safety Book (ref HS 178) can be purchased via their online shop. See: **www.rospa.com**.

Home security

It is important for every householder to make sure they are not at risk from crime. Your local crime prevention officer should be able to advise you on home security arrangements and whether there are any local 'neighbourhood watch' schemes in operation.

Should you be leaving your property empty for a time due to holidays, the Royal Mail's 'Keepsafe' service will store your mail. This avoids mail piling up and alerting potential burglars to your absence. There is a charge for the service. See: **www.royalmail.com/personal/help-and-support**.

There is some excellent security advice to be found on the website of The Master Locksmiths Association – see **www.locksmiths.co.uk/faq/security-advice-for-your-home-top-13-tips**. In brief, these include:

- *Home exterior*: Check any broken windows or access via garages or conservatories. Tools and ladders should be locked away.
- *Door and window locks*: All windows and doors should have locks that are in good condition, properly fitted to comply with insurance requirements.

- *Beware opportunist thieves*: Should your home look unoccupied, using time switches to control inside lighting is a good deterrent.
- *Sensor lights*: Dusk to dawn or sensor lighting to the front and rear of your home will deter potential thieves.
- *Security alarms*: Remember to regularly change the code as this gains you the maximum benefit.
- *Security grilles or bars*: Can protect side windows, or use reinforced glass if window cannot be blocked.
- *Key replacement*: If you haven't replaced locks recently it's possibly time you did. If you ask a professional locksmith to fit a patented system, you will have the reassurance that keys can only be copied with proof of ownership.
- *Garden shed*: A good quality lock or padlock will protect your garden shed and its contents.
- *Car keys at risk*: Statistics show that thieves are increasingly breaking into homes to steal car keys. Don't make it easy for them by leaving keys in view.

If you want to know of a reputable locksmith, you should contact the Master Locksmiths Association; website: **www.locksmiths.co.uk**.

The BBC's *Crimewatch Roadshow* (**www.bbc.co.uk/crimewatchroadshow**) also offers tips on staying safe.

Age UK Advice provide a booklet, *Staying Safe*. See website: **www.ageuk.org.uk**.

Insurance

Apparently about 6.8 million households in the UK are under-insured. Hopefully yours is not one of them. It is vital to ensure your insurance cover is adequate for both buildings and contents. Reassessing your policy annually makes sense: you may have made improvements to your property, or added to your home contents. A number of insurance companies now give discounts on house contents premiums if proper security precautions have been installed.

If you are planning to move into accommodation that has been converted from one large house into several flats or maisonettes, check with the landlord or managing agent that the insurance on the structure of the total building is adequate. When buying a new property you are under no obligation to insure your home with the particular company suggested by your building society.

Owners of properties in flood-prone areas in the UK have difficulty getting insurance. It is advisable to check whether you live in a high-risk area and, if so, take steps to protect your property. Information on flood-risk areas and how to get help in obtaining insurance can be found on the Environment Agency website: **www.gov.uk/government/organisations/environment-agency**. Further information can be obtained from the National Flood Forum: **www.nationalfloodforum.org.uk**.

The latest help for flood victims, and homes that are at risk, can be found on the Flood Re website (**www.floodre.co.uk**) which went live on 4 April 2016. This is a national scheme to help provide better access to affordable flood insurance cover. An important part of the Flood Re scheme will be to offer help to people to increase their understanding of their level of flood risk and explaining how, where possible, they can take action to reduce that risk. The scheme is in place for 25 years and is authorized by the Prudential Regulatory Authority and Financial Conduct Authority.

Buildings insurance

If your buildings and contents insurance was originally arranged through your building society, it may cease when your mortgage is paid off. If you buy a house with cash – for instance when moving to a smaller home – it is advisable to get a qualified assessor to work out the rebuilding costs and insurance value of your new home. The cost of replacing the fabric of your house, were it to burn down, could possibly be significantly greater than the amount for which it is currently insured. Remember, you must insure for the full rebuilding cost: the market value may be inappropriate. Your policy should also provide money to meet architects' or surveyors' fees, as well as alternative accommodation for you and your family if your home were completely destroyed by fire.

If you rent your home, it is up to your landlord to arrange buildings insurance. If you own your own home, it is up to you. Even if you no longer have a mortgage, make sure your home is insured. The Royal Institution of Chartered Surveyors' Building Cost Information Service provides cost information on all aspects of construction. It has an online calculator at **www.rics.org/uk** to estimate how much cover you need.

Contents insurance

It is important to have the right level of cover. Once you stop work, you may need to review the value of your home contents. With older possessions, you should assess the replacement cost and make sure you have a 'new for old' or 'replacement as new' policy. Cancel items on your contents policy that you no longer possess and add new valuables that have been bought or received as presents. In particular, do check that you are adequately covered for any home improvements you may have added.

Where antiques and jewellery are concerned, a professional valuation is wise. See the British Antique Dealers' Association website: **www.bada.org**; or the Association of Art and Antiques Dealers, website: **www.lapada.org**. Photographs of particularly valuable items can help in the assessment of premiums and settlement of claims. Property marking, for example with an ultraviolet marker, is another useful ploy, as it will help the police trace your possessions should any be stolen.

Further advice can be obtained from the Association of British Insurers: **www.abi.org.uk** and the British Insurance Brokers' Association: **www.biba.org.uk**. Some insurance companies offer home and contents policies for older people at substantially reduced rates:

- **www.rias.co.uk**;
- **www.castlecover.co.uk**;
- **www.ageukinsurance.com**;
- **www.staysure.co.uk**;
- **www.50plusinsurance.co.uk**;
- **www.saga.co.uk**.

There is an excellent article to be found on the This is Money website on general insurance advice; see **www.thisismoney.co.uk/money/bills/article-3266640/Are-life-s-precious-possessions-risk-check-insured.html**.

Financial institutions are keen on 'loyalty marketing' but loyalty should work both ways. Don't stay with a provider out of loyalty. Nowadays *disloyalty* pays because the winners are those customers who constantly switch from one provider to another.

If you feel you have been unfairly treated by an insurer you can take your grievance to the Financial Ombudsman Service. It receives about 350 complaints about buildings insurance a month, about half relating to damage caused by bad weather.

Earning money from your home

Your home doesn't have to be a drain on your finances. If you need some spare cash or a regular source of income, there are several ways you could make money from your home. Some good ideas can be found on the Moneywise website: **www.moneywise.co.uk/work-wages/make-more-money/10-ways-to-turn-your-home-goldmine**.

Here are some ideas to consider:

- *Rent a room scheme*: This is the Government's incentive which allows owner-occupiers and tenants to receive tax-free rental income if furnished accommodation is provided in the main – or only – home. The amount you can earn is £7,500 per year. For more information, see HMRC website: **www.gov.uk/government/organisations/hm-revenue-customs**. If you live in a suitable area, you could find a commuting lodger who only wants the room on week nights – see websites such as Monday to Friday: **www.mondaytofriday.com**.
- *Rent out your drive*: Some areas of the United Kingdom are chronically short of available parking for people going to work or travelling from a nearby airport. A useful and informative article to read is: **www.moneysavingexpert.com/shopping/cheap-parking-rental**.
- *Your home in lights*: It is possible to rent out your home as a film or TV set, particularly if it is quirky or charming. You can list your home via an online agency, such as Film Locations, **www.filmlocations.co.uk**, or Amazing Space, **www.amazingspace.co.uk**, though agencies will take a fee if your home is used.
- *Host students*: Offer your home as a base for a foreign language or exchange student. This pays typically £100 per week. Contact your local language schools, colleges and universities to see if they offer a pairing service for would-be lodgers and hosts.
- *Holiday lets*: If you own a home in the country, renting it out for holiday lets can be profitable as long as certain conditions are met. To qualify, the property must be in the UK, be available for at least 140 days during the tax year and actually be let for at least 70 days. For more information on financial responsibilities see Money Advice Service: **www.moneyadviceservice.org.uk/en**.

Further information on this subject can be found in *The Complete Guide to Letting Property* by Liz Hodgkinson, published by Kogan Page (**www.koganpage.com**).

And finally, make money from clearing your clutter. The first national Clear Your Clutter Day took place on 19 March 2016. It was the brainchild of Jasmine Birtles, founder of MoneyMagpie.com; see website:

www.moneymagpie.com/clear-your-clutter-day. Some of us may be magpies and have overflowing piles of surplus possessions that could be converted into cash. An obvious outlet is eBay but you could also try **www.preloved.co.uk**.

Should the idea of saving money appeal to you as much as making money from your home, a book crammed with thrifty ideas for penny pinching pensioners is *Tips for Meanies: Thrifty Wisdom from The Oldie* by Jane Thynne. Makes a good present and is brimful of clever suggestions (**www.penguin.co.uk/vintage**).

Benefits and taxes

Housing Benefit

More than a quarter of a million pensioners who are tenants could get their rent reduced by claiming Housing Benefit, some could be missing out on an average of more than £60 per week. The biggest reductions are for those on Pension Credit. If you have less than £16,000 in savings you may be able to get this financial help from your local council. For advice contact your Local Authority or Citizens Advice Bureau. The amount of benefit you receive depends on several factors: the number of people in the household, your eligible rent, your capital or savings, your income and your 'applicable amount' (which is the amount the government considers you need for basic living expenses). If you think you may be eligible, contact your council for an application form or apply on line. For further information see **www.gov.uk** – Benefits.

Council Tax

This is based on the value of the property you live in and also consists of a personal element. Most domestic properties are liable for Council Tax, including rented property, mobile homes and houseboats. The value of the property is assessed according to a banding system. Not everyone pays Council Tax. The bill, which is sent out in April each year, is normally sent to the resident owner or to the tenant. The valuation of each property assumes that two adults are resident. The charge remains the same if there are more adults. However, if there is a single adult only living in the property, the bill is reduced by 25 per cent. For further information see **www.gov.uk** – Council Tax.

Exemptions from Council Tax include:

- Property that has been unoccupied and unfurnished for less than six months.
- The home of a deceased person; the exemption lasts until six months after the grant of probate.
- A home that is empty because the occupier is absent in order to care for someone else.
- The home of a person who is or would be exempted from Council Tax because of moving to a residential home, hospital care or similar.
- Empty properties in need of major repairs or undergoing structural alteration can be exempt for an initial period of six months, but this can be extended for a further six months. After 12 months, the standard 50 (or possibly full 100) per cent charge for empty properties will apply.
- Granny flats that are part of another private domestic dwelling may be exempt, but this depends on access and other conditions. To check, contact your local valuation office.

Disputes

If you are responsible for paying the Council Tax on a property that you feel has been wrongly banded, you have six months to appeal and can request that the valuation be reconsidered. If you have grounds for appeal, you should take up the matter with the Valuation Office. If the matter is not resolved, you can then appeal to an independent valuation tribunal. For advice and further information, contact your local Citizens Advice Bureau.

Council Tax Benefit

When the Government last did the statistics, there were around two million pensioners who didn't claim the help with Council Tax they could get – missing out on an average of more than £725 a year. If you get Pension Credit, your Council Tax should be zero. Even if you are not receiving any other social security benefit, you may still qualify for some Council Tax Benefit. The amount you get depends on your income, savings, personal circumstances, who else lives in your home (in particular whether they would be counted as 'non-dependants') and your net Council Tax bill (after any deductions that apply to your home). For further information see Citizens Advice, **www.citizensadvice.org.uk**.

Applying for both Housing Benefit and Council Tax Benefit is complicated. But you can find out what you might get via the very useful website: **www.entitledto.com**.

Chapter Six
Health

'The Japanese eat very little fat and suffer fewer heart attacks than the British or Americans. The French eat a lot of fat and also have fewer heart attacks than the British or Americans. The Japanese drink very little red wine and suffer fewer heart attacks than the British or Americans. The Italians drink excessive amounts of red wine and also suffer fewer heart attacks than the British or Americans. Conclusion: Eat and drink what you like. What kills you is speaking English.'

MICHAEL FITZPATRICK

According to recent research (published in *Mature Times* magazine) the over 50s now consider 76 as the start of their twilight years. People no longer feel 'over the hill' at around 50, and the research study, conducted by Argos to launch their Independent Living range, shows that old age doesn't begin until well into our 70s. Being mobile, mentally stimulated, living independently in our own home, taking regular exercise, using technology and still enjoying gardening are some of the reasons given by many of us for feeling younger than our birth age.

The media is full of information about important advances in medical research, with breakthroughs in diagnosis or treatment for serious illnesses. Additionally, clinical trials and tests are helping to find cures for diseases that would previously have been fatal. It is heartening to know that all these new discoveries have the power to improve our health and longevity. Despite this, remaining healthy after the age of 50 is, it seems, to a large extent in our own hands. It is no surprise to read that current evidence suggests eating a healthy and balanced diet, not smoking, reducing alcohol intake, staying physically and mentally active and keeping fit can help us enjoy life to a ripe old age.

Key points in this chapter

This chapter is important reading, if for no other reason that taking on board some of the advice it contains could literally add years to your happy retirement. As we age, it gets harder to change one's habits. However, if we do as we've always done, we'll get what we've always got. So for starters, have a think about what you would like to do differently now you are in retirement. As the saying goes, 'If you don't use it, you lose it.'

- *Keep fit at all costs.* Get moving as much as you can. Exercise is one of the greatest benefits to good health, so fight the urge towards a sedentary lifestyle in retirement. This chapter shows you what options and choices you have and how achievable they are.
- *You are what you eat.* Is this true of you? Be honest! There is a great section on fitness and diet, as well as suggestions on how to eat more healthily now that you have time to spare. Don't avoid the issue – taking action could add years to your life.
- *Be weather wise.* Tips included in this chapter cover what to do in the heat and suggestions on food safety. All sensible advice and it is well worth adopting some of these recommendations if you value your health and well-being.
- There are sections on *drink (alcohol) and smoking*, as well as *accident prevention*: You can never be too careful. Aches, pains and other abnormalities are also highlighted, as prevention is always better than cure.
- If you already have, or are considering taking out, *health insurance*, there is some good advice on this topic. In addition, you will find information about long-term care insurance, and income protection insurance.
- You may already have had some *health screening checks.* If not, when new to retirement taking action in this way may well give you some peace of mind. There are also sections on the NHS and advice about going into hospital.
- *Complementary and alternative medicine* may not be for you, but should you want to find out more about it, there are paragraphs on this that might provide interesting reading.
- *It pays to look after what you've got.* Give some attention to the sections on eyes, feet, hearing, sleep, teeth, and personal relationships.
- Finally, this chapter covers the issue of *depression* (which can affect a large number of newly retired people) and also gives information on some common disorders.

Five top tips for older adults to help us achieve a healthy retirement:

1. *Eating at least five servings of fruits and vegetables a day* is important, along with whole grains, fish, low fat dairy and healthy fats.
2. *Being active*. Mild to moderate physical activity helps control weight, improve balance, posture and mood.
3. *Using a smaller glass*. Excessive drinking can increase depression, and your chances of falling, and can also cause trouble sleeping and interfere with any medication you may be taking.
4. *Giving your brain a workout*. The more you use it the better it will perform. Any cerebral stimulation helps, from crossword puzzles, Sudoku, or socializing to taking some form of adult education course – many of which are free for the over 65s.
5. *Feeling down or anxious* about anything, or sensing things are not quite right? Speak up, and take remedial action. Don't delay: the earlier your GP learns about your symptoms the more effective your treatment is likely to be.

In retirement, one of the most important things is to keep fit and healthy for as long as we can. A lot of useful reading and informative articles can be found on two senior websites: **www.maturetimes.co.uk** and **www.laterlife.com** as well as the website **nidirect.gov.uk**.

So perhaps a few changes in your daily routine (now that you've retired and have a little more time) could go a long way to improving your physical and mental health. It makes sense for all of us to look after ourselves as best we can, and not take our health for granted.

Keeping fit

Staying physically active improves our health and quality of life, and can help us live longer. Physical activities like housework, gardening or dog walking are easy to incorporate into our daily routine. But specific exercise like swimming, golf, gym-based activities or sports such as tennis or football may be more appealing to some of us. Actually, anything that makes us a bit out of breath, and gets our hearts and pulses pumping faster than usual, is beneficial.

Among the advantages of keeping active are a reduced risk of developing a life-threatening disease, a better chance of avoiding obesity, maintaining or reaching a healthy weight, improved sleep and increased day-time energy, feeling happier and keeping your brain sharp. The more physically active you are, the longer you are likely to remain independent. Exercise makes you stronger, boosts confidence and increases your sense of well-being.

We hear much about the obesity crisis, which costs the NHS millions each year. While not being unhealthily overweight, many of us could probably benefit from taking more exercise. If you haven't done any exercise for years, and are feeling like taking the plunge, do speak to your doctor before starting any fitness programme. It is best to start slowly and build up gradually. Experts recommend 30 minutes of moderate exercise a day about five times a week. It's easy to boost your physical activity by incorporating some of the following into your everyday life:

- Avoid lifts and escalators – take the stairs instead.
- Get off the bus a stop or two earlier and walk home.
- Vacuum the house.
- Clean the car by hand.
- Play games with the grandchildren.
- Take a walk with friends.
- Park further away from your destination if you have to drive somewhere.

(Source: **nidirect.gov.uk**)

Organized activities

There are lots of ways of staying fit and loads of classes to help you do it. In most local areas there may be free, or cut-price sessions, at your sports or community centre or local park. Find out what's available for you in your area. There are all sorts of activities, including boxercise, pilates, table tennis, circuit training, swimming, running, cycling, walking groups and bowling.

The following three websites are where you can find online exercise classes if this appeals to you:

- *Fitness Blender* offers more than 400 free workout videos, ranging from high-intensity interval training to yoga: **www.fitnessblender.com**.
- *Crunch Live* is the online outpost of New York's Crunch Gym. The classes put a premium on high-energy 'entertainment' but they also cover more sensible basics, including aerobics and core fitness: **www.crunchlive.com**.
- *Pilatesology* covers classes for all needs, the only kit required is a mat: **www.pilatesology.com**.

(Source: *The Sunday Times*)

Three of the most recent fitness trends for the over 50s, as suggested by **www.high50.com**, the lifestyle website for the 50 plus generation, are:

- *Body weight training*: This doesn't use complicated gym equipment, but involves exercises such as push-ups, squats and planks. A versatile option for those who can't always get to the gym, and can be performed almost anywhere.
- *Ballet classes*: As we get older are excellent, as many of us lack core strength. Ballet improves posture, strengthens the body and lengthens muscles that don't get used on a daily basis. Classes are a low-impact but high-intensity workout suitable for both men and women.
- *Treadmill training*: This involves interval training on treadmills: mixing speed, duration, incline and recovery. Similar to spinning classes but with treadmills instead of bikes.

If these don't tempt you, the following websites will give you information on classes and other choices available to you

- Extend: **www.extend.org.uk**;
- Fitness League: **www.thefitnessleague.com**;
- Fitness Over Fifty: **www.fitnessoverfifty.co.uk**;
- Keep Fit Association: **www.keepfit.org.uk**;
- Medau Movement: **www.medau.org.uk**;
- Pilates Foundation: **www.pilatesfoundation.com**;
- British Wheel of Yoga: **www.bwy.org.uk**;
- Yoga for Health and Education Trust: **www.yoga-health-education.org.uk**;
- Yoga Village UK: **www.yogauk.com**.

Healthy eating

Bad habits, like beds, are easy to get into but difficult to get out of. Some of us, without realizing, can neglect our body's nutritional needs. If you want to improve your quality of life and avoid obesity and diseases associated with ageing, sensible eating is the best way forward. As we age our metabolic rate slows down so age-related weight gain will occur if we don't adjust our diet or increase the amount we exercise. We need fewer calories in our 50s and 60s than we did in our 30s. Eating a balanced diet and not over-eating is important. To get the best from your diet, follow these suggestions:

- Eat at least five portions of fruit and vegetables a day.
- Base meals on starchy foods like bread, potatoes, rice or pasta.
- Drink plenty of water and cut out fizzy, sugary drinks.
- Limit consumption of saturated fats.
- Eat more fish.
- Drink less alcohol.
- Limit your salt intake.

(Source: **nidirect.gov.uk**)

Some tips to help you include:

- *Keep a food diary*: This helps you track what you eat and will identify any bad habits you may have developed.
- *Say 'no' to unhealthy food*: If you have a tendency to over-indulge and lack willpower, it's best to avoid having tempting treats such as cake, biscuits or chocolate in your kitchen.
- *Portion control is key*: Cutting down on the amount you eat, and making sure each meal contains a variety of protein, carbs and vegetables – colourful plates are usually healthier.

Should you be advised to lose weight by your GP or nutritionist, there are weight loss programmes to help you. Here are two websites, should you want to kick-start a weight-loss regime: Slimming World: **www.slimmingworld.com**; Weight Watchers: **www.weightwatchers.co.uk**.

How to keep healthy in the heat

In the very hot weather there are certain groups of people who are at risk: the very young, the elderly and the seriously ill, as heat can make heart and breathing problems worse. As long as we take sensible precautions, most of us can safely enjoy hot weather. The main risks posed by a heatwave are dehydration (not having enough water), overheating, heat exhaustion and heatstroke. The website **www.nhs.uk/Livewell/Summerhealth** offers some tips for coping in hot weather:

- Shut windows and pull down blinds when it is hot outside.
- Stay inside during the hottest time of the day.
- Take cool baths or showers.

- Drink cold drinks regularly: avoid tea, coffee and alcohol.
- Wear loose, cool clothing and take a sun hat when outdoors.
- Keep an eye on friends, relatives and neighbours who may be less able to look after themselves.

Food safety

One disadvantage of age is that we become more vulnerable to bugs and germs from incorrectly prepared food. As our immune system weakens, it is harder to fight off bacteria and serious illness. Once a food-borne illness is contracted, the infections can be difficult to treat. Many such illnesses have virus-like symptoms, which could lead to dehydration if not properly treated. The good news is there are some simple, sensible precautions that can be taken to avoid such happenings. The Food Standards Agency recommends the four 'Cs':

- cleaning;
- cooking;
- chilling;
- cross-contamination (avoiding it).

They also recommend that you stick to a food's 'use by' date and the storage instructions on the packet.

For detailed information on prevention of food poisoning, see the NHS Choices website: **www.nhs.uk/Conditions/Food-poisoning/Pages/Prevention.aspx**. In summary, their suggestions include:

- *Cleaning*: The spread of harmful bacteria and viruses can be minimized by maintaining good personal hygiene standards and keeping work surfaces and utensils clean. Regularly wash hands with soap and warm water before preparing food, after handling raw food and after touching bins or pets. If you are ill with stomach problems, *do not* handle food.
- *Cooking*: In order to kill any harmful bacteria that might be present, it is important to cook food thoroughly, particularly meat and most types of seafood. Food that is cooked thoroughly should be steaming hot in the middle. When re-heating food, make sure it is steaming hot all the way through. Do not re-heat food more than once.

- *Chilling*: Certain foods need to be kept at the correct temperature to prevent harmful bacteria from growing and multiplying. Your fridge should be set to 0–5°C (32–41°F). Cooked leftovers should be cooled quickly and then put in the fridge or freezer.
- *Cross-contamination*: This occurs when bacteria are transferred from raw foods to other foods. To prevent cross-contamination, always wash your hands after handling raw food. Raw meat should be stored in sealable containers at the bottom of the fridge so it cannot drip on to other foods. Chopping boards, knives and other utensils should be thoroughly washed after using them with raw food. *Do not wash raw meat or poultry* – any harmful bacteria will be killed by thorough cooking, and washing may splash harmful bacteria around the kitchen.

Drink (alcohol)

There is so much reported about over-indulgence with alcohol, that this topic may seem too obvious to mention. If unwinding at the end of the day with a glass of wine is something you have been used to, there's no reason to give up this pleasure. However, the more you drink, the greater the risk to your health.

For many strong-willed people, 'Dry January' is now an annual event. It forms part of their New Year resolutions, saving money they would otherwise spend on booze and donating it to charity. It also gives their liver a well-earned rest and reduces the chances of contracting liver disease. In fact all the reasons for cutting alcohol consumption are positive: feeling better in the mornings, having more energy and being less tired in the day, saving money and reducing your calorie intake. If you drink every day and feel you don't want to give up, you could try the 5 : 2 method – having two 'dry' days a week when you don't drink alcohol.

However, should you want to check how many units of alcohol you are drinking each week to see if you are overdoing things, use the NHS Change4Life drinks checker on: **www.nhs.uk/change4life**.

For people who suspect they may have a drinking problem, the first point of contact should be their GP. There are organizations to help those in need of support, such as:

- Al-Anon Family Groups UK & Eire: **www.al-anonuk.org.uk**.
- Alcohol Concern: **www.alcoholconcern.org.uk**.
- Alcoholics Anonymous: **www.alcoholics-anonymous.org.uk**.

Smoking

It's no secret that smoking is bad for your health and quitting makes life better, according to the NHS website: **www.nhs.uk/Livewell/smoking**. You will find good reasons to stop smoking here, and information on stop smoking treatments available on the NHS. The benefits for stopping smoking include slower facial ageing, healthier teeth and gums, improved lung capacity and longer life. There's a lot of help for those thinking of giving up the habit, and many websites to check. The following have good advice:

- National Centre for Smoking Cessation and Training: **www.ncsct.co.uk**;
- Quit: **www.quit.org.uk**;
- Smokefree: **quitnow.smokefree.nhs.uk**;
- Smokeline (Scotland only): **www.canstopsmoking.com**;
- Stop Smoking UK: **www.stopsmokinguk.org**.

Accident prevention

The prevention of accidents – particularly those likely to occur in the home – is something we should all be aware of. There is a section in Chapter 5, which deals with this in detail. There is further advice on safety issues to be found in Chapter 10. For anyone who feels at risk of accidents, the best advice is to consult your GP. He/she will be able to assess whether any medical problems you suffer from could make you more vulnerable, such as sleep disorders, diabetes or epilepsy. There is some good general advice to be found on this website: **www.patient.co.uk/doctor/accidents-and-their-prevention**.

Prevention of falls is something worth highlighting here. Did you know that one in three over 65s have a fall each year? Across the UK every year 1.2 million people end up in A&E after a fall, costing the NHS £1.6 billion. Falls prevention is an important challenge, and a guide called 'Get up and Go' which provides examples of exercises, and tips on how to fall-proof their home can be found on Chartered Society of Physiotherapy website: **www.csp.org.uk/publications/get-go-guide-staying-steady** (*Mature Times*, January 2016).

The Royal Society for the Prevention of Accidents also has some excellent safety advice: **www.rospa.com/home-safety/advice/general**.

Should you be unlucky enough to be injured in an accident, whether in the street or elsewhere, the National Accident Helpline, may be able to help with claiming compensation: **www.national-accident-helpline.co.uk**.

Aches, pains and other abnormalities

Recognizing signs of illness, at whatever age, is difficult. We are warned that it can take up to three weeks to get an appointment to see our GP, yet we are told not to clog up the nearest hospital's A&E department with minor complaints. How can we recognize serious warning signs when things are wrong? These can vary hugely from person to person. For example, chest pain is the most common symptom of a heart attack in both men and women, yet some people will not experience chest pain at all. Heartburn can in some cases be so severe it may be mistaken for a heart attack.

Knowing the signs and what to look out for is essential. Use the NHS 111 service for non-emergency calls. Trained advisers, supported by health care professionals, will ask you questions to assess your symptoms and immediately direct you to the best medical care for you. NHS 111 is available 24 hours a day, 365 days a year. Calls are free from landlines and mobile phones. For less urgent health needs, contact your GP or local pharmacist for advice.

The following symptoms should always be investigated by a doctor:

- any pain that lasts more than a few days;
- lumps, however small;
- dizziness or fainting;
- chest pains, shortness of breath or palpitations;
- persistent cough or hoarseness;
- unusual bleeding from anywhere;
- frequent indigestion;
- unexplained weight loss.

Health insurance

The United Kingdom is one of the few places in the world that has a universal free health service, so why would anyone choose to pay for medical care?

The main reasons (according to BUPA) are avoidance of long waiting lists, fear of catching super-bugs and concerns about hospital cleanliness.

Around 5.1 million UK residents have private medical insurance (PMI), with the industry paying out £7 million in claims every day, according to the Association of British Insurers (ABI). Health insurance pays out for private treatment if you fall ill, it also allows you to avoid long queues for treatment, receive fast-track consultations, and be treated privately in an NHS or private hospital. PMI is not essential, but if you have disposable income and your finances are in order, it can buy you peace of mind. Not every eventuality is covered by PMI, so it is important to check your policy details. The following are some of the best known organizations that provide PMI cover:

- Aviva: **www.aviva.co.uk**;
- AXA PPP Healthcare: **www.axappphealthcare.co.uk**;
- BUPA: **www.bupa.co.uk**;
- The Exeter: **www.the-exeter.com**;
- Vitality Health: **www.pruhealth.co.uk**;
- Saga: **www.saga.co.uk**;
- Simply Health: **www.simplyhealth.co.uk**.

Choosing a scheme

With so many plans on the market, seeking advice from a specialist insurance broker or intermediary is the best way to ensure you get the right health insurance policy for you. Here are two websites to investigate: Association of Medical Insurance Intermediaries (AMII): **www.amii.org.uk** and Private Healthcare UK: **www.privatehealth.co.uk**.

Private patients – without insurance cover

If you do not have private medical insurance but want to go into hospital in the UK as a private patient, there is nothing to stop you, provided your doctor is willing and you are able to pay the bills from your savings. The choice if you opt for self-pay lies between the private wings of NHS hospitals or hospitals run by charitable or non-profit-making organizations, such as: BMI Healthcare: **www.bmihealthcare.co.uk** and Nuffield Health: **www.nuffieldhealth.com**.

Medical tourism

The term 'medical tourism' refers to travellers who have chosen to have medical/dental/surgical treatment abroad. Cosmetic surgery, dental procedures and cardiac surgery are the most common procedures that medical tourists undertake.

Since the standards of medical treatments and available treatments vary widely across the world, anyone considering undertaking medical treatment abroad should carry out their own independent research. Further information and advice can be found here:

- **www.nhs.uk/NHSEngland/Healthcareabroad;**
- **www.themedicaltouristcompany.com;**
- **www.treatmentabroad.com.**

Long-term care insurance

Paying for care in old age is a growing issue. Long-term care insurance provides the financial support you need if you have to pay for care assistance for yourself or a loved one. Although government state benefits can provide some help, the level of support you receive will depend on where in the UK you live.

There are a number of different types of long-term care plans, which makes it difficult to know what would be best. Future planning involves anticipating unknowns: who is most likely to need long-term care, and for how long. Before deciding what you need, it is essential to obtain good advice. The Society of Later Life Advisers can help (**www.societyoflaterlifeadvisers.co.uk**), or an IFA through the Association of Professional Financial Advisers (**www.apfa.net**). In addition, there are three main providers of care annuities:

- Partnership Assurance: **www.partnership.co.uk;**
- Just Retirement: **www.justretirement.com;**
- Friends Life: **www.friendslife.co.uk.**

A useful booklet, *A Brief Guide to Long Term Care Insurance: Choosing the Right Option for You*, is available from the Association of British Insurers: **www.abi.org.uk.**

A possible alternative to a conventional long-term care policy is *critical illness insurance*, which pays a lump sum if you are unfortunate enough to suffer from cancer or have a stroke.

Hospital care cash plans

A hospital health care cash plan is an insurance policy that helps you pay for routine health care treatment, such as eye tests, dental treatment and physiotherapy. They are totally different to private medical insurance and can be a cheap way of paying for everyday health costs. You pay a monthly premium, depending on how much cover you want. When you receive the treatment you pay upfront, send the receipt to the insurer and it reimburses you, depending on the terms of your policy. More information is available from British Health Care Association: **www.bhca.org.uk**.

Income protection

Income protection insurance used to be known as Permanent Health Insurance. It is a replacement-of-earnings policy for people who are still in work. While highly recommended for the self-employed, many employees have some protection under an employer's policy. Either way, if you are close to retirement, income protection is unlikely to feature on your priority list.

Health screening

Personalized health assessments are a wise investment because they give an overview of your current general health and aim to identify any future health risks. Private health screening, outside the NHS, can give people peace of mind that they are not suffering from a serious health problem. There are a number of health assessment options depending on your personal needs, covering key lifestyle and health risks. For more information see:

- **www.bmihealthcare.co.uk**;
- **www.bupa.co.uk**;
- **www.privatehealth.co.uk**.

National Health Service

Choosing a GP

If you need to choose a new GP for whatever reason, it is important to find a good one. There was a great article in *The Oldie* magazine (December

2014) by Dr Tom Stuttaford entitled 'How to spot a bad physician'. The essential quality of a good GP, according to him, is 'one who is interested in individual patients, their minds as well as their bodies. They must enjoy meeting and talking with them, whatever their background, age, intellect, gender and supposed vices or beliefs. In short, an effective GP is one who cares enough to listen'.

The best way to find such a paragon is to ask for recommendations. Otherwise following the advice given on the website: **www.nhs.uk/choiceintheNHS** is a good starting point. It will help you find a suitable practice, and give you the information you need before registering with your new doctor.

Changing your GP

If you want to change your GP, you go about it in exactly the same way. Since January 2015 all GP practices in England have been free to register new patients who live outside their boundary area. (These arrangements are voluntary for GP practices. If the practice has no capacity at the time or feels that it is not clinically appropriate for you to be registered, it can refuse registration and explain its reasons for so doing.) If you know of a doctor whose list you would like to be on, you can simply turn up at his or her surgery and ask to be registered. You do not need to give a reason for wanting to change, and you do not need to ask anyone's permission. For further information see: **www.nhs.uk/NHSEngland/AboutNHSservices/doctors/Pages/patient-choice-GP-practices.aspx**.

NHS 111 service

111 is the NHS non-emergency number. It's fast, easy and free. When you call 111, you will speak to an adviser, supported by health care professionals, who will ask a number of questions to assess symptoms and direct you to the best medical care available. NHS111 is available 24 hours a day, 365 days a year. Calls are free from landlines and mobile phones. For further information see: **www.nhs.uk**.

Help with NHS costs

Although treatment on the NHS is free, there may be some additional costs, such as your journey to hospital. The NHS Low Income Scheme or Universal Credit may be able to help you.

There is more information to be found here:

- for England: **www.nhs.uk/NHSEngland/Healthcosts**;
- for Wales: **www.healthcosts.wales.nhs.uk**;
- for Northern Ireland: **www.citizensadvice.org.uk/nireland/healthcare**;
- for Scotland: **www.scotland.gov.uk/healthcosts**.

Prescriptions

The current prescription charge is £8.40, but both men and women aged 60 and over are entitled to free NHS prescriptions. Certain other groups are also entitled to free prescriptions, including those on low incomes. Leaflet HC12 NHS 'Help with Health Costs' gives full information. There are also Prescription Prepayment Certificates, which can save you money if you require a lot of medication on a regular basis.

Going into hospital

Going into hospital can cause people a lot of anxiety. You may be admitted as an outpatient, a day patient (day case), or an inpatient. Many patients are unaware that they can ask their GP to refer them to a consultant at a different NHS trust or even, in certain cases, help make arrangements for them to be treated overseas. Before you can become a patient at another hospital, your GP will need to agree to your being referred. Those likely to need help on leaving hospital should speak to the hospital social worker, who will help make any necessary arrangements. Help is sometimes available to assist patients with their travel costs to and from hospital.

If you go into hospital you will continue to receive your pension as normal. Your pension – as well as Employment and Support Allowance, Severe Disablement Allowance, Income Support and Pension Credit Guarantee Credit – will continue to be paid in full, without any reductions, for the duration of your stay. For full information see **www.nhs.uk/choiceinthenhs**. You can access NHS Northern Ireland, NHS Scotland and NHS Wales websites and information from this site.

Complaints

If you want to make a complaint about any aspect of NHS treatment you have received or been refused, go to the practice or the hospital concerned and ask for a copy of their complaints procedure. This is the same for GPs, opticians, dentists, hospitals and any care given in the NHS. Full details of how to do this can be found on NHS Choices: **www.nhs.uk/choiceinthenhs/rightsandpledges/complaints**.

You can take the matter to the Health Services Ombudsman should you be dissatisfied after an independent review has been carried out. For further details see:

- Parliamentary and Health Service Ombudsman for England: **www.ombudsman.org.uk**;
- Public Services Ombudsman for Wales: **www.ombudsman-wales.org.uk**;
- Scottish Public Services Ombudsman: **www.spso.org.uk**.

An alternative would be to get in touch with your local Patient Advice and Liaison Service office in the event of a problem with the health service. Details can be found via the NHS Choices website: **www.nhs.uk/choiceinthenhs**.

Complementary and alternative medicine

Complementary and alternative medicines are treatments that fall outside mainstream health care. Although 'complementary and alternative' medicines are often used as a single category, there are distinct differences between them. Complementary medicine is a complementary treatment that is used alongside conventional medicine, whereas alternative medicine is a treatment used in place of conventional medicine. The best known of these practices are homoeopathy, reflexology, osteopathy, chiropractic, aromatherapy, herbal remedies and hypnosis. For further information and fuller descriptions see NHS Choices website: **www.nhs.uk/Livewell/complementary-alternative-medicine**.

Information on the most popular forms can be found on the following websites:

- Association of Reflexologists: **www.aor.org.uk**;
- British Acupuncture Council: **www.acupuncture.org.uk**;
- British Chiropractic Association: **www.chiropractic-uk.co.uk**;
- British Homoeopathic Association: **www.britishhomeopathic.org**;
- British Hypnotherapy Association: **www.hypnotherapy-association.org**;
- General Osteopathic Council: **www.osteopathy.org.uk**;

- Incorporated Society of Registered Naturopaths: **naturecuresociety.co.uk**;
- National Institute of Medical Herbalists: **www.nimh.org.uk**.

Eyes

Did you know that eyes rarely hurt when there's a problem? Because our eyesight changes as we get older, almost all of us will need to wear glasses or contact lenses by the age of 65. Like most other parts of the body, we neglect them at our peril. Regular eye tests are a sensible precaution as we get older. You will find out a lot more than whether or not you need new glasses – your sight test is an important eye health check. If you are a keen driver who needs to wear glasses when behind the wheel, it is essential to ensure that your current prescription is accurate. Some of the most common eye problems include: difficulty reading, floaters, cataracts, glaucoma, and macular degeneration. Some people on low incomes can get help with costs of eye tests, people with mobility problems can request an eye test in their own home. People who are registered blind are entitled to a special tax allowance – for 2016/17 it is £2,290.

For more information on matters relating to sight, see:

- Royal National Institute of Blind People (RNIB): **www.rnib.org.uk**;
- International Glaucoma Association: **www.glaucoma-association.com**;
- Partially Sighted Society: **www.partsight.org.uk**;
- BT: **www.bt.com/includingyou**;
- British Wireless for the Blind: **www.blind.org.uk**;
- Calibre Audio Library: **www.calibre.org.uk**;
- Talking News Federation: **www.tnf.org.uk**.

Feet

You only get one pair of feet so it's essential to take good care of them. Looking after your feet is one of the most important aspects of personal health care whatever your age, as unhappy feet can cause mobility problems. Foot health is particularly significant for people with diabetes. To make sure your feet stay fit you need to keep them clean, warm and well supported. Many of us will develop some foot problems with age, simply as a result of wear and tear. Most common problems can be treated successfully by a chiropodist or podiatrist. You can find some good advice for 'fitter feet' on the Age UK website: **www.ageuk.org.uk**.

The professional association for registered chiropodists and podiatrists has a list of over 10,000 private practitioners. Society of Chiropodists and Podiatrists: **www.scpod.org**.

Hearing

Deafness is on the rise in the UK, recent research showing that more than 800,000 people are severely or profoundly deaf, and one in six of us suffer from some form of hearing loss. Signs of hearing loss can be subtle and emerge slowly, so when changes occur to this sense, it is not immediately apparent to ourselves or to others. But over time you may find social situations more stressful and this may affect you emotionally.

If you're concerned about hearing loss, early tests are advisable before deafness adversely affects relationships and your quality of life. Deafness can be socially isolating and 4 million people in the UK have undiagnosed hearing loss, according to the UK charity Action on Hearing Loss. Hearing aids are now so discreet as to be almost undetectable, and hearing aid technology is advancing constantly. If you think you are losing your hearing, take a free hearing test. Your GP can then refer you, if necessary, for further tests and advice.

Here are some of the specialist organizations that can help on hearing aids and other matters:

- Action on Hearing Loss (formerly RNID): **www.actiononhearingloss.org.uk**;
- British Deaf Association: **www.bda.org.uk**;
- British Tinnitus Association: **www.tinnitus.org.uk**;
- Hearing Link: **www.hearinglink.org**.

Sleep/insomnia

A good night's sleep elevates your mood, keeps you alert and gives you a feeling of well-being. Experts suggest that most healthy adults require seven to nine hours of sleep every night. Yet over one-third of the population suffer with insomnia or have difficulty getting to sleep. But it is difficult to define what 'normal' sleep is, because everyone is different. Sleeping problems tend to increase with age, and women are more likely to be affected than men. Many things can help you get a good night's sleep, such as controlling the light, and shutting out noise. Some tips to help you get a good night's sleep include: don't eat too close to your bedtime; avoid stimulants (alcohol, caffeine, TV and computer) if you have trouble getting to sleep; drink water before you go to sleep and on waking; open the bedroom window to get fresh air; sleep when you are actually tired rather than at a particular time. Alternatively, should your bed or mattress have seen better days, why not consider investing in new ones, which could give you more comfort and aid better sleep.

If you have difficulties sleeping, it is important to speak to your GP. There is some good advice to be found on the following websites: **www.nhs.uk/Livewell/insomnia** and **www.sleepcouncil.org.uk**.

Teeth

Did you know that World Oral Health Day is celebrated each year on 20 March? It promotes worldwide awareness of the importance of oral health and hygiene. For more information see: **www.worldoralhealthday.com**. Oral health is important because it can affect our general health. Recent research reveals that infections in the mouth can cause problems in other parts of the body. Exercise, eating a healthy diet, and keeping a normal body weight will help you maintain healthy teeth. Should you experience any of the following, visit your dentist or hygienist to have a check up: inflammation of the gums, unpleasant taste in the mouth, bad breath, loose teeth or regular mouth infections. Dentistry is one of the treatments for which you have to pay under the NHS, unless you are on a very low income. This also applies to the hygienist, should you need to see one. To find a dentist in your area, search NHS Choices: **www.nhs.uk**.

Prevention is always better than cure. If you want free, independent and impartial advice on all aspects of oral health, and free literature on a wide range of topics, including patients' rights, finding a dentist and dental care for older people, see British Dental Health Foundation: **www.dentalhealth.org**.

For those who like to be able to budget ahead for any dental bills, the best advice is to take out a dental health plan. Denplan (**www.denplan.co.uk**), one of the UK's leading dental payment plan specialists, has over 6,500 member dentists and over 2 million patients across the UK.

Personal relationships

Reaching retirement age is something many people look forward to, but it is a major lifestyle change. The first few months of retirement can be both exciting and a challenge for people. If you are a couple, personal relationships can be affected, particularly if one of you is looking forward to giving up work, and the other doesn't relish hours of free time with no idea how to fill the new-found leisure. A bit of time spent on planning and preparing for this change can ensure that any difficulties are minimized. The key to keeping personal relationships harmonious depends on your ability to share, compromise and be flexible. No one wants to join the ranks of the 'silver splitters', those whose relationships fracture after the age of 60.

Personal relationships are a key factor in determining how happy our retirement years will be, according to Relate's recent survey. According to their research, 91 per cent of people aged over 50 in the UK said that a close personal relationship is as important as good health and financial security. This emphasizes the fact that as we grow older strong and healthy personal relationships do matter. Should the need arise, the following organizations can offer help and advice:

- Marriage Care: **www.marriagecare.org.uk**;
- The Spark (formerly Scottish Marriage Care): **www.thespark.org.uk**;
- Relate: **www.relate.org.uk**;
- Relationships Scotland: **www.relationships-scotland.org.uk**.

Help for grandparents

Grandparenting is a hugely important role and around three-quarters of adults become grandparents eventually. Most people will be a grandparent for about a third of their lives. Currently grandparents get a rather good press, because more and more couples are now relying on them for help with money, time, wisdom and support with bringing up their children. This is being proved beneficial to both younger and older generations.

Being responsible but not 'in charge' requires both delicacy and tact. Mutually reliant relationships where each side has power and vulnerability can take a while to settle down, but in most cases the advantages outweigh the disadvantages. Should this extended relationship be impossible to maintain, for whatever reason, grandparents may need support. This organization can offer practical help and support when difficulties occur: Grandparents Plus: **www.grandparentsplus.org.uk**.

Depression

According to the Royal College of Psychiatrists:

> Everyone feels sad sometimes, but later life can give you more reasons to feel down. Ceasing work, having less income, health problems, death of parents, partner or friends, can all contribute to depression. Yet most older people cope well in spite of these difficulties.
>
> (Source: **www.rcpsych.ac.uk/healthadvice/problemsdisorders/depressioninolderadults.aspx**)

It has also recently been recognized that depression can occur when other health problems are diagnosed, such as hearing loss and people with visual impairment. While being treated for the condition itself, more than half the patients suffer symptoms of clinical depression but are not being diagnosed or given the treatment they need.

Undiagnosed depression is a serious matter, so if you think someone is depressed, encourage them to seek help. Outwardly it may be noticeable that they do not enjoy things as they used to; refuse opportunities to socialize; may lose their appetite and suffer weight loss; feel irritable and be sleeping badly. In such cases they should see their GP. Depression is a debilitating illness, not a sign of weakness, and requires the right help and support. Fortunately there are numerous treatments available. More information is available from these websites:

- Depression Alliance: **www.depressionalliance.org**;
- Mind: **www.mind.org.uk**;
- Samaritans: **www.samaritans.org**;
- Sane: **www.sane.org.uk**.

Some common disorders

The rest of this chapter deals with some common disorders, such as back pain and heart disease. If you are unfortunate enough to be affected, or have a member of your family who is, there are some organizations that provide information and support.

Aphasia

Aphasia is an impairment of language, affecting the production or comprehension of speech and the ability to read or write. It is due to an injury to the brain, most commonly from a stroke, particularly in older people. This condition affects a person's ability to *communicate*, but not their intelligence. The national charity that can help is the National Aphasia Association: **www.aphasia.org**.

Arthritis

There are about 200 different musculoskeletal conditions. Arthritis is a term used by doctors to describe inflammation within a joint, while rheumatism is a more general term that's used to describe aches and pains in or around the joints. The two most common forms are *osteoarthritis* and *rheumatoid arthritis*.

Osteoarthritis affects over 8 million people, and mostly affects adults over the age of 40. It is characterized by gradually worsening symptoms, including sore or stiff joints, stiffness after resting (which improves with movement), and pain that worsens after activity or towards the end of the day. The most commonly affected joints are: hands, spine, knees and hips.

Rheumatoid arthritis affects more than 400,000 people and often starts around the age of 40 or 50. Women are three times more likely to be affected than men. RA is caused by the body attacking its own tissues, producing symptoms that vary but often involving pain, fatigue, and warm, swollen, inflamed-looking joints. Although arthritis is often thought of as an older person's complaint, it accounts for the loss of an estimated 70 million working days per year in Britain.

You don't have to put up with the pain of arthritis, as there are a number of organizations that can help:

- Arthritis Action: **www.arthritisaction.org.uk**;
- Arthritis Care: **www.arthritiscare.org.uk**;
- Arthritis Research UK: **www.arthritisresearchuk.org**.

Asthma

Asthma is a common long-term condition that can cause coughing, wheezing, chest tightness and breathlessness. The severity of these symptoms varies from person to person. Asthma can be controlled well in most people most of the time. Occasionally asthma symptoms can get gradually or suddenly worse; this is known as an 'asthma attack'. Asthma is caused by inflammation of the small tubes, called bronchi, which carry air in and out of the lungs. Common asthma triggers include: house dust mites, animal fur, pollen, cigarette smoke, exercise and viral infections. Asthma can develop at any age. Full details of this condition can be found on the NHS website: **www.nhs.uk/conditions/asthma/Pages/Introduction.aspx**.

For more information and advice, see Asthma UK's website: **www.asthma.org.uk**.

Back pain

Back pain is a common problem that affects most people at some stage of their lives. It may be triggered by bad posture while sitting or standing, bending awkwardly or lifting incorrectly. In most cases back pain will improve within a few weeks or months, although some people experience long-term pain that keeps recurring. Regular exercise such as walking or swimming, or activities such as yoga or pilates, are an excellent way of improving flexibility and strengthening back muscles. There is good advice to be found at **www.nhs.uk/Conditions/Back-pain**, and more information is available from Back Care: **www.backcare.org.uk**.

Blood pressure

As we get older, we need to watch our blood pressure. The higher our blood pressure becomes the higher the risk of (at some stage) a heart attack or a stroke. Having high blood pressure (hypertension) is not usually something we feel or notice. The only way to find out the level of our blood pressure is to have it measured. Even if we do not have high blood pressure at the moment, it is important that we keep blood pressure as low as we possibly can.

The good news is that if it is found that you do have high blood pressure, healthy lifestyle changes will help to bring it down. Recommendations for keeping blood pressure low include: reduce salt intake, eat more fruit and vegetables, keep to a healthy weight, reduce alcohol and keep active. A lot of information and advice can be found on the website for Blood Pressure UK: **www.bloodpressureuk.org**.

Cancer

Cancer has such a high profile today that the media report frequently about new research and survival statistics. Nearly all of us are or have been affected by this disease either directly or indirectly. According to Cancer Research UK, cancer survival in the UK has doubled in the last 40 years. One in 30 people living in the UK either has cancer or is in remission. More men are surviving prostate and bowel cancer, and women with breast cancer have a better outlook than ever before. But the UK still lags behind other European countries in terms of cancer survival. Cancer Research UK says that part of the problem is unhealthy lifestyles. It is estimated that about a third of cancers are caused by smoking, diet, alcohol and obesity. Early diagnosis is paramount, so it goes without saying that anyone with a lump or swelling, or unexplained tiredness or weight loss, should have it investigated by their doctor.

There are now over 300 cancer charities in existence, each researching or focusing on a particular variant of the disease. Here are a few, but to find a list of all of them consult **www.charitychoice.co.uk**:

- Beating Bowel Cancer: **www.beatingbowelcancer.org**;
- Bowel Cancer UK: **www.bowelcanceruk.org.uk**;
- Breast Cancer Care: **www.breastcancercare.org.uk**;
- Cancer Research UK: **www.cancerresearch.org**;
- Macmillan Cancer Support: **www.macmillan.org.uk**;
- Marie Curie Cancer Care: **www.mariecurie.org.uk**.

Chest and heart diseases

New research found that 70 per cent of people aged 45 and over say they are not worried about their heart health, despite the fact that over 2.3 million people are thought to be living with some form of coronary heart disease in the United Kingdom. The survey (commissioned by Sirco – the first scientifically proven drink to help maintain cardiovascular health) also questioned people as to what lifestyle changes they have made to help improve their heart health. The two main causes of heart disease are unhealthy blood and high cholesterol.

Keeping your heart healthy, whatever your age, is the most important thing you can do to help prevent and manage heart disease. The earlier sections on smoking, diet, drink and exercise list some of the most pertinent 'dos and don'ts' that can help. More information on heart disease can be found on: **www.nhs.uk/conditions/Coronary-heart-disease**.

The following charity plays a leading role in the fight against diseases of the heart and circulation: British Heart Foundation: **www.bhf.org.uk**.

Constipation

According to recent research, 66,000 people were admitted to hospital with constipation in 2014/15 – that's 182 people per day. Of those, 48,409 were unplanned emergency admissions, meaning they went to A&E for a condition that's easily preventable or could be treated at home. In other words, Britons' embarrassment over their bowel movements costs the NHS £145 million a year (*Mature Times*, April 2016, **www.maturetimes.co.uk/constipation-costs-nhs-145-million-year**). Before becoming too alarmed, there are some simple steps that can be taken to avoid constipation or to relieve it:

- Drink plenty of water.
- Include lots of fibre in your diet.
- Eat little and often.
- Chew food slowly and thoroughly.
- Establish a routine (bodies are creatures of habit).
- Keep a food diary (if you suspect a certain food is causing problems).
- Visit your GP for treatment if the condition persists.

Diabetes

Diabetes is a common lifelong health condition where the amount of glucose in the blood is too high. Symptoms occur because some or all of the glucose stays in the blood, and isn't being used as fuel for energy. New figures released by the charity Diabetes UK, show that 700 people a day are diagnosed with diabetes in the UK – that's one person every two minutes.

There are two main types of diabetes: type 1 and type 2. In type 1 diabetes the signs and symptoms are very obvious and develop quickly over a few weeks. In type 2 diabetes the signs and symptoms are not so obvious, as the condition develops slowly, possibly over a number of years, and may only be picked up at a routine medical check-up.

The main symptoms of diabetes are: feeling very thirsty; urinating more frequently than usual (especially at night); extreme tiredness; weight loss and loss of muscle bulk; cuts or wounds that heal slowly; blurred vision. To help people get a better understanding of their diabetes, Diabetes UK have produced a free book, *100 Things I Wish I'd Known About Diabetes*, written by people living with diabetes for people living with diabetes. For further information see Diabetes UK: **www.diabetes.org.uk**.

Migraine

A migraine is usually a severe headache felt as a throbbing pain at the front or side of the head. Some people have other symptoms, such as nausea, vomiting, and increased sensitivity to light and sound. Migraine is a chronic health condition that affects over 10 million people in the UK. Most of the time migraines are not a threat to your overall health but they can interfere considerably with your day-to-day quality of life. Migraines are more common in women but often become less severe and less frequent with age. More information can be found **www.nhs.uk/conditions/migraine**.

The Migraine Trust funds research, provides evidence-based information, campaigns for and supports people affected by migraine in the United Kingdom. See: **www.migrainetrust.org**.

Osteoporosis and menopause problems

Osteoporosis is a disease that causes bone tissue to thin and become less dense. Maximum bone density and strength are achieved around the age of 30. From the age of 35 our bones begin to weaken gradually as most of us become less active. For women, bone loss is usually most rapid during the first few years after menopause, during which time women's levels of the hormone oestrogen naturally decrease. This can lead to osteoporosis, a condition in which bones become so fragile that they can break very easily. The most common injuries from falls affect the spine, hip and wrist. One in two women (and one in five men) suffers from osteoporosis.

Age UK has compiled a list of ways to boost bone health:

- Weight-bearing exercise is important to help keep your bones strong. Walking, tennis, aerobics and dancing strengthen your bones.
- Enjoy a balanced diet. Milk, cheese, yoghurt, baked beans, lentils and dried apricots are great sources of calcium.
- Taking a stroll in the summer sun (just 10 minutes will help) is a great way of absorbing vitamin D, which keeps bones healthy.
- Avoid smoking. Smokers lose bone density at a faster rate than non-smokers.
- Drink moderately.

The following websites may be useful:

- National Osteoporosis Society: **www.nos.org.uk**;

- The British Menopause Society: **www.thebms.org.uk**;
- Women's Health Concern: **www.womens-health-concern.org**.

Stroke

A stroke is a serious, life-threatening medical condition that occurs when the blood supply to part of the brain is cut off. Strokes are a medical emergency and urgent treatment is essential because the sooner the person receives treatment for a stroke, the less damage is likely to happen. Every year over 150,000 people in England alone suffer a stroke. People over 65 are most at risk and it has recently been discovered that iron deficiency may lead to an increased risk of suffering a stroke. Prevention is similar to the steps you can take to avoid heart disease.

A stroke has a greater disability impact than any other medical condition. Most people experience a faster period of recovery just after a stroke; this is followed by a longer period of slower rehabilitation. If you come across someone who may be having a stroke, remember the word 'FAST'. This stands for face – arms – speech – time. Look out for:

- *Face*: If the person's face droops on one side, or they cannot smile evenly.
- *Arms*: If the person cannot lift one or both arms and keep them up because of weakness or numbness.
- *Speech*: If speech becomes slurred or garbled, or if the person finds it difficult to talk.
- *Time*: If you see any of these symptoms and suspect a stroke, dial 999 immediately. A stroke is a medical emergency that requires immediate professional attention.

(Source: **www.nhs.uk/conditions/stroke**)

The Stroke Association is the only UK-wide charity solely concerned with combating stroke in people of all ages. See Stroke Association: **www.stroke.org.uk**.

Disability

Disability is covered in Chapter 10. If you or someone in your family has a problem not mentioned here, you may look there to find the answer you need.

Chapter Seven
Starting your own business

'Screw it – let's do it!'

SIR RICHARD BRANSON

'I have always found that plans are useless but planning is indispensable.'

GENERAL EISENHOWER

The number of small businesses now account for over 15 per cent of occupations. More and more people are setting up their own business and becoming their own boss. Whether it is earning £2,000 to supplement a pension, or building a business that can keep you earning and occupied for years to come beyond your intended retirement date, this is the chapter for you. While financially rewarding, this is not the only reason people want to start a business, as social and emotional benefits also feature. It may even be a route to providing more freedom than that available in corporate structures, where endless meetings may start to lose their appeal for the 50-plus age group and at a time when there is still time to learn a new trick or two. It may even rekindle a passion for work and a can-do attitude. Importantly, you will not be alone and this chapter will signpost you to plenty of help and support – and most of it is free (it is just a matter of knowing where to look!).

Key points in this chapter

This chapter will give you the confidence to get started and has plenty of straightforward advice. The key issues covered are:

- Starting a small business in just one page.
- Understanding the differences between starting a small business and employment, especially if both options are still open to you.
- Do I need to bother with a business plan?
- Getting off to a good start – practical and emotional tips and buying your first equipment.
- Administration, finance and tax – keep on top of the paperwork or it will keep on top of you!
- Filling the diary with work, and some clever tips for marketing that will make a difference.
- The trading format – should you set up your own limited liability company, work as a sole trader or maybe go into partnership?
- Other ways of getting started and operational issues.
- Where you can go for further help – remember you are not alone and these are enterprising times in the United Kingdom.
- A summary checklist to help you tick off the key issues once you decide to get started in business.

Start a small business – in one page

This one section will get you on the way to starting a small business as a sole trader – just follow this step-by-step guide:

- Find something you enjoy doing and/or goods or services that you know you can sell.
- Register as self-employed with Her Majesty's Revenue & Customs (HMRC) on 0300 200 3500, or for customers who are deaf or hard of hearing on 0845 915 3519 (textphone) and say you're calling to register as self-employed. Or register via **www.gov.uk** (then go to 'Set up as a sole trader').
- You will then have to complete HMRC's self-assessment form each year and declare your taxable income. Check **www.gov.uk/government/**

organisations/hm-revenue-customs for guidance on the basics of Income Tax.

- Acquire some files and keep a list of your income and costs, sales invoices, purchases receipts, bank statements, cash books. If it 'proves' your business transactions, you must keep it for six years.
- The big lesson: HMRC don't like people evading tax (it is illegal!). If you have acted honestly, kept your records and help HMRC with their questions you will have little to worry about. But if you can't prove your transactions then you will be charged the tax that HMRC believe they were due, plus a penalty of up to an extra 100 per cent plus interest. They can go back six years without much fuss and even longer if they believe your errors were deliberate.
- If you are self-employed and keep good records you may be able to prepare the year-end accounts and self-assessment tax return by yourself. In time your business may generate enough to pay an accountant or a bookkeeper for some assistance or to handle all accounts and tax on your behalf.
- To help your business grow (the vital bit!), jump to the marketing section. The tips should take you to the next level and, in time, you may benefit from delving into even more of this chapter and our hints and tips.

The secret ingredient

Co-editor, chartered accountant and business adviser Allan Esler Smith, has helped hundreds of people set up in business. Here he offers his advice on the secret ingredient for starting your own business and bringing in potentially a vital extra income:

> Of all the businesses I see, the ones that seem to do better have a secret ingredient. It's actually quite simple and is the 'can do' and positive attitude of the business owner. They also have the ability to press on with their vision and deliver on what they say. They seek out and are good at listening to others who have experience of running their own businesses and listen to their advisers (old dogs can learn new tricks!). However, they recognize, at the end of the day, it's down to them.
>
> On the other hand, the businesses that falter seem to do the opposite and never quite reach their potential.

Maybe some of those reading this chapter will follow Richard Branson's mantra 'Screw it – let's do it', ie take a view on the risk, weigh it up against the opportunity and then get on with it (or out of it). Again, recognition that, at the end of the day, it's down to you is worth repeating here for a second time as it is so important!

Some of the differences between starting a small business and employment

In some cases where there is an opportunity to start a small business there could be a similar opportunity to take a full- or part-time employed position. Which route is right for you?

Here are some of the reasons for starting a small business:

- focus on what you are best at or enjoy;
- be your own boss and therefore benefit from very rapid decision making;
- flexibility (around other interests/responsibilities);
- freedom to organize things your way;
- no commuting;
- less involvement in internal politics and no more pointless meetings;
- enjoy working on your own;
- developing a unique idea or delivering a better solution/product;
- provide a legacy for your children;
- the more you put in, the more you get out.

On the other hand, here are some of the reasons for seeking a part- or full-time employed position:

- a local employer with known travel requirements;
- security of income;
- benefits of holiday pay, pension, paid sick leave, and perhaps private health and life cover;
- bonuses and perhaps a car;
- team aspect and friendship of colleagues;
- no personal liability if things go badly wrong;
- staff discounts or other perks.

Why bother with a plan?

There are thousands of success stories about those who took the plunge nearing or post-retirement to build a business that provided involvement, fun and income and maybe even a legacy for their children. However, for every three success stories there is a business that does not work out and your money could disappear fast if you set up in the wrong way or over-stretch yourself. Worst of all, you could lose your home if things go really badly wrong, so the reasons below and tips throughout this chapter should help you understand and deal with the risks.

Why businesses fail – learning the lessons

Businesses can fail for many reasons. Learn from the mistakes of others and you will be doing yourself a favour. The number one reason why businesses fail is that *the market moves on and you are left behind*. Take time out to think and keep abreast of what your customers really want (have you tried asking them recently?). Where are your competitors and what are they doing to keep on top of or ahead of the market and, overall, how is the market moving?

A second reason (and one that will continue to increase in 2017 as HMRC increases its resources on tackling tax evasion and avoidance) is the *failure to deal with tax affairs properly*. The implications of penalties and interest levied by HMRC are often ignored and only hit home when it is too late. Keep your books properly and retain all records for seven years after the year end – in brief, if you can't prove it, you may lose the tax benefit and pay additional tax, penalties and interest. If there is a problem, HMRC can go back and inspect previous years' accounts (for up to six years or even longer). If you fail to pay your tax fully when it is due, HMRC will pursue you vigorously and you are giving them a reason to have a closer look at you and your business. On the other hand, if you have genuine cash flow difficulties and cannot pay your tax on the due date, talk to HMRC and you may find their attitude refreshing (especially if it is the first time you have stumbled).

Other reasons include a failure to plan and also bad debts (where the customer goes bust and cannot pay your invoices), as this will come off your bottom-line profit and can really hurt. There are a few simple steps that you can take to reduce the potential of taking such a hit. What are your credit terms and have you encouraged all customers to pay electronically? Do you contact them as soon as your invoices become overdue? Do you require cash on delivery or prepayment? PayPal and mobile credit card machines are transforming the payment services. In some cases it is worth remembering that a bad customer is sometimes worse than no customer at all.

So 'why bother' when it comes to planning? The answer should now be evident from the above – you are improving your chances of succeeding and may even do rather better than you first thought.

What goes into a plan?

'I have always found that plans are useless but planning is indispensable.' This is a quote from General Eisenhower and is about planning for battle. We can draw a couple of lessons from this but the starting point is to make a promise that you will put your plan in writing. Too many people run a mile when the subject of a plan comes up, especially the notion of a grand-sounding business plan. Some new businesses – perhaps armed with confidence gained from a book on setting up a business, business banking literature, or even after attending a setting-up-in-business course – start a plan but never get it finished.

The reason for this is twofold: first, fear of the planning process and, second, intimidation by daunting plan templates and spreadsheets seen in some books or banking literature. The prescription is a three-stage plan that will get you started and then, with experience, you can tweak it and make it that bit slicker.

Stage 1 of the plan: objectives

What, financially, do you need to set as objectives to bring you in that £2,000 or £20,000 or £60,000 which you need to help reach and attain the lifestyle you desire? This takes a bit of thinking through but you should be able to come up with two or three simple objectives based on income, gross profit (if you sell stock) and overheads.

For someone who sells advice-based services and who does not sell stock there could be just two objectives.

Objective 1: I aim to invoice £30,000 in my first year of trading based on working at least 100 days at an average billing rate of £300 per day. I will review my billing rates quarterly and my performance monthly.

Objective 2: I will aim to keep my overheads (after expenses recharged to clients) in my first year to £5,000.

Then, for the more complicated businesses, for example one that trades in buying and selling stock, you will need a further objective based around the difference between sales price and purchase price. *Objective 3* will be something like: I will aim to achieve the following gross profit percentages:

- product line A: 30 per cent;
- product line B: 40 per cent;
- product line C: 50 per cent;
- gross profit percentages are calculated using: (sales price less cost of materials/product sold ÷ sales price) × 100.

The key point with objectives is that less gives more: you don't want a long list of objectives.

Stage 2 of the plan: your market research

The next page of your plan should be all about your marketing effort: this is a topic that is often misunderstood and mistaken for advertising. Think about approaching this section under the following three headings: products, customers and competitors.

Products

Start with your main product or service and think about the features and benefits of what you are selling. Understanding these and discussing them with your trusted advisers will allow you to start thinking about other related services or goods that you could offer.

Customers

For each main product area ask lots of questions to tease out your research. Who are my customers? Where are they based? When do they tend to buy? How and where do they tend to buy and at what price? How should I contact them? Keep asking those important questions of who, what, why, where, when and how – as they tease out all sorts of quality research information that you can action.

Competitors

Again, ask yourself who, what, why, where, when and how? This should lead to a series of activities that you can do to help secure new quality work and customers (note that the marketing section later on in this chapter has further tips). If you end up with a jumble of unfocused ideas try ranking each idea on the basis of priority, impact and cost (free is good!).

Stage 3 of the plan: your income and expenditure forecast

This is your income and expenditure forecast for the year and this third stage is the tricky one. It is your map for the year ahead financially and will allow you to monitor your actual performance against the plan. You can then do something about it when you are off target. You should be able to do this yourself, but if it becomes a struggle ask your accountant or a friend who has their own business to help.

Is there more?

Once you have completed your first plan keep it alive and keep reviewing how you are doing against it; even if the plan is useless you will find, as Eisenhower did, that the planning process itself teases out things that will make things that little bit better – guaranteed!

Practical and emotional tips

Your partner's attitude is crucial. Even if not directly involved, he or she may have to accept (at least initially) the loss of some space in the house to give you an office. Do you have space available to work from home initially or would you need/prefer to rent accommodation? There will be the added distractions of out-of-hours phone calls and, perhaps, suddenly cancelled social engagements depending on your business. Can your family/partner cope with having you and your business in the house? Can you cope without the resources/back-up provided by an employer (IT/HR/training/administrative support) – as you will have to do it yourself or buy it in.

Keep on top of the paperwork

Generally, this one topic causes the most groans! But simple bookkeeping, if done properly, is just a by-product of your business and flows naturally from raising sales invoices or receipts to track income and tracking what you pay for, when and how. As a bonus, you will never miss an unpaid sales invoice if you are on top of your bookkeeping.

An even more compelling reason for doing your own bookkeeping is that HMRC has a 'prove it or lose it' view of enquiring into an aspect of your tax return. Under the system of self-assessment, HMRC relies on you completing your tax returns. In the case of an enquiry, HMRC tells you precisely what part of your tax return is under investigation and you are expected to be able to validate sample payments or receipts. If you are unable to prove the expenditure, you lose it as far as HMRC is concerned, resulting in, for example, fewer purchases being accepted as a deduction from your profits and more tax to pay. There will be penalties and interest to pay and the scope of HMRC's enquiries will be widened, which means more time, distraction from your business and, probably, stress.

Basic bookkeeping

All incoming and outgoing payments need to be recorded throughout the year. Records of outgoings need to be categorized according to type; examples of some categories you might need to consider are: stock, subscriptions/meeting fees, office equipment, office supplies, post and courier costs; travel fares, parking and subsistence; telephone and internet; sundry; accountancy and professional fees; and insurance.

Many small business owners opt to do their own bookkeeping, with or without the help of a computer software package. If you opt for a software package choose one that your accountant understands as their fees should then be less. For many small businesses your accountant should be able to provide some Excel spreadsheets that will do the job, together with a bookkeeping guide to help get you started.

If you are really averse to bookkeeping yourself, consider hiring a bookkeeper. Bookkeepers currently charge between about £16 and £23 per hour, depending on geographical location and experience, and can be found by recommendation from your accountant or business network contacts.

Accountants

Depending on qualifications and experience, accountants assisting new small start-up businesses could charge from £35 to about £120 per hour to assist you in setting up in business and to prepare your accounts and tax.

Anyone can call themselves an accountant so it can be a bit hit and miss with very variable quality when things go wrong at the lower end of the spectrum (and sometimes even with seemingly respectable firms claiming to have thousands of clients). Unreturned calls and not dealing factually with enquiries and questions, vague verbal assurances and not dealing with formal complaints are all part of the 'deal' when you end up with a lower-end accountant. If there are mistakes in your accounts and tax you will also find that you are very much on your own when it comes to dealing with HMRC enquiries. Lower-end accountants may neither be regulated by a professional body nor have professional indemnity insurance. What should you look for? The letters ACA or FCA after the accountant's name mean that you can be assured that you are dealing with a Chartered Accountant.

Some accountancy firms offer a combination of bookkeeping, accountancy and tax services and, if so, you can expect to pay a premium on the bookkeeping hourly rates quoted above. Ask your trusted family members or friends if they can recommend an accountant. Then ensure you get clarity on three things: 1) confirmation of the accountant's qualifications (the type of qualification); 2) the professional body you would complain to if there is ever a problem; and 3) check that they hold professional indemnity insurance. These three points would usually be clarified by an accountant; if you have to actually ask for them it probably tells you a lot. It is advisable to meet at least two accountants and see how you feel about rapport and the availability of proactive hints and tips. Make sure you believe you can get on with the accountant you select as it is likely to be a long and mutually beneficial relationship. Will the person you meet be the person who does your accounts and tax and provides proactive advice? Get written confirmation of hourly rates plus an estimate of fees for the year, and get clarity on what happens if you decide to change accountants halfway through the year if fees are paid up front or monthly. Most accountants would be used to providing clients with a 'retainer', clarifying the above and what you and the accountant will do and by when. A good accountant who knows your industry area will be able to help with general guidance and offer input to your plan on marketing and pricing, drawing on experience beyond accounting and tax.

Finally, there is sometimes some confusion over the term 'audit of accounts'. Many years ago, smallish companies in the UK had to have an audit of their accounts. The turnover threshold (one of three thresholds) for being required to have an audit has been increased and currently stands at £10.2 million, so the vast majority of start-ups need not concern themselves with audited accounts.

Paying tax and National Insurance

Sole traders

Self-employed individuals running their own businesses are usually called 'sole traders'. All new businesses that trade as sole traders need to register as self-employed with HMRC on 0300 200 3500, or for customers who are deaf or hard of hearing on 0845 915 3519 (textphone) and say you're calling to register as self-employed. Or register via **www.gov.uk** (then go to 'Set up as a sole trader').

While tax can be daunting, some sole traders with relatively straightforward billing and overheads do their own tax returns and pay income tax on their profits. With Income Tax, you first have a Personal Allowance, which gives you a tax-free amount, and then any excess income (including your profits) is taxed at 20 per cent, then over a certain limit at 40 per cent and then 45 per cent. The precise yearly limits are available from the HMRC website or your accountant. In very broad terms, if you are under 65, you currently (summer 2016) have a tax-free allowance of £11,000 which will rise to £11,500 in April 2017 as part of this government's commitment to increase the level at which individuals start to pay tax to £12,500 by 2020.

You are then taxed on the *next* £32,000 at 20 per cent (rising to £33,500 in April 2017) as part of the Government's commitment to increase the level at which an individual pays tax at 40 per cent to £50,000 by 2020. For 2017/18 an individual will be able to earn £45,000 before having to pay tax at 40 per cent (ie £11,500 Personal Allowance at 0 per cent tax and then £33,500 at 20 per cent). Then 40 per cent tax applies to further taxable income up to £150,000. Anything above £150,000 gets taxed at 45 per cent.

Many sole traders choose to run their bookkeeping for the year to 5 April to coincide with the tax year end (or 31 March, which HMRC effectively accepts as equivalent to 5 April).

If you are past the state retirement age there will be no National Insurance Contributions (NICs) to pay. Subject to this, sole traders are liable for Class 2 NICs (currently a nominal amount of £2.80 per week, which will be abolished from 6 April 2018). You are also liable for the much more significant Class 4 NICs that are assessed and collected by HMRC at the same time as assessing your Income Tax on profits. Currently (summer 2016) these are at 9 per cent on profits between £8,060 and £43,000 and this reduces to just 2 per cent on profits over £43,000.

The payment of sole-trader Income Tax is reasonably straightforward but there is a twist in your first year of trading. Assuming that you have a year end of 5 April 2018, the first payment will be due by 31 January 2019 so you have a long period of (effectively) interest-free credit, as some of the profits on which the tax is due may have been earned as long ago as May 2017. With the first payment, however, you get a 'double whammy' as you also have to pay on 31 January 2019 a payment on account of your second year's trading. Then on 31 July 2019 you have to make a second on-account payment of the second year's trading. Both on-account payments are set by default on the basis of your year 1 profits. You can 'claim' a reduction if year 2 is proving to have lower profits than year 1; your accountant will help you with this if it is appropriate.

After the initial tax famine, followed by (effectively) a double payment of tax, you will thereafter pay tax twice a year. Payments need to be made by 31 January (during the tax year) and then by 31 July after the end of that tax year, with any overpayment or underpayment sorted out by the following 31 January. Many sole-trader businesses set up a reserve bank account in addition to their current account, and place a percentage of their income aside, which is earning interest each month (albeit not amounting to much in the current climate). This tactic should help you resist the temptation to raid money that is not for spending – and ensure you can pay your tax on time.

Additionally, as a self-employed person you are allowed certain other reliefs. Ask your accountant, but the following expenses and allowances are usually tax deductible:

- *Business expenses*: These must be incurred 'wholly and exclusively' for the purposes of the trade. Office supplies that you buy will probably qualify; however, any business entertaining will not.
- *Partially allowable expenses*: These mainly apply if you are working from home. They include such items as the part of your rent (or mortgage interest), heating, lighting and telephone usage that you devote to business purposes, and also possibly some of the running expenses on your car, if you use your car for your business.
- *Spouse's wages*: If you employ your partner in the business, his or her pay (provided this is reasonable) qualifies as a legitimate expense, in the same way as any other employee's, but must be accounted for through a PAYE system.
- *Pension contributions*: Tax relief is generally available for pension contributions at the higher of £3,600 (gross) or 100 per cent of relevant earnings up to a maximum of £40,000 (this is subject to a tapered reduction for taxpayers with 'adjusted income' in excess of £150,000).
- *Capital allowances*: This is a tax break for expenditure on equipment.

Partnerships

Partnership tax is broadly similar to the process described above for a sole trader, with the exception of some more paperwork due to submitting each partner's individual personal self-assessment tax return and a composite partnership tax return.

Limited company

Companies pay corporation tax on their profits (currently at summer 2016 at 20 per cent and reducing to 19 per cent in April 2017 and then 17 per cent in April 2020). Your company accounts need to be finalized and any corporation tax paid nine months after your year end.

The key point with a company is that the money coming in is not your money – it is the company's money – so how do you extract your money? The first option is salary and this means running a Pay As You Earn (PAYE) system: another form of tax with a rigorous calculation regime and payments that have to be made to HMRC. PAYE carries the income tax rates as featured for the sole trader, but NICs (National Insurance Contributions) are much higher as these are a composite of employee *and* employer NICs (as the company is an employer). Currently these are 12 per cent employee NICs on £8,060 to £43,000, reducing to 2 per cent for amounts above £43,000 and then an additional 13.8 per cent employer NICs on everything above £8,112. Salary and employer's NICs are deductible when calculating corporation tax.

The second option for extracting funds is dividends, but these are not deductible when calculating your corporation tax. From April 2016, significant changes were introduced to the dividend tax regime. The change is designed to reduce what the government perceived to be an incentive for companies to extract profits through a dividend due to (until then) lower overall rates of tax. The following was implemented:

- There is now a new annual dividend allowance of £5,000 that is tax-free.
- The 1/9 Tax Credit has disappeared.
- The new rates of tax on dividend are 7.5 per cent if the dividend falls in the basic rate tax band, 32.5 per cent if it falls in the higher-rate tax band (£43,000 to £150,000) and 38.1 per cent if it falls in the additional rate tax band (£150,000 plus).

For some contracting or consultancy type businesses that trade as companies there is a further possible 'tax trap' for the unwary known as HMRC regulation number 35 (IR35) that came into force in April 2000. HMRC is particularly interested in ex-employees setting up service companies that work exclusively for their former employer or for just a few clients (sometimes called 'personal service companies' to use an HMRC term – and sometimes called 'freelancers'). This is an extremely wide-ranging and difficult subject but, in very simplified terms, IR35 is to be avoided if at all possible and it only applies to companies (not sole traders).

There are many hints and tips and some urban myths about IR35 all of which are outside the scope of this guide. It is a big issue and one that you have first got to recognize and then, if potentially applicable, do something about. One of the key players in helping freelancers guide themselves through the minefield of IR35 is the Association of Independent Professionals and the Self Employed (IPSE) at **www.ipse.co.uk**. This organization, working in conjunction with a chartered accountant who understands IR35, is probably your next step if you are concerned. Briefly, if you fall foul of IR35, the tax inspector will seek to set aside the dividends you have paid and treat the dividend payment as if it were subject to PAYE and NICs (including employer NICs) and the tax advantage you thought you may have had could disappear.

Registering for VAT

Value Added Tax (VAT) was introduced in 1973 and it seems that many people have lost sight of the name of this tax and especially the word 'added'. You are, in effect, adding a tax and are an unpaid tax collector.

If your taxable turnover is likely to be more than £83,000 in a 12-month period, you must register for VAT unless your supplies/services are outside the scope of VAT. Any expenses that you recharge to clients need to be included in the calculation of taxable turnover.

UK business clients are invariably registered for VAT so are not concerned about having VAT added to your invoice as they can reclaim the VAT. For that reason, some businesses register for VAT before reaching the £83,000 compulsory registration limit so that they can claim VAT on their purchases. If your turnover is less than £83,000 and before voluntarily applying consider whether registration will really be of benefit to you, that is, whether reclaiming the VAT paid on items needed for your business (such as office equipment) is worth the trouble of sending in mandatory, quarterly VAT returns and keeping separate VAT records.

You can claim back VAT on pre-start/pre-registration expenditure involved in setting up the business. If you elect for 'cash accounting' status, this means that VAT only becomes payable or reclaimable when invoices are actually paid. It avoids having to pay the VAT on your own sales invoices before slow-paying clients pay you, which creates cash-flow problems. One final positive if you do register for VAT is that it seems to give you added credibility with clients.

VAT flat-rate scheme

HMRC introduced the flat-rate scheme in 2004, with the aim of simplifying record keeping for small businesses. This allows you to charge VAT to your clients at the standard rate of 20 per cent and to pay VAT as a percentage of your VAT-inclusive turnover (instead of having to work out the VAT payable on your sales less purchases). You can apply to join the scheme if your taxable turnover (excluding VAT) will not be more than £150,000 in the next 12 months.

HMRC publishes a list of business categories from which you need to decide which best describes your business. A further bonus is that you can deduct 1 per cent from the flat rate that you use for your first year of VAT registration. As a tip, do not do anything without checking it out with your accountant as there are a few twists and turns that could make the VAT flat-rate scheme unsuitable. But, at face value, it seems to have been beneficial to many small businesses.

Marketing tips to fill your diary

It is a sad fact that many new business owners believe that marketing simply means placing an advert in some well-known directory. This will achieve only a fraction of the sales of any comparable business with a decent grasp of marketing. So how can you generate sales for a new business? The following tips should start to help you along.

1 *Your own website and/or social media.* Business and the public rely heavily on the internet and a presence is vital either through a website and/or harnessing social media. Is there a vital domain name (website unique address) that you need to secure and register? If this one question alone fills you with fear the solutions are nearer than you think – just try asking friends and don't ignore help that is right in front of your nose: young friends or relatives may know more than you.

   It is also worth checking out websites run by trade or professional associations that may allow you to register and set up a profile. You can set up profiles on various social media 'networking websites' such as LinkedIn. Depending on your business, Facebook and Twitter can provide the benefits of building your online contacts and allow you to showcase your expertise in a certain area. Social media (very like networking, below) is not about sell, sell, sell. It is more about building relationships and trust with an ever-increasing contact list.

2 *Personal contacts and networking.* Once you decide to set up your own business, your personal contacts, ex-colleagues or other small business owners are a potential source of work. Too many small businesses forget that behind every contact there is another layer of potential contacts, who are just one introduction away; so ignore this multiplier effect at your peril. In your first year you should be re-educating your contacts to think of you not as 'Jane who used to work at IBM' but 'Jane who now runs her own business advising small businesses on their IT needs'. Do not be afraid to pick up the phone or send business cards explaining your new business and what you can offer. Joining the best trade or professional association you can find will be a great way of networking, with the added bonus of research facilities, information and other fringe benefits.

3 *Discounts and offers.* These can be used to great effect during seasonal dips, introducing a new service or clearing old stock. Whether it is 20 per cent off, a buy-one-get-one-free offer or the numerous variations of this basic approach, there are three golden rules:

Always state the original or usual price (to show the value in the offer).

Always specify an expiry date.

Always explain that the offer is subject to availability.

4 *Flyers and business cards.* Generally speaking, a response rate of 1 per cent to a flyer is considered fairly good. With some clever thinking you can increase the response rate. Have you targeted the flyer? A good example would be a wedding gown designer who neatly persuades a sought-after wedding location hotel to keep a flyer dispenser in their foyer. Are you able to include your professional or trade association logo on your flyer and business cards? Have you asked if this is possible? There are two sides to a flyer and business card – have you thought about putting information on the blank reverse side? Could this contain some useful tips or, perhaps, a special offer or discount? Anything that ensures the card or flyer is kept rather than dumped will help your business to edge ahead.

5 *Testimonials*. People generally buy on trust, and testimonials show prospective customers that you have done a good job and can be relied upon. Positive testimonials can be powerful and should never be underestimated.

6 *Agencies*. Agencies will be especially important for prospective consultants or contractors, as many recruitment agencies also place full- and part-time contracts (as opposed to employed positions). The contract market is growing and offers dynamic and fast-moving industries the opportunity to hire (and fire) swiftly. When marketing yourself through an agency the same rules apply as when marketing yourself to a potential employer. Good personal and written presentation will help the agency to sell you on to its clients – and it is in their interest to find you work, given the fee they receive for placing you.

7 *Advertising*. There are many options for advertising yourself and your business, such as website banners, free and paid-for directory listings. Another approach could be 'free' advertising through a press release that you forward to local or trade press with an interesting story. A clever variant is advertising yourself and your skills by writing articles in professional or trade journals – what do you have that is news or novel or leading edge?

8 *Sponsorship*. Another subset of advertising is sponsorship. The driving instructor who sponsored the playing shirts on the local under-17s football team is a great example of cost-effective and rather clever sponsorship.

9 *Awards*. Business awards can offer new businesses an opportunity to make a splash in the local area, introduce you to other vibrant businesses, and there may even be a category for mature business owners newly starting up. These are often sponsored by local press and the Federation of Small Businesses (**www.fsb.org.uk**), where more information can be found.

Learn when to say 'no'

This is one of the hardest lessons to learn and comes with experience. The fear of losing a sale to a competitor, or the uncertainty of where the next piece of work or sale will come from if you reject this one, may induce you to overstretch or undercut yourself. If you continually face this dilemma the resulting stress means you may not survive in business for long. So learning how to say 'no' in a way that does not burn bridges is important.

Business alliances

Business alliances can work well and when you first start up in business all sorts of folk and businesses may approach you. Lord Alan Sugar's words on what makes an entrepreneur, in his book *The Way I See It: Rants, Revelations and Rules for Life*, published by Pan Macmillan (2011, website: **www.panmacmillan.com**) gives a clear and simple lesson on this: 'If you have partners, they have to bring something to the party.'

Trading formats

Sole trader

A self-employed person is someone who works for him/herself, instead of an employer, and draws an income from their personally run business. If the profits from the work are accounted for on one person's tax return, that person is known as a sole trader. If the profits are shared between two or more people, it is a partnership (see below).

There is no clear definition of self-employment. Defining an employee, on the other hand, is slightly easier as it can generally be assumed that if Income Tax and NICs are deducted from an individual's salary before they are paid, then that individual is an employee.

Importantly, the business has no separate existence from the owner and, therefore, all debts of the business are debts of the owner, who is personally liable for all amounts owed by the business. This strikes fear into the hearts of many business owners. You only need to think of the number of business owners who go bust every time a recession comes around and lose their house. Should this be a worry?

First and foremost, you must consider the risk to you in any work that you do. Could it go wrong and could you be sued? Is that a realistic prospect or so remote that it does not even warrant thinking about? Or is it somewhere in the middle? Can insurance help? (On this, see the relevant section later in this chapter.) Remember that such insurance is only as good as the disclosures you make and the levels of cover provided. At the end of the day you know your business, your customers and the work that you do, so the risk assessment can only be done by you.

How to start up as a sole trader

- You can start trading immediately.
- You can trade under virtually any name, subject to some restrictions that are mostly common sense, such as not suggesting something you are not (connection to government, royalty or international pre-eminence). A B Jones trading as Super Lawns is fine.
- The full name and address of the owner and any trading name must be disclosed on letters, orders and invoices.
- Make a phone call to HMRC's helpline for the newly self-employed (0300 200 3500) and say you're calling to register as self-employed. Or register via **www.gov.uk** (then go to 'Set up as a sole trader').

Partnership

Two or more self-employed people who work together on a business and share the profits are trading in partnership. The profits from the work are accounted for on a partnership tax return and extracts from that partnership tax return are then copied into the partners' individual tax returns.

The business has no separate existence from the partners and, therefore, all debts of the business are debts of the partners, so they are personally liable for all amounts owed by the business. In addition, partners are jointly and severally liable for the debts of the business or, put more simply, the last person standing pays the lot. There is a saying that you need to trust your business partner better than your husband/ wife/civil partner.

As with sole traders, the first consideration is the potential for business risk, since your personal wealth is backing the debts of the business. First and foremost you must consider the risk to you in any work that you do and, given the 'joint and several liability' point explained above, the trust and faith you have in your business partner. As mentioned above, could it go wrong and could you be sued? Is that a realistic prospect or so remote that it does not even warrant thinking about? Or is it somewhere in the middle? Can insurance help? Again, remember that such insurance is only as good as the disclosures you make and the levels of cover provided. At the end of the day you know your business, your business partner, your customers and the work that you do, so the risk assessment can only be done by you.

How to start up as a partnership

- You can start trading immediately.
- You can trade under virtually any name, subject to some restrictions that are mostly common sense, such as not suggesting something you are not (connection to government, royalty or international pre-eminence). A B Jones and A B Smith trading as J & S Super Lawns is fine.
- You will need to consult a solicitor to assist with the preparation and signing of a partnership deed. The partnership deed is for your protection and is essential because it sets out the rules of the partnership including, for example, the profit or loss split between partners, what happens if one partner wishes to leave or you wish to admit a new partner.
- The full name and address of the partners and any trading name must be disclosed on letters, orders and invoices.
- Make a phone call to HMRC's helpline for the newly self-employed (0300 200 3504) explaining that you are starting a partnership or visit the website via **www.gov.uk** (then go to 'Running a business partnership').

Limited company

A limited liability company (often the shorthand of 'limited company' is used to describe this trading format) is a company whose liability is limited by shares and is the most common form of trading format. The company is owned by its shareholders. The company is run by directors who are appointed by the shareholders.

The shareholders are liable to contribute the amount remaining unpaid on the shares – usually zero as most shares are issued fully paid up. The shareholders therefore achieve limited liability.

How to start up a limited company

- A company needs to be registered with Companies House and cannot trade until it is granted a Certificate of Incorporation. The registration process is quick and inexpensive using Companies House's web incorporation service (it currently costs £15 and is completed within 24 hours). Some people use a company formation agent (Google this term to find such an agent – there are plenty of them) and the process should cost less than £50.

- The company name needs to be approved by Companies House. No two companies can have the same name and approval is usually completed in a day. Names that suggest, for instance, an international aspect will require evidence to support the claim and certain names are prohibited unless there is a dispensation (for example 'Royal').
- You must appoint a director and this 'officer' of the company carries responsibilities that can incur penalties and/or a fine. The appointment of directors should therefore not be done lightly. The full range of responsibilities is set out in The Companies Act; further guidance is available from the Companies House website (**www.gov.uk/government/organisations/companies-house**). Some examples of the responsibilities include the duty to maintain the financial records of the company, to prepare accounts, to retain the paperwork and to avoid conflicts of interest. Small businesses no longer require a separate company secretary but it can be useful to have another office-holder signatory and the risks associated with this position are relatively light. In addition you will need to appoint a registered office, which is a designated address at which official notices and communications can be received. The company's main place of business is usually used as the registered office but you could also use the address of your accountant or solicitor (there may be a charge for this).

Alternative ways of getting started

Rather than start a new business, you could buy into one that is already established, or consider franchising.

Buying a business

Buying an established business can be an attractive route to becoming your own boss, as it eliminates many of the problems of start-up. The enterprise is likely to come equipped with stock, suppliers, an order book, premises and possibly employees. It is also likely to have debtors and creditors. Take professional advice before buying any business, even one from friends. In particular, you should consider why the business is being sold. It may be for perfectly respectable reasons – for instance, a change of circumstances such as retirement. But, equally, it may be that the market is saturated, that the rent is about to go sky-high or that major competition has opened up nearby.

Before parting with your money, verify that the assets are owned by the business and get the stock professionally valued. You should also ensure that the debts are collectable and that the same credit terms will apply from existing suppliers. Get an accountant to look at the figures for the last three years and have a chartered surveyor check the premises. A solicitor should be engaged to vet any legal documents, including staff and other ongoing contracts.

The value of the company's assets will be reflected in its purchase price, as will the 'goodwill' (or reputation) that it has established. For more information, agents specializing in small business sales have useful guides (for instance, see **www.christie.com**).

Franchising

Franchising continues to be a popular form of business entry route with attractions for both franchisor and franchisee. The franchisor gains, as their 'brand' is able to expand quickly. The advantage to the franchisee is that there are normally fewer risks than starting a business from scratch.

A franchisee buys into an established business and builds up his or her own enterprise under its wing. In return for the investment, plus regular royalty payments, he or she acquires the right to sell the franchisor's products or services within a specified geographic area and enjoys the benefits of its reputation, buying power and marketing expertise. As a franchisee you are effectively your own boss. You finance the business, employ the staff and retain the profits after the franchisor has had its cut. You are usually expected to maintain certain standards and conform to the broad corporate approach of the organization. In return, the franchisor should train you in the business, provide management support and give you access to a wide range of backup services.

The amount of capital needed to buy a franchise varies enormously according to the type of business, and can be anywhere between a few hundred pounds and £500,000 or more. The franchisee is normally liable to pay an initial fee, covering both the entry cost and the initial support services provided by the franchisor, such as advice about location and market research.

The length of the agreement will depend both on the type of business involved and on the front-end fee. Agreements can run from three to 20 years and many franchisors include an option to renew the agreement, which should be treated as a valuable asset.

Many franchises have built up a good track record and raising money to invest in good franchises may not be too difficult. Most of the leading high-street banks operate specialist franchise loan sections. Franchisors may also be able to help in raising the money and can sometimes arrange more advantageous terms through their connections with financial institutions.

The British Franchise Association (BFA) represents 'the responsible face' of franchising, and its members have to conform to a code of practice. When considering opportunities a good franchisor will provide a great deal of invaluable help. However, some franchisors may be less helpful and this will usually tell its own story. Make careful enquiries before committing any money: as basic information, you should ask for a bank reference together with a copy of the previous year's accounts. Also check with the British Franchise Association whether the franchisor in question is a member, and visit some of the other franchisees to find out what their experience has been. Before signing, seek advice from an accountant or solicitor. For more information, see the British Franchise Association website: **www.thebfa.org**.

Operational and other issues

Inventions and intellectual property

If you have a clever idea that you would like to market, you should ensure that your intellectual property is protected. For information about patenting an invention, and much more, look at the UK Intellectual Property Office website: **www.gov.uk** (and go to 'Intellectual Property Office').

Licences

Certain types of business require a licence or permit to trade; these include pubs, off-licences, nursing agencies, pet shops, kennels, minicabs or buses, driving instructors, betting shops, auction sale rooms, cinemas, street traders and, in some cases, travel agents and tour operators. You will also require a licence to import certain goods. Your local authority planning office will advise you whether you require a licence, and in many cases your council will be the licensing authority.

Permissions

Depending on the nature of your business, other permissions may need to be obtained, including the environmental health department, licensing authorities and the fire prevention officer. In particular, there are special requirements concerning the sale of food, and safety measures for hotels and guest houses. Your local authority will advise you on what is necessary.

Employing staff

Should you consider employing staff, you will immediately increase the complexity of your business. As well as paying salaries, you will have to account for PAYE, keep National Insurance records and conform to the multiple requirements of employment legislation. If you are worried or don't want the bother of doing the paperwork yourself, your accountant is likely to be able to introduce you to a payroll service, which will cost you money but will take some of the burden off your shoulders. Keeping personnel records will bring you into the scope of data protection; see **ico.org.uk**.

Employment legislation

As an employer, you have certain legal obligations in respect of your staff. The most important of these cover such issues as health and safety at work, terms and conditions of employment, and the provision of employee rights including, for example, parental leave, trade union activity and protection against unfair dismissal. Very small firms are exempt from some of the more onerous requirements, and the government is taking steps to reduce more of the red tape. However, it is important that you understand in general terms what legislation could affect you. You will usually find free support on this subject via membership of a trade association or organization such as the Federation of Small Businesses (**www.fsb.org.uk**). The Health and Safety Executive has a useful website: **www.hse.gov.uk**.

An employer, however small the business, may not discriminate against someone on the grounds of sex, race, disability, religion, marital status, sexual orientation or age. This applies to all aspects of employment, including training, promotion, recruitment, company benefits and facilities. More information at: **www.equalityhumanrights.com**.

Disputes

If you find yourself with a potential dispute on your hands, it is sensible to approach the Advisory, Conciliation and Arbitration Service (ACAS), which operates an effective information and advisory service for employers and employees on a variety of workplace problems, including employment legislation and employment relations. It also has a wide range of useful publications, giving practical guidance on employment matters. See website: **www.acas.org.uk**.

Insurance

Insurance is more than just a wise precaution. It is essential if you employ staff, have business premises or use your car regularly for commercial purposes. Many insurance companies now offer 'package insurance' for small businesses, which covers most of the main contingencies in a single policy. This usually works out cheaper than buying a collection of individual policies. An insurance broker should be able to guide you through the risks and insurance products available:

- *Employers' liability*: This is compulsory if you employ staff. It provides indemnity against liability for death or bodily injury to employees and subcontractors arising in connection with the business.
- *Product and public liability*: This insures the business and its products against claims by customers or the public.
- *Professional indemnity*: This is essential if a client could suffer a mishap, loss or other damage in consequence of advice or services received.
- *House insurance*: If you operate your business from home, check that you have notified your house insurer of this fact.
- *Motor risks*: Check that you have notified your insurer if you use your motor vehicle for your business.
- *Life assurance*: This ensures that funds are available to pay off any debts or to enable the business to continue in the event of your death.
- *Permanent health insurance*: Otherwise known as 'income protection', it provides insurance against long-term loss of income as a result of severe illness or disability.

- *Key person insurance*: This applies to the loss of a key person through prolonged illness as well as death. In small companies where the success or failure of the business is dependent upon the skills of one or two key executives, key person insurance may be demanded by lenders.

You should discuss these points with your insurance company or a broker. To find an insurance broker, see the British Insurance Brokers' Association website: **www.biba.org.uk**; or the Association of British Insurers website: **www.abi.org.uk**.

Property investment

A frequent avenue that some people explore when nearing retirement is property investment, either in the UK or abroad. Since they may be armed with spare funds and perhaps have the advantage of more time available and perhaps even some maintenance skills, you can understand why this happens. Key focus points are around minimizing your property tax bill in an era when the government has made successive attacks on the buy to let market (where there is money there is tax!), deciding whether to use a letting agent or not, complying with all the red tape and avoiding 'tenants from hell'.

Remember that there are many players in this market – including mortgage lenders, mortgage brokers, developers, property syndicates and letting agents – and that most will know more than you and all will want some of your money. Some even pay for your flights and travel expenses to visit property abroad and then play on this in a subsequent high-pressure sales environment. You are strongly advised to consider carefully before signing up – there will always, of course, be another day, another deal. For anyone thinking about property investment you would be wise to invest in David Lawrenson's bestselling property book *Successful Property Letting: How to Make Money in Buy-to-Let* (published by Constable & Robinson, website: **www.littlebrown.co.uk**) and review his website, **www.lettingfocus.com**. This will open your eyes to some of the issues touched upon here and will give you straightforward and clear advice and information on this market. For instance, one of David's candid tips is: 'You must like property. So, if houses bore you stiff, you're probably better off doing something else.'

Armed with this and advice from friends and relatives who have invested in property, you might then be ready to put your toe in the water and start to explore this area.

Further help, advice and training

Small businesses are well served when it comes to general help and training. Some of the best available feature below.

Organizations providing free or subsidized help

Government resources

The government website (**www.gov.uk**) contains the government's online resource for businesses.

Regional- or country-specific support is also available at:

- Northern Ireland: **www.nibusinessinfo.co.uk**;
- Scotland: **www.mygov.scot/business**;
- Wales: **www.business.wales.gov.uk**.

Business is Great

Business is Great has been set up by the government to help you with support, advice and inspiration for growing your business including advice on imports and exports, finance, employment, intellectual property and regulation. It includes a 'business support tool' and after answering a few questions you get a report of resources and schemes to start to support your business. Further information is available from: **www.greatbusiness.gov.uk**.

Start-up Britain

Start-up Britain has been set up by the government to help you find information about starting a business and contains offers and discounts available to new business start-ups. Further information is available from: **www.startupbritain.org**.

Adult education centres

Short courses in specific business skills are run by business schools and colleges of higher and further education. Further information is available from **www.learndirect.co.uk** and the Workers Education Association, website: **www.wea.org.uk**.

Other useful organizations

- *Solicitors*: Many solicitors offer a free initial consultation and advice can be sought on a range of issues. To find solicitors in your local area use the 'find a solicitor' section at the website: **www.lawsociety.org**.
- *The Federation of Small Businesses* (**www.fsb.org.uk**): The networking opportunities and benefits of the Federation of Small Businesses make it a 'must have' for most new small businesses.
- *Association of Independent Professionals and the Self Employed* (**www.ipse.co.uk**): Its *Guide to Freelancing* is free and can be downloaded from its website. The organization's knowledge of and guidance on IR35 for freelancers and contractors is second to none.
- *Business start-up websites*: These are packed with free hints and tips and a useful one is **www.bstartup.com**; their exhibitions are free, well attended and have some excellent free workshops and guest speakers.

Useful reading

An extensive list of books for small and start-up businesses is published by Kogan Page, website **www.koganpage.com**, including *Start Up and Run Your Own Business* and *Working for Yourself: An Entrepreneur's Guide*, both by Jonathan Reuvid; *Soul Trader: Putting the Heart Back Into Your Business*, by Rasheed Ogunlaru; and *The Rebel Entrepreneur: Rewriting the Business Rulebook*, by Jonathan Moules.

Starting and running a business – checklist

When starting or running a business you will encounter a vast range of information and this can lead to you feeling swamped. This checklist has been developed to help you on the journey. Try annotating each item – N: not applicable; W: work on now; A: review with accountant; C: complete.

- If you want to travel somewhere you use a map. In business it's just the same except you get yourself a *plan*. Commit it to writing and don't expect to get it right first time (no one does!). A few pages are fine to start with based on objectives, a profit-and-loss forecast and your marketing research and action plan. Review it with your accountant and a trusted friend, then build it up.

- Choose your *trading format*, ie company (usually signified by 'limited') or sole trader or partnership or limited liability partnership. This is an important step and one to talk through with your accountant or a business adviser. You can set up a company for £15 at Companies House (**www.companieshouse.gov.uk**) 'web incorporation service'. Understand the personal liability risks of sole trader/partnership and, indeed, joint and several liability if trading in partnership ('last person standing pays the lot'!). If things go badly wrong your personal wealth could be at risk – but perhaps insurance could help (see below).
- Choose your *accountant*. There are many accountancy organizations; chartered accountants can be found at **www.icaew.co.uk** (England and Wales); **www.icas.org.uk** (Scotland) and **www.charteredaccountants.ie** (Ireland). Accountants are usually prepared to see you for an initial 'no obligation' meeting. Be clear about who your regular contact will be, their qualifications and knowledge of your industry, their hourly rates and whether they have professional indemnity insurance.
- Make sure you have a source of *legal help*. Could your local solicitor help? Alternatively, your trade association may offer a free legal helpline that may suffice initially. An early legal question that will usually arise is about your terms and conditions of trade or contracts.
- There is some *free government help* that you will find at **www.gov.uk**, which contains the government's online resource for businesses.
- You should also check out the government-backed initiative **www.startupbritain.org** and **www.greatbusiness.gov.uk** for inspiration and ideas. Regional or country-specific support is also available at:

  Northern Ireland: **www.nibusinessinfo.co.uk**;

  Scotland: **www.mygov.scot/business**;

  Wales: **www.business.wales.gov.uk**.
- Join the best *trade or professional association* that you can identify and consider the extra benefits each provides in the areas of research information, networking events, helplines, tax investigation help and insurance offerings.
- Choose and, if appropriate, protect your *business name*. There is some useful free help available on intellectual property (patents, brands, etc) at the Intellectual Property Office at **www.gov.uk/government/organisations/intellectual-property-office**.

- Choose a *business bank account*. Shop around for the best deal that suits your business (often a trade-off between the convenience of a local 'bricks and mortar' branch accompanied by internet banking versus free or reduced charges for internet-only accounts).
- Assess your *pension* needs. See **www.unbiased.co.uk** to find an independent financial adviser (IFA).
- Sort out your *tax and record keeping* (documents need to be kept for seven years and you need to become a receipt/invoice hoarder with a logical 'system for filing'); as the taxman might say, 'Prove it or lose it.' Check with your accountant that your proposed bookkeeping and record-keeping systems are acceptable before you buy them.
- Understand the implications of failing to deal with your *tax* affairs properly. This can be penalties ranging from 30 per cent to 100 per cent plus interest. Some trade associations include 'free' tax investigation cover – a very useful benefit.
- Understand your key *tax obligations* and deadlines. For companies you are obliged to file your annual accounts at Companies House nine months after your year end and your *annual return* on the anniversary of setting up a company each year. There is good-quality free help at Companies House, **www.companieshouse.gov.uk**.
- Understand your obligations on *VAT*. The current (summer 2016) registration threshold for compulsory registration is £83,000. Consider VAT schemes, especially the VAT flat-rate scheme for small businesses.
- Set up your *premises* so that you can work effectively. If you work from home, manage your family's and neighbours' expectations – suddenly the phrase 'time is money' takes on a new meaning.
- Set up your *suppliers* (set up contracts and bills in the company or business name) and, if appropriate, set up stock control and delivery systems.
- Consider *insurance* policies for identified business risks (professional indemnity, public liability, product liability, etc). An insurance broker can advise on this and you should also consider policies available via trade associations as these can provide increased cover at less cost.
- Consider protecting the income you take from your business (especially if you have dependants) in the event of long-term *illness* or *death* (**www.unbiased.co.uk** for finding an independent financial adviser).

- If running your *business at home* you must tell your insurer that you run a business from home.
- *Marketing and selling* will be massively important to your success. If you are not from a selling/marketing background, talk to trusted friends who run their own business and your accountant/adviser or mentor about your market research and marketing plan. Understand your customers and what they need.
- Do not underestimate the importance of networking.
- Plan the *pricing* strategies for your product or service. A different package means a different price. How have you benchmarked your price and how have you differentiated your offering (features and benefits) to allow you to charge that little bit more? Conversely, what features and benefits have you stripped out to allow you to offer a headline price that comes in beneath the competition?
- Plan your *marketing promotion strategy*. Remember that 'folk are different' and that it is a bit like fishing – you use different hooks depending on what you are trying to catch.
- Get paid promptly for your sale. What are your *payment terms* (terms and conditions)? Follow up on outstanding debts. If you sell stock have you included a reservation of title clause to help you retrieve unpaid stock if your client goes bust?
- Set up your *IT system* and support and have a system to back up your data securely. Check whether you need to notify the Information Commissioner under the *data protection* laws (**ico.org.uk**).
- Consider other *red tape*, especially if your area is a specialized sector (food, health and safety, etc). Investigate and apply for the licences and permits that your business may need.
- Review and update your business plan in the light of experience and keep it a living document.

Chapter Eight
Working for others
Volunteering and paid work

'Many people take no care of their money till they come nearly to the end of it, and others do just the same with their time.'
JOHANN WOLFGANG VON GOETHE

We already know that we're living longer than our parents' generation, but more than that, many of us are also working a lot longer than they did. With the abolition of the default retirement age, we can now work as long as we wish. Indeed, for some of us that's quite a lot longer than might be expected, as the example of 89-year-old Bill Dudley of Mold, North Wales, proves. Bill is Europe's oldest McDonald's employee and is hoping to continue working into his 90s. He's a great-grandfather and was awarded a medal in 2015 for his heroism during the Second World War where he served in the navy. Another outstanding example is 72-year-old great-grandmother Pat Thomson, who braves 90 mile per hour winds and lightning storms and works half way around the world as Britain's oldest oil rig worker (see **www.dailymail.co.uk/news/article-2602347**).

Now whether you're keen to carry on working to a ripe old age is entirely up to you. But in 2015 the government published the report *A New Vision for Older Workers: Retain, Retrain, Recruit*, highlighting the value of older people remaining in the workplace. Baroness Altmann was the coalition government's Business Champion for Older Workers when this report was published. It can be downloaded from **www.gov.uk/government/uploads/system/uploads/attachment_data/file/411420/a-new-vision-for-older-workers.pdf** and makes interesting reading. The report was commissioned because the landscape of the workforce is changing rapidly as we live longer.

By 2022 the number of people in the workforce aged 50 and over will have risen to 13.8 million, while the number aged 16–49 will have reduced by 700,000. An Age UK study showed that older workers are as productive and willing to work flexibly as their younger counterparts. Encouraging and enabling those who want to work longer is vital, because mature workers have so much to offer. Taking advantage of their skills and experience boosts the economy as many employers recognize the over 50s' excellent work ethic. The primary reason for many continuing to work beyond 65 is to augment disappointing pension pots. However, many of us wish to continue working for reasons other than purely financial.

Working beyond retirement provides a boost to our self-esteem, a social life and much-appreciated mental stimulation. Wanting to have something to do to avoid boredom, and a desire to feel useful are other key reasons many people continue working, whether paid or unpaid. And why not? If they enjoy it, feel they are too young to stop, or want to try their hand at becoming 'grand-trepreneurs' – adults of State Pension age who are choosing to use their new-found freedom to set up or invest in businesses – they should be encouraged to do so. Whether you are contemplating remaining fully employed, working part-time, or working voluntarily is something well worth considering.

Maybe it's time to rethink your later life working plans, and look for purpose, structure and fulfilment by doing something different. It is incorrect to think of work as just a source of income; it also gives us a goal, identity, social connections and (for many) dignity. Whether you are considering working for yourself (see Chapter 7), volunteering or looking for paid employment, working in our 50s and beyond gives us the opportunity to try new things, meet new people and keep our minds, bodies and spirits in good shape. This is an important consideration for us all if we wish to age well.

Key points in this chapter

In this chapter we cover options available when working for others, either voluntarily or by taking paid employment. The advice contained here applies across the spectrum, whether you are thinking of working for just a few hours a week, per month or longer. So, whatever your inclination this chapter is for you.

- The first section is about volunteering opportunities (because so many early retired people enjoy working in the not-for-profit sector – we really are a generous bunch!) It is very important to choose the right type of work for you, so read this section carefully – it could save you hours of frustration. This year we shine a spotlight on Citizens Advice – there could be a role for you!

- There is also a section on long-term volunteering and opportunities for volunteering overseas.
- If you are considering getting a job because you wish for paid employment, read the section on how to find a job, to give yourself some ideas on how to plan your job search. If you don't prepare, you could waste hours of your precious time, and end up wondering why you are bothering.
- There is also information and advice on training opportunities and other employment ideas, including finding public appointments, which can be satisfying and financially rewarding. Once you start reading, you will be on the way to finding the ideal occupation for you.

Volunteering opportunities

One of the many good things about retirement is the flexibility – it gives us the time to do what we want when we want. If there is no need to work to earn more money, some people find volunteering brings heightened benefits, simply because they are working without financial reward. The feeling of contributing to society in later life is enhanced because they do it for free.

According to a poll conducted by the Royal Voluntary Service, two-fifths of the older generation are doing their bit for charities and their communities by engaging in voluntary work. That's around 2.2 million people over the age of 60 volunteering with one or more good causes. Eighty-three per cent of the volunteers polled said they liked to help because they believe charity work is important, and more than half of those polled said they enjoyed having a purpose in life.

Mature volunteers make a huge difference to the lives of others in communities across the country. If you do make a commitment to volunteering, you should consider carefully how much time you wish to devote to it. There are voluntary roles that allow more flexibility than others. Getting the balance between flexibility and commitment can sometimes be difficult, so it's important to bear in mind where you want the balance and then choose an appropriate voluntary role that fits. For those with professional skills, these can be used to help train and mentor others.

The range of jobs in the voluntary sector is enormous, from the predominantly physical, to cerebral, sedentary or active, indoors or outdoors, interacting with other people, or working alone. You may not find your ideal role immediately but with patience and persistence you should discover the right one for you. Someone who becomes a volunteer at the age of 60 could have two decades or more of positive contribution to make. The most frequently cited reasons why people volunteer include:

- maintaining friendships, teamwork, status and a sense of belonging;
- wanting to 'make a difference' to other people's lives;
- enjoying using their skills in new and valuable ways;
- feeling better both physically and mentally;
- supporting local activities and neighbourhood organizations;
- being a committed member of social and charitable projects;
- actively participating in democratic institutions – such as parish/community councils, boards of school governors, or neighbourhood watch;
- finding opportunities to help in education, sport, culture, leisure, conservation and the environment.

There are so many types of work available to volunteers, depending on what you enjoy doing and what skills you have – you should be able to find something to suit. It is entirely dependent on you what you choose – the range is enormous, from the large international or national charities to much smaller organizations. Always play to your strengths: you should be able to find many opportunities in your local community to volunteer. Types of work could include:

- *Administrative*: Any active group is likely to need clerical help, from stuffing and labelling envelopes to organizing committees. This may involve a day or so a week or occasional assistance at peak times. Many smaller charities are desperate for help from individuals with IT expertise and accountancy experience.
- *Committee work*: This can cover anything from very occasional help to a virtually full-time commitment as chair, treasurer or secretary. People with business skills or financial or legal backgrounds are likely to be especially valuable, and those whose skills include minute-taking are always in demand.
- *Direct work*: Driving, delivering 'meals on wheels', counselling, visiting the housebound, hospital visiting, working in a charity shop, helping

with a playgroup, respite care for carers: the list is endless and the value of the work incalculable. There are many interesting and useful jobs for those without special training. As regards time commitment, only do what you feel comfortable with. Whether one morning per month, or a certain number of hours per week, it is far better to be reliable than to over-promise and have to cancel or let people down.

- *Fundraising*: Every voluntary organization needs money, and when donations are static or falling, more creativity and ingenuity are required to help bring in funds. Events are many and varied, but anyone with energy and experience of organizing fundraising events would be welcomed with open arms as a volunteer.
- *Overseas*: Many more people in later life are now combining volunteering with travel. There are many in their 50s and 60s who are seizing this opportunity as they may have missed their 'gap year' when they were young. Further information on long-term voluntary work and working overseas will be found later in this chapter.

If you are serious about volunteering, as with paid work, do your research. Before you start, think carefully about what volunteering jobs would suit you and what would fit in best with your family and other commitments: there are a variety of openings as described above.

Then you will need to ask questions of the organization, such as: who you will be working with; what is expected; when you will be needed; if expenses are paid – and if so, what for and how much. Once you have all this mapped out you will find that volunteering can be very rewarding. It is a serious commitment, so finding the right role is essential, otherwise you may be less than enthusiastic about it. Voluntary work is not only rewarding in its own right but also allows you to make a real contribution to the community.

Should you consider working with vulnerable people (young or old) you will need to have a full Disclosure and Barring Service (DBS) (formerly CRB) check. For further information about this see the government website: **www.gov.uk** – Employing people (select the 'Recruiting and hiring' link).

Citizens Advice – now there's a thought, and maybe an opportunity for you!

Have you ever had a problem or crisis in your life when you needed advice? Citizens Advice provides people with advice for all kinds of problems without judging them and the organization is powered by an army of volunteers who make a difference and benefit from all that volunteering brings. And there is probably a role for you at your local Citizens Advice outlet.

But first some context. Citizens Advice provides a reliable and consistent service by sticking to a few key aims and principles:

- Providing advice people need for the problems they face.
- Trying to improve the policies and practices that affect people's lives by showing the people who make the decisions what people's experiences are.

Citizens Advice is independent and provides free, confidential and impartial advice to everyone regardless of race, sex, disability, sexuality or nationality. It is the largest advice-giving network in the United Kingdom, with over 3,000 outlets (there should be one near you) and 20,000 volunteers. They help people deal with nearly 6 million problems every year by phone, email and outreach sessions. The volunteers come from all walks of life and are committed to providing an independent advice service. The advice is based on four principles. It is:

- *Independent*: They will always act in the interests of their clients, without influence from outside bodies.
- *Impartial*: They won't charge their clients or make assumptions about them. The service is open to everyone and they treat everyone equally.
- *Confidential*: They will not pass on anything a client tells them or even the fact that they visited without their permission.
- *Free*: No one has to pay for any part of the service they provide.

Putting these principles into action enables them to provide a vital service to millions of people each year. They, and therefore you, can help make a real difference to people in your community.

What do their volunteers do?

There are lots of different roles and a few are summarized below – there really is something for everyone.

- *Caseworkers/advisers*: An adviser will assist clients at drop-in sessions, appointments in the outlet, over the phone or at outreach sessions explaining the choices and consequences clients face. They may refer clients to other agencies. They need to be good at listening, work as a team, be open-minded and non-judgemental and enjoy helping people.

- *Administrators*: Help ensure everything runs smoothly. There are many different roles that may match your skills and time availability. These can include developing administrative systems, helping to arrange events, receptionist activities such as greeting clients and arranging appointments.
- *IT support coordinators*: Support training and troubleshoot hardware and software problems, develop networks, designing spreadsheets, databases and websites.
- *Campaigners*: Train staff and volunteers, conduct research on local issues and manage media campaigning.

Each area is run autonomously as a separate charity. For instance, in Citizens Advice North Hertfordshire they have 70 volunteers ranging in age from 18 to 89 undertaking roles from receptionist to caseworker. Volunteering times vary according to what people can give, ranging from about four hours a week upward.

So what training will I receive if I volunteer?

You will initially receive a briefing lasting about two hours, which will explain more about your local Citizens Advice and the potential opportunities that are available. At this session you will be with six to ten other potential volunteers and have an opportunity to ask lots of questions (although numbers can vary regionally). It is a very comfortable session without any obligation. Following this session, if you do wish to volunteer, you then undergo the initial stage of training which lasts about eight weeks and takes about half a day per week. After that it's up to you on what you want to give and how your new volunteering will progress. To find out more just check out **www.citizensadvice.org.uk** and the volunteering section of their website where you can search for opportunities by entering your postcode.

Choosing the right voluntary work

Once you've decided that you might take on some volunteering, doing the research to see what is available in this huge sector is essential. You could ask friends who are experienced volunteers for their advice and recommendations. Locally there are a number of options: the local council should have someone who liaises with local voluntary organizations; the library; local newspaper; church and shop noticeboards should carry information on possible opportunities.

The organization REACH has been connecting charities and non-profits with skilled volunteers for over 35 years. Last year Reach placed 710 skilled volunteers into charities and non-profits. They have worked with 10,000 organizations across the UK. To find out more, see **www.reachskills.org.uk**.

The following UK-wide general websites will give you lots of help and information:

- Volunteering Matters: **www.volunteeringmatters.org.uk**;
- Volunteering England: **www.volunteeringengland.org.uk**;
- Volunteer Scotland: **www.volunteerscotland.net**;
- Volunteering Wales: **www.volunteering-wales.net**;
- Volunteer Now (Northern Ireland): **www.volunteernow.co.uk**;
- Business in the Community: **www.bitc.org.uk**;
- Citizens Advice: **www.citizensadvice.org.uk**;
- Do-it Trust: **www.doittrust.org**;
- Lions Clubs International (British Isles and Ireland): **www.lionsclubs.co**;
- Royal Voluntary Service: **www.royalvoluntaryservice.org.uk**;
- The Media Trust: **www.mediatrust.org**;
- TimeBank: **www.timebank.org.uk**.

The following are just a few specialist areas for which you could consider volunteering. There are no descriptions given because they are self-explanatory. The websites listed are the more well known ones for each category, though there are many, many smaller charities you could research via such sites as **www.charitychoice.co.uk**.

Animals

- Blue Cross: **www.bluecross.org.uk**;
- Cats Protection: **www.cats.org.uk**;
- Cinnamon Trust: **www.cinnamon.org.uk**;
- Dogs Trust: **www.dogstrust.org.uk**;
- Horse Trust: **www.horsetrust.org.uk**;
- PDSA: **www.pdsa.org.uk**;

- Pets As Therapy (PAT): **www.petsastherapy.org**;
- RSPCA: **www.rspca.org.uk**;
- Royal Society for the Protection of Birds (RSPB): **www.rspb.org.uk**;
- Wildfowl & Wetlands Trust (WWT): **www.wwt.org.uk**;
- World Wildlife Fund UK: **www.wwf.org.uk**.

The elderly

- Age UK: **www.ageuk.org.uk**;
- Age International: **www.ageinternational.org.uk**;
- Carers Trust: **www.carers.org**;
- Carers UK: **www.carersuk.org**;
- Contact the Elderly: **www.contact-the-elderly.org.uk**;
- Independent Age: **www.independentage.org.uk**;
- Royal Voluntary Service: **www.royalvoluntaryservice.org.uk**.

Armed and ex-services

There are over 2,200 armed forces charities. To find them, search Armed Forces Charities: **www.armedforcescharities.org.uk**. Well-known armed forces charities include:

- ABF The Soldiers' Charity: **www.soldierscharity.org**;
- Blind Veterans UK: **www.blindveterans.org.uk**;
- Combat Stress: **www.combatstress.org.uk**;
- Help for Heroes: **www.helpforheroes.org.uk**;
- Royal Air Force Benevolent Fund: **www.rafbf.org**;
- Royal British Legion: **www.britishlegion.org.uk**;
- Royal Marines Charitable Trust Fund: **www.rmctf.org.uk**;
- Seafarers UK: **www.seafarers-uk.org**;
- SSAFA: **www.ssafa.org.uk**.

Bereavement

- Bereavement UK: **www.bereavementuk.co.uk**;
- Cruse Bereavement Care: **www.cruse.org.uk**;
- Grief Encounter: **www.griefencounter.org.uk**;
- Rainbow Trust: **www.rainbowtrust.org.uk**;
- The Compassionate Friends: **www.tcf.org.uk**;
- Winston's Wish: **www.winstonswish.org.uk**.

Children and young people

- Action for Children: **www.actionforchildren.org**;
- Barnardo's: **www.barnardos.org.uk**;
- Beanstalk Charity: **www.beanstalkcharity.org.uk**;
- Children's Society: **www.childrenssociety.org.uk**;
- Children's Trust: **www.thechildrenstrust.org.uk**;
- Girl Guiding: **www.girlguiding.org.uk**;
- Marine Society and Sea Cadets: **www.ms-sc.org**;
- NSPCC: **www.nspcc.org.uk**;
- Save the Children: **www.savethechildren.org.uk**;
- Scout Association: **www.scouts.org.uk**;
- UNICEF: **www.unicef.org.uk**.

Conservation

- Architectural Heritage Society of Scotland: **www.ahss.org.uk**;
- Campaign to Protect Rural England: **www.cpre.org.uk**;
- Churches Conservation Trust: **www.visitchurches.org.uk**;
- Friends of the Earth: **www.foe.co.uk**;
- Greenpeace: **www.greenpeace.org.uk**;
- Ramblers: **www.ramblers.org.uk**;
- The Conservation Volunteers: **www.tcv.org.uk**.

Family

- CoramBAAF Adoption and Fostering Academy: **corambaaf.org.uk**;
- Family Action: **www.family-action.org.uk**;
- Marriage Care: **www.marriagecare.org.uk**;
- Relate: **www.relate.org.uk**.

Health and disability

- British Deaf Association: **www.bda.org.uk**;
- British Heart Foundation: **www.bhf.org.uk**;
- Cancer Research UK: **www.cancerresearchuk.org**;
- Diabetes UK: **www.diabetes.org.uk**;
- Guide Dogs: **www.guidedogs.org.uk**;
- Leonard Cheshire Disability: **www.leonardcheshire.org**;
- Marie Curie Cancer Care: **www.mariecurie.org.uk**;
- Mind: **www.mind.org.uk**;
- Parkinson's UK: **www.parkinsons.org.uk**;
- Riding for the Disabled Association: **www.rda.org.uk**;
- Royal National Institute of Blind People: **www.rnib.org.uk**;
- St John Ambulance: **www.sja.org.uk**;
- Scope: **www.scope.org.uk**.

Heritage

- Ancient Monuments Society: **www.ancientmonumentssociety.org.uk**;
- Architectural Heritage Fund: **www.ahfund.org.uk**;
- Council for British Archaeology: **new.archaeologyuk.org**;
- English Heritage: **www.english-heritage.org.uk**;
- National Trust: **www.nationaltrust.org.uk**;
- SPAB (Society for the Protection of Ancient Buildings): **www.spab.org.uk**.

Politics

- Conservative Party: **www.conservatives.com**;
- Green Party: **www.greenparty.org.uk**;
- Labour Party: **www.labour.org.uk**;
- Liberal Democrats: **www.libdems.org.uk**;
- Plaid Cymru: **www.plaidcymru.org**;
- Scottish National Party: **www.snp.org**;
- UKIP: **www.ukip.org**;
- Ulster Unionist Party: **www.uup.org**.

Social welfare

- British Red Cross: **www.redcross.org.uk**;
- Turn2Us: **www.turn2us.org.uk**;
- Oxfam: **www.oxfam.org.uk**;
- Salvation Army: **www.salvationarmy.org.uk**;
- Samaritans: **www.samaritans.org**;
- Shelter: **www.shelter.org.uk**.

Long-term and overseas volunteering

Are you perhaps considering taking a 'gap year' before settling down to full time retirement? Volunteering overseas offers a large and ever-expanding wealth of opportunities. Depending on the organization you choose, projects vary in length from five weeks to up to two years. As long as you are in good health, many organizations welcome volunteers up to the age of 70 and some beyond that. This sort of work requires a different kind of commitment; but there is a wide range of opportunities. Some volunteering roles require specialist skills such as engineering or medicine, while others essentially need people with practical qualities, common sense and enthusiasm. Each organization has a minimum period of service.

Before committing yourself, it is worth checking that you are volunteering for an ethical organization. See website: **www.ethicalvolunteering.org**.

General conditions are similar; travel is paid, plus a living allowance or salary that is based on local levels rather than on expatriate rates. Couples without dependent children are welcome, as long as both have the necessary skills. National Insurance contributions are provided, and a resettlement grant is paid on completion of the tour. If you are up to the challenge, it can be immensely rewarding. See:

- AidCamps International: **www.aidcamps.org**;
- Helpx: **www.helpx.net**;
- Inspire Volunteer: **www.inspirevolunteer.co.uk**;
- Over 50 and Overseas: **www.over50andoverseas.com**;
- Progressio ICS: **www.progressio.org.uk**;
- Projects Abroad: **www.projects-abroad.co.uk**;
- The Conservation Volunteers: **www.tcv.org.uk**;
- Voluntary Service Overseas: **www.vso.org.uk**;
- Workaway.info: **www.workaway.info**;
- Worldwide Opportunities on Organic Farms: **www.wwoof.net**.

Searching for paid employment

According to *Saga Magazine*, official figures show there are now 850,000 women over the age of 60 in employment – the highest figure since records began. Also, the number of older women workers is growing faster than any other age group. This greying trend is set to continue because by 2020 one-third of the workforce will be aged over 50 and by 2025 almost half the adult population in the UK will be 50 years or over.

Indeed, according to Aviva's *Working Lives Report 2016*, a third of people aged over 50 who are employed in the private sector are now planning to retire later than they previously hoped. More than one in three of those interviewed suggested it would be by an average of eight years later. The main reasons people gave for working longer included:

- lack of pension savings;
- the amount available through the State Pension;
- debts to pay off (including mortgage);
- still having something to offer;

- job satisfaction and being valued by their employer;
- need to financially support children or elderly relatives.

Job opportunities for people in their 50s and 60s are increasing. There are a number of global companies becoming known for employing people beyond the normal age of retirement, including IKEA, Coca Cola, Barclays, Tesco and Asda. But some people find, having left employment, perhaps due to redundancy, that it is difficult to get re-employed. So, if you currently have a job that you enjoy, hang on to it, even if you have to negotiate to work fewer hours and consequently earn less money. It's a fact: the longer people are out of work, the harder it is to get back into it. If this is a situation someone is facing, the previous section on volunteering is particularly relevant, as showing that you have worked as a volunteer rather than remaining unoccupied whilst unemployed, effectively and efficiently fills a gap in your CV. Indeed, volunteering roles can, on occasion, lead to paid jobs within the organization or charity.

If you wish to remain in the workplace, never turn down the chance of any sort of training. Opportunities to refresh skills or add new ones will make you a valuable resource in whatever job you take. You may not realize how many skills you have attained over your working life. Spend some time considering what these are, as a number of them will be transferable and useful in a whole host of jobs.

Should a change of direction (and employer) appeal to you, you will need to start your research. There is a lot of useful information on how to obtain work to be found on the Laterlife website: **www.laterlife.com**.

If you are seeking work while coping with redundancy, you will find some excellent independent advice on Redundancy Help's website: **www.redundancyhelp.co.uk**.

Some other organizations with lots of useful advice include:

- Employers Forum on Age: **www.efa.org.uk**;
- Forties People: **www.fortiespeople.com**;
- Retired 4 Hire: **www.Retired4Hire.co.uk**;
- Skilled People: **www.skilledpeople.com**;
- The Age and Employment Network: **www.taen.org.uk** (the national employment, learning and skills charity Shaw Trust acquired the brand and intellectual property of TAEN in May 2015).

Top tips for preparing your job search campaign

- *Do the sums*: Particularly important if you are currently unemployed. Work out how long you can manage financially without getting into difficulties. With regard to salary, decide what is your acceptable and your minimum level.
- *Get organized*: Your job-hunting campaign needs planning. Don't leave something so important to chance. Set aside a study area in your home, and devote a number of hours each day to job searching.
- *Assess yourself*: What do you have to offer to a potential employer? List things you've achieved and excelled at throughout your career, including your outside interests. In addition to work skills, what are your personal strengths?
- *CV writing*: This is so important, and presentation is key. If it's a few years/decades since you've updated your CV, make sure it's current and contains the following sections: personal and contact information; education and qualifications; work history and/or experience; relevant skills to the job in question; personal interests, achievements and hobbies, and referees. Use assertive, positive language, emphasizing the skills you have gained from past work. Referees are important: one should be a previous employer, the other someone who can vouch for you personally. NB: this shouldn't run to more than two pages of A4 paper.
- *Let the (internet) force be with you*: The ability to use the internet to get a job is vital. Social media sites such as Twitter, LinkedIn, and Facebook will show that you are up to speed with technology. It will also show interviewers that you are able to connect with younger colleagues and keep abreast of the ever-changing technological advances.
- *Who you know is often more important than what you know*: It's true – more older people get back into work through people they know than any other method. Essentially the people in your network are people you know who may be able to help with advice, information or eventually a potential job lead. Decide what the best means of approach will be for each one of them – personal contact, email, telephone or letter.
- *Remember the '3 Rs'*: While looking for paid work, regularly review results. Check how much progress you make each week on your work-seeking campaign: how many contacts have you added to your network, what results have these have yielded and how you plan to follow them up.

Training opportunities

Knowing what you want to do is one thing, but before starting a new job you may want to brush up existing skills or possibly acquire new ones. Most professional bodies have a full programme of training events, ranging from one-day seminars to courses lasting a week or longer. Additionally, adult education institutes run a vast range of courses or, if you are still in your present job, a more practical solution might be to investigate open and flexible learning, which you can do from home.

Open and flexible learning

There are a number of vocational education and training opportunities for individuals of all ages. You are more likely to be successful if you learn at a time, place and pace best suited to your own particular circumstances. The following organizations offer advice and an excellent range of courses:

- Adult Education Finder: **www.adulteducationfinder.co.uk**;
- Home Learning College: **www.homelearningcollege.com**;
- Learn Direct: **www.learndirect.co.uk**;
- National Extension College: **www.nec.ac.uk**;
- Open and Distance Learning Quality Council: **www.odlqc.org.uk**;
- Open University: **www.open.ac.uk**.

IT skills are essential, so make sure your skills are current. These websites could help: Computeach, **www.computeach.co.uk**; Home and Learn, **www.homeandlearn.co.uk**.

Employment ideas

Consultancy and contracting

If the idea of hiring yourself out as a consultant or contractor appeals, you may be able to build up a steady stream of assignments and be recommended to other companies who could use your skills. More in Chapter 7, and the following websites:

- Association of Independent Professionals and the Self Employed: **www.ipse.co.uk**;

- Consultancy UK: **www.consultancy.uk**;
- Institute of Consulting: **www.iconsulting.org.uk**;
- Mindbench: **www.mindbench.com**;
- Top Consultant: **www.top-consultant.com**.

Interim management

Interim management is the temporary provision of senior or director level management resources and skills. It is a short-term assignment of a proven heavyweight interim executive manager to manage a period of transition, crisis or change within an organization. Assignments could be full time or involve just one or two day's commitment per week.

For more information here are some of the UK's top websites:

- Alium Partners: **www.aliumpartners.com**;
- Executives Online: **www.executivesonline.co.uk**;
- Institute of Interim Management: **www.iim.org.uk**;
- Interim Management Association: **www.interimmanagement.uk.com**;
- Interim Partners: **www.interimpartners.com**;
- Odgers Interim: **www.odgersinterim.com**;
- Penna Interim: **www.penna.com**.

Non-executive directorships

A non-executive director, or external director, is a member of the board of directors of a company or organization who does not form part of the executive management team. They are not employees and they do not participate in the day-to-day management of the organization. Instead, they are expected to monitor and challenge the performance of the executive directors and the management. Such appointments carry heavy responsibilities and people who are qualified to take on such a role are usually chosen for their breadth of experience and personal qualities. See the following:

- Executives Online: **www.executivesonline.co.uk**;
- FT Non-Executive Directors' Club: **www.non-execs.com**;
- First Flight: **www.nonexecdirector.co.uk**;
- NED on Board: **www.nedonboard.com**;

- NED Works: **www.nedworks.net**;
- Non Executive Directors: **www.nonexecutivedirectors.com**.

Public appointments

There are a large number of advisory and other public bodies or quangos (quasi-autonomous non-government organizations) that have responsibility for a raft of public services at national, regional and local level. Those services cover a vast spectrum, including health, education, the environment, agriculture and food, defence, policing, legal/judicial, culture, media, sport, science and technology, transport. The list is by no means exhaustive and further detail can be found on the Cabinet Office website **publicappointments.cabinetoffice.gov.uk** which outlines opportunities throughout the whole of the UK.

Most of the bodies have a large staffing complement and a managing board or executive of senior administrative and professional staff. However, as public bodies, most are also required to have non-executive directors or board members drawn from the general public. The role of these external appointments is to bring outside experience and expertise to the table and also to bring a degree of external challenge to the work and decisions of the executive body or board. There are also purely advisory bodies designed to give external advice in a wide range of areas.

It is not necessary to have been in the public sector in order to be able to make a contribution as a non-executive member. Indeed, in many instances the body will be looking for the sort of practical experience that people gain in business or commerce outside of the public sector. The skill set will vary from body to body and, in addition to a lay person's interest in the subject matter, experience in areas such as finance, human resources and change management, along perhaps with specialist knowledge, will often be seen as valuable.

The time commitment can vary, but on average it is probably one or two days per month. Likewise, the remuneration varies from body to body – from a very modest attendance allowance to several thousand pounds per year. But for some people the idea of being involved in an area of particular interest may be as attractive as any financial reward. For the post of chairperson, the time commitment is likely to be much greater, but so too will be the remuneration.

There is a rigorous and open appointments procedure for all posts. That usually involves the extent to which any candidate measures up to the specific competence-based criteria that the appointment requires. Full details of the appointment, the criteria relating to it and general advice on applying will be available to those who apply. It is important that this information should be looked at in detail as the short list for final interview will be based on an objective assessment of the extent to which the information provided in the application form meets the specific criteria relating to the post.

Virtually all posts are now publicly advertised in the national, regional or local press – so anyone interested should keep an eye on this. Further information, including vacancies, is also available on the Cabinet Office website mentioned earlier or at a regional level from **www.gov.scot/public-bodies** for Scotland; and **www.nidirect.gov.uk/public-appointments** for Northern Ireland.

Market research

Market research provides relevant data to help solve marketing challenges that a business will most likely face, enabling that business to maintain competitiveness over its competitors. The work involves the capture and analysis of consumer, competitor and market trend data. See websites:

- MrWeb: **www.mrweb.com**;
- Market Research Society: **www.mrs.org.uk**;
- National Centre for Social Research: **www.natcen.ac.uk**;
- Research Job Finder: **www.researchjobfinder.com**.

Paid work for charities

If you are thinking of working (for money) in the third sector, it might be helpful to work as a volunteer before seeking a paid appointment. Anyone thinking of applying for a job with a charity must be sympathetic to its aims and style. The following organizations may help:

- CF Appointments: **www.cfappointments.com**;
- Charity Job: **www.charityjob.co.uk**;
- Charity People: **www.charitypeople.co.uk**;
- Harris Hill: **www.harrishill.co.uk**;
- ProspectUs: **www.prospect-us.co.uk**;
- Third Sector Jobs: **jobs.thirdsector.co.uk**;
- TPP Not for Profit: **www.tpp.co.uk**.

Jobs with tourism and travel

The travel and tourism sector comprises many different industries such as tour operators, tourist boards, passenger transport (coach, aviation, waterways and rail) and visitor attractions, such as museums, theme parks, zoos and heritage sites. This industry is not just for the young, mature and experienced people are also sought after. If you have stamina, enjoy meeting the general public and like travelling, working in the tourism sector could be interesting. It requires an academic mind and involves a certain amount of study. Tour guides need an interest in history and culture, and in many cases an aptitude for languages. Some people with specialist knowledge sign on as a lecturer with one of the travel companies offering special interest holidays, others specialize in tourist attractions nearer to home. Air courier jobs are also good for people who like travelling abroad. See the following websites:

- Guild of Registered Tourist Guides: **www.britainsbestguides.org**;
- Travel Job Search: **www.traveljobsearch.com**;
- Travel Weekly: **jobs.travelweekly.co.uk**;
- Overseas Experience: **www.overseas-experience.com**.

Teaching and tutoring

If you have experience of teaching, there are a number of possibilities open to you, both in the United Kingdom and abroad. With examinations becoming more competitive many parents require private tutors to help their children prepare for public examinations. There is always a demand for people to teach English to foreign students at the many language schools. Most UK universities offer language courses during the summer. For more information see:

- Gabbitas Education Consultants: **www.gabbitas.co.uk**;
- Home Tutors: **www.hometutors.org.uk**;
- British Council: **www.britishcouncil.org**;
- Intensive TEFL Courses: **www.tefl.co.uk**.

House sitting

If you like the idea of saving money, having a paid holiday, enjoying new horizons, staying in a beautiful home and making friends with the family pets, why not consider house-sitting? This is something mature, responsible people can do. There are opportunities throughout the United Kingdom and abroad. Agencies prefer car owners, non-smokers, with no children or pets of their own. Companies who specialize in this kind of work include:

- Homesitters Ltd: **www.homesitters.co.uk**;
- House Sitters UK: **www.housesittersuk.co.uk**;
- Rest Assured House Sitters: **www.restassuredhousesitters.co.uk**;
- Trusted House Sitters: **www.trustedhousesitters.com**.

Caring for others

A good carer can make an immeasurable difference to someone's life. Caring for others includes working with young as well as old people, and those with mental or physical disability. If you are a good communicator, patient, have excellent problem solving skills and are physically fit, you will find numerous opportunities for paid work in this field. You may be required to have a full Disclosure and Barring Service (DBS) check if you are considering working with vulnerable people (young and old). For further information about DBS checks, see **www.gov.uk** – Employing people.

The Lady magazine, England's longest-running weekly magazine for women, published every Wednesday, has classified advertisements for domestic help. Have a look to see what job opportunities are offered there. In addition a number of agencies specialize in finding temporary or permanent companions and housekeepers for elderly, disabled people, or for those who are convalescing. Some of these include:

- Bunbury Care Agency: **www.bunburyagency.com**;
- Consultus Care and Nursing Agency: **www.consultuscare.com**;
- Country Cousins: **www.country-cousins.co.uk**;
- Home Instead Senior Care: **www.homeinstead**;
- Universal Aunts Ltd: **www.universalaunts.co.uk**.

Chapter Nine
Hobbies and holidays

'In our leisure we reveal what kind of people we are.'

OVID

What would you like to do in retirement? Go on a world cruise? Enrol on an educational course? Read all the books that have piled up by your bedside over the preceding years? Take up a new sport and get fit? Spend quality time with family and friends? Or enjoy the luxury of idleness and watch lots of daytime television? For many of us there's almost too much choice, but for those who are grandparents, or who have young relatives or friends, here are some ideas. McCarthy & Stone (the UK's leading retirement housebuilder) have published *The Ultimate Guide to Grandparenting* (**www.mccarthyandstone.co.uk/global/ultimategrandparent.pdf**). This comprises a list of 20 activities every grandparent should *do* with their grandchild and a further 20 things every grandparent should *know*. It makes interesting reading.

The first list – twenty things grandparents should do – isn't too scary: such activities include baking a cake, kicking up leaves, finding the best bridge for playing Pooh Sticks and riding on a steam train. But the second list – twenty things grandparents should know – could prove more challenging for some: knowing the difference between Peppa Pig and Mr Tumble, how to play Angry Birds and Candy Crush, how to facetime the grandchildren, and knowing the name of the latest *X-Factor* or *Strictly* winner. If you are comfortable with all the above, you are obviously in great shape and your leisure time in retirement already looks to be well structured and in good order.

However, if you think idleness could become the norm in retirement, *Mature Times* (March 2016) recommends signing up with the University of the Third Age. This organization could almost be described as a 'one size fits all' because it is committed to lifelong learning, can help combat loneliness with social interaction and offers a huge range of activities and courses both cerebral and physical. There are at present 935 U3A branches around the United Kingdom, so you should be able to find one near you. For more information, visit **www.u3a.org.uk**. For further ideas and suggestions, read on.

Key points in this chapter

- Joining a reading group, planning a parachute jump or travelling to the other side of the world: the array of hobbies and holidays on offer today is second to none. Also the friendships and enjoyment to be gained from taking up a new interest or discovering hitherto unfamiliar experiences are added rewards and can propel you down all sorts of stimulating avenues. Many leisure activities are great for keeping your brain challenged and/or your body fit and healthy. So, what's not to like? As a well-known branded sports firm says: 'Just do it'. In reading this chapter you might surprise yourself at finding a hidden talent that has lain dormant until now.
- Other nuggets of information in this chapter include how to access free 'big name' entertainment through signposts to accessing TV audience tickets – and we all like quality and free (and those two words do not often go hand in hand).
- Holidays are, for some people, the oasis in an otherwise unremarkable calendar. The range of holidays for the disabled, singles or those wishing to learn is often untapped and our book will help you navigate the options and direct you to some great further help.
- The flip side is that our perfect 'oasis' can be spoilt by others and there is good help around for dealing with bust holiday companies, cancelled flights, etc. Our tips about paying by credit card and always carrying the Consumer Council's 'Plane Facts' in your hand luggage could just help get you out of a pickle.
- This chapter deals with all types of hobbies and holidays. It is brimming with ideas for activities – some you can do without leaving home, and other choices where a special interest can include a vacation and opportunities for learning and exploring new places. Here we go...

So, let's get started. Age, far from being an excuse not to be adventurous, is in fact, for many of us, a spur to drive us on, to see what we can achieve. Some outstanding examples include a grandmother, Ann Bebbington, who proved she's fighting-fit by taking up boxing at the age of 70 to keep herself active. Another super-healthy pensioner, Bill Mitchell, started running as a hobby when he retired, and has just completed his hundredth marathon, aged 71. Since he began pounding the roads in 2010 he has clocked up an astonishing 2,620 miles (*Mature Times*, January 2016).

Arts and culture

Arts and culture enrich our lives, whether we participate or appreciate the performance of others. There is one umbrella organization, The Arts Council, that champions, develops and invests in artistic and cultural experiences that enhance people's lives. For more information see: **www.artscouncil.org.uk**.

Arts and crafts

The following organizations offer residential arts and crafts holidays:

- Art and Craft Holidays in the Scottish Highlands: **www.artandcraftholidays.co.uk**;
- Field Studies Council: **www.field-studies-council.org**;
- Marlborough College Summer School: **www.mcsummerschool.org.uk**;
- Missenden Abbey: **www.missendenabbey-al.co.uk**;
- National Association of Decorative and Fine Arts Societies: **www.nadfas.org.uk**;
- West Dean College: **www.westdean.org.uk**.

Creative arts

To study creative arts, the Open College of Arts is an educational charity whose purpose is to widen participation in arts education. For further information see: **www.oca.ac.uk**.

Cultural holidays

One of the best ways to enjoy luxurious travel with the opportunity to explore beautiful places – if you choose a cultural holiday it offers a combination of visits to places of artistic, historic, musical and architectural interest, with lectures given by professional academics, writers and curators. They are carefully researched and provide high standards of customer service, including comfortable hotels and authentic restaurants. Here are a few to consider:

- Abercrombie & Kent: **www.abercrombiekent.co.uk**;
- Ace Cultural Tours: **www.aceculturaltours.co.uk**;
- Andante Travels: **www.andantetravels.com**;
- Cox and Kings: **www.coxandkings.co.uk**;
- Cultural Breaks: **www.cultural-breaks.com**;
- Kirker Holidays: **www.kirkerholidays.com**;
- Martin Randall Travel: **www.martinrandall.com**;
- Opera Tours Italy: **www.operatoursitaly.com**;
- Peter Sommer Travels: **www.petersommer.com**;
- Specialtours: **www.specialtours.co.uk**;
- Travel for the Arts: **www.travelforthearts.com**;
- Voyages Jules Verne: **www.vjv.com**.

Festivals

There are a huge number of annual festivals to experience, if you wish to feast on music, drama, literature and the arts. This is not confined to the UK and Europe; festivals are to be found all over the world. When going on holiday many people plan their trips around a festival – be it folk music in the mountains in Bulgaria, or a horse fair in Portugal. Depending on your purse, you can arrange your trip as a budget break, or a more comfortable holiday. There are literally hundreds of festivals across Britain and many of them are free. From the internationally renowned such as the Edinburgh Festival, to music festivals like The Three Choirs which started in 1715 and is the oldest continuous music festival in Europe, to flower festivals in many of the beautiful ancient cathedrals, literary and poetry festivals and the obscure ones like Cheese Rolling and Black Pudding Throwing. To find out what is going on where, in your local area or any other part of the UK, contact the Arts Council or your regional Arts Council office.

One of the best websites to look at for upcoming events, anniversaries and festivals in Britain is Project Britain – British Life and Culture: **www.projectbritain.com/calendars**. Another useful source of information is the booklet *Go Away Great Britain: The Oldie's Guide to Britain Through Its Festivals*, which provides a comprehensive list; see: **www.theoldie.co.uk**.

And did you know... if you are making your way around the country to attend festivals, there's a cheap alternative to hotel accommodation: youth hostels! Some readers may be surprised to know that youth hostels are popular with oldies. Although the Youth Hostels Association's primary purpose is to enable young people 'of limited means' to explore the countryside, there is no upper age limit for membership. YHAs are part of the leisure and hospitality industry and their accommodation is comfortable yet minimal, though the rooms are centrally heated, with TV and free wi-fi. Why not try one sometime? See **www.yha.org.uk**.

Film

Cinema is a hugely popular art form, and the choices include your local community cinema, local film society or visiting the National Film Theatre. Discounts are often available for seniors: Odeon Silver Cinema (**www.odeon.co.uk/silvercinema**), for instance, offers tickets from just £3 for the over 55s with free tea, coffee and biscuits before the film. Similarly, Vue Cinemas (**www.myvue.com/offers-competitions/senior-vue**) offers Seniors Cinema Club screenings for the over 60s.

For more information see the following websites:

- British Federation of Film Societies: **cinemaforall.org.uk**;
- British Council Film: **film.britishcouncil.org**;
- British Film Institute (BFI): **www.bfi.org.uk**.

Museums

If you enjoy lectures and guided tours on collections and special exhibitions, one of the best ways to absorb culture is by visiting museums and galleries when travelling, wherever you are in the world. The UK has a wealth of excellent choices, and you can join as a friend and benefit from certain advantages, such as private views, visits to places of interest, receptions and other activities. Even if you just drop in when you are free, there is always much to be gained from a visit. Apart from the famous national museums, there are many smaller ones around the country, depending on your area of interest. Here are a few well-known ones to consider:

- British Association of Friends of Museums: **www.bafm.org.uk**;
- Ashmolean Museum of Art and Archaeology: **www.ashmolean.org**;
- British Museum: **www.britishmuseum.org**;

- Fitzwilliam Museum: **www.fitzmuseum.cam.ac.uk**;
- National Museums of Scotland: **www.nms.ac.uk**;
- Natural History Museum: **www.nhm.ac.uk**;
- Royal Museums Greenwich: **www.rmg.co.uk**;
- Science Museum: **www.sciencemuseum.org.uk**;
- Victoria and Albert Museum: **www.vam.ac.uk**.

For information on museums in Northern Ireland, visit: **www.discovernorthernireland.com/museums**. For information on museums in Scotland, visit: **www.scotland.org/experience-scotland/museums-and-galleries**. For information on museums in Wales, visit: **www.visitwales.com/things-to-do/attractions/museums-galleries**.

Opera, ballet and concerts

Classical music, ballet or opera can be enjoyed by anyone at any age. There are venues throughout the country, as well as the more obvious ones listed here:

- Covent Garden: **www.roh.org.uk**;
- English National Opera: **www.eno.org**;
- Royal Albert Hall: **www.royalalberthall.com**;
- Sadler's Wells: **www.sadlerswells.com**;
- Scottish National Opera: **www.scottishopera.org.uk**;
- Southbank Centre: **www.southbankcentre.co.uk**;
- Welsh National Opera: **www.wno.org.uk**.

TV and radio audiences

Participating as members of studio audiences and contributions to programmes may be for you. If so, here are a couple of websites to look at: Applause Store, **www.applausestore.com**, and BBC Shows, **www.bbc.co.uk/showsandtours/tickets**.

Theatre

Keeping up with current and forthcoming productions for national and regional theatres, as well as reviews, is easily done on the internet. The following websites are useful for all keen theatregoers:

- ATG Tickets: **www.atgtickets.com**;
- Barbican: **www.barbican.org.uk**;
- Donmar Warehouse: **www.donmarwarehouse.com**;
- National Theatre: **www.nationaltheatre.org.uk**;
- National Theatre Wales: **www.nationaltheatrewales.org**;
- Official London Theatre: **www.officiallondontheatre.co.uk**;
- Theatre Network: **www.uktheatre.net**;
- The Old Vic: **www.oldvictheatre.com**;
- TKTS: **www.tkts.co.uk**.

Coach and rail holidays

Exploring can be done easily and comfortably if you allow others to take the strain. Whether you prefer travelling by road or rail, coach tours and train journeys can offer a huge variety of destinations for fat or slim purses. You can choose from hundreds of coach and rail holidays and short breaks to many popular destinations across Britain, Europe and further afield.

Don't forget that the over 60s can travel for less, by obtaining a free bus pass. Londoners do especially well as they get all travel free within the capital. The senior railcard can save a third of the cost on standard or first class fares (**www.senior-railcard.co.uk**) and National Express offers a Senior Coachcard that entitles you to a third off ticket prices (**www.nationalexpress.com**).

Just while we're on the subject of transport, it's worth drawing attention to The Campaign for Better Transport (**www.bettertransport.org.uk**) which campaigns for communities to have affordable transport that improves quality of life and protects the environment. One particularly endangered species is the rural bus service, which faces further drastic cuts by many local authorities. Buses are the favoured mode of transport for lots of older people, particularly those living in the country, where often it is their only means of getting from A to B if they don't, or cannot, drive. Buses support independent living, have a direct impact on social exclusion and play a huge part in ensuring people do not become isolated. So when you can, catch the bus: once again, it's a matter of 'if you don't use it, you may well lose it'.

If you're interested in coach holidays, start your research by looking at:

- Find A Coach Holiday: **www.findacoachholiday.com**;
- Grand UK Holidays: **www.grandukholidays.com**;

- National Express: **www.nationalexpress.com**;
- National Holidays: **www.nationalholidays.com**;
- Shearings: **www.shearings.com**.

Taking the train is often cheaper than flying, and can even be cheaper than travelling by bus – particularly if you invest in a Global InterRail pass for seniors. This offers major savings on long journeys plus flexibility. For more information visit: **www.voyages-sncf.com**.

For rail travel safety, *Mature Times* recommends that you book in advance on scenic routes if you want a window seat; try to travel light – luggage racks are not spacious; keep wallets and travel documents secure at all times; and, helpfully, most information desks at major stations speak English.

The following tour operators offer rail holidays:

- Danube Express: **www.danube-express.com**;
- Etrains4u: **www.etrains4u.co.uk**;
- Ffestiniog Travel: **www.ffestiniogtravel.com**;
- French Travel Service: **www.f-t-s.co.uk**;
- Great Rail Journeys: **www.greatrail.com**;
- Holidays By Rail: **www.holidaysbyrail.com**;
- Planet Rail: **www.planetrail.co.uk**;
- Rail Trail: **www.railtrail.co.uk**;
- Railway Holidays: **www.railwayholidays.com**;
- The Man in Seat 61: **www.seat61.com**;
- Venice Simplon-Orient-Express: **www.orient-express.com**.

Cruising

The cruise market has broken new records, according to figures released recently by the Cruise Lines International Association. A record 1,789,000 passengers from the UK and Ireland took an ocean cruise in 2015, a 9 per cent rise year on year and the highest increase in seven years (reported in *Mature Times* weekly e-bulletin, 14 April 2016).

The reasons so many people enjoy cruising include: the good value; seeing multiple destinations but unpacking only once; the wide choice as cruise ships come in all shapes and sizes. Cruise vacations are easy to plan, it's social and there are continuous activities and entertainments galore. Finding a cruise to suit you has never been easier. If you are interested, visit the following: Cruise Critic, **www.cruisecritic.co.uk**, and The Cruise Show, **www.cruisingshow.com**.

Top tips for cruising

- *Avoid an inside cabin*: It will be cheaper because there is no natural light, but it plays havoc with your body clock.
- *Don't pay the brochure price*: Protect yourself by booking your cruise through an ABTA agent.
- *Remember that prices usually include extras*: If you think the cost is high, remember that food and non-alcoholic drinks are included.
- *Watch out for on-board credit offers*: Cruise lines tempt customers with on-board credit that can only be spent on the ship.

From among the hundreds of companies offering cruise travel advice and tours, here are just a few websites to look at.

- Alastair MacKenzie's Travel Lists: **www.travel-lists.co.uk**;
- Amawaterways: **www.amawaterways.co.uk**;
- Avalon Waterways: **www.avaloncruises.co.uk**;
- Blue Water Holidays: **www.bluewaterholidays.com**;
- Celebrity Cruises: **www.celebritycruises.co.uk**;
- Cunard: **www.cunard.co.uk**;
- Fred Olsen Cruise Lines: **www.fredolsencruises.com**;
- Grand Voyages: **www.voyagestoantiquity.com**;
- Hebridean Island Cruises: **www.hebridean.co.uk**;
- Hurtigruten Norwegian Cruises: **www.hurtigruten.co.uk**;
- Norwegian Cruise Line: **www.ncl.co.uk**;
- Noble Caledonia: **www.noble-caledonia.co.uk**;
- P&O Cruises: **www.pocruises.com**;
- Princess Cruises: **www.princess.com**;
- Regent Seven Seas Cruises: **www.rssc.com**;

- Royal Caribbean International: **www.royalcaribbean.co.uk**;
- SeaDream Yacht Club: **www.seadream.com**;
- Silversea: **www.silversea.com**;
- Six Star Cruises: **www.sixstarcruises.co.uk**;
- Viking River Cruises: **www.vikingrivercruises.co.uk**;
- Voyages of Discovery: **www.voyagesofdiscovery.co.uk**;
- Windstar Cruises: **www.windstarcruises.com**.

Cargo ship cruises

Seeing the world by cargo ship doesn't offer the trappings of a conventional cruise, but being aboard a freight ship as a paying passenger is like being in another world. Many carry up to 12 non-crew members on routes from a week to months long. Securing a berth can be complicated, and periods in port tend to be brief, but life on board is uneventful – perfect for reading and writing. See Cargo Ship Voyages: **www.cargoshipvoyages.com**; The Cruise People: **www.cruisepeople.co.uk**.

Although it's not strictly cruising, it is worth drawing attention to the ferries that travel daily from the UK to the Channel Islands. The latest fast ferry takes only three hours to reach Guernsey from Poole, the onward journey to Jersey just one hour longer. A day trip, or mini cruise island hopping, is a great experience. Exploring Guernsey (25 square miles) and Jersey (46 square miles) offers a huge variety of history, natural beauty, great walks, good food and beautiful beaches. What's not to like? See **www.condorferries.co.uk**.

Education at home and learning holidays

A bit of cerebral stimulation is good for everyone, it wards off memory loss and, as they say, it's never too late to learn. Your local community will offer various social and learning activities, so visit your leisure centre, church, community centre or library to find out what's available. If possible, use your local library as your first point of reference and resource. Libraries are a somewhat endangered species these days and need as much footfall as possible.

Before we move on to the choices, a word about reading groups. Joining one can be a great source of friendships and interest. Reading Groups for

Everyone is the UK's largest reading group network. Anyone who is in a reading group or interested in setting one up can sign up at **www.readinggroups.org** for helpful information.

If you look online, you will be presented with myriad choices for educational courses. Whether it's a simple occasional class or something more ambitious such as a degree course, you should be able to find what suits you. Here are just a few suggestions to whet your appetite:

- Adult Education Finder: **www.adulteducationfinder.co.uk**;
- Birkbeck, University of London: **www.bbk.ac.uk**;
- Home Learning College: **www.homelearningcollege.com**;
- National Extension College: **www.nec.ac.uk**;
- Open University: **www.open.ac.uk**;
- University of the Third Age: **www.u3a.org.uk**.

For those who enjoy absorbing knowledge and enlarging the mind while enjoying a relaxing break, the range is enormous. There is nothing you cannot accomplish if you are prepared to do your research. The following is a small and eclectic selection of learning holidays to get you started:

- Arblaster & Clarke Wine Tours: **www.winetours.co.uk**;
- Centre for Alternative Technology: **www.cat.org.uk**;
- Corrie Cook School: **www.corriecookschool.com**;
- Dana Holidays: **www.danaholidays.com**;
- Denman College: **www.denmancollege.org.uk**;
- Field Studies Council: **www.field-studies-council.org**;
- Forestry Commission: **www.forestry.gov.uk**;
- Go Learn To: **www.golearnto.com**;
- Grape Escapes: **www.grapeescapes.net**;
- HF Holidays: **www.hfholidays.co.uk**;
- Inland Waterways Association: **www.waterways.org.uk**;
- National Association of Flower Arrangement Societies: **www.nafas.org.uk**;
- National Trust Working Holidays: **www.nationaltrust.org.uk**;
- Painting and Cooking in Italy: **www.paintinginitaly.com**;
- Smooth Red: **www.smoothred.co.uk**;
- SwimTreck: **www.swimtrek.com**.

Gardens and gardening

Visiting beautiful and historic gardens has always been a popular pastime, with so many people being enthusiastic about horticulture. If it's a hobby you would like to take up, whether you enjoy watching gardening programmes on TV from the comfort of your armchair, have acres of garden yourself, or simply yearn to have an allotment of your own, there is a vast choice on the horticultural landscape. You can take courses, visit historic homes and gardens, attend shows and learn about garden charities. The following organizations have information for you:

- English Gardening School: **www.englishgardeningschool.com**;
- Garden Organic: **www.gardenorganic.org.uk**;
- Gardening for Disabled Trust: **www.gardeningfordisabledtrust.org.uk**;
- National Gardens Scheme: **www.ngs.org.uk**;
- National Allotment Society: **www.nsalg.org.uk**;
- Northern Ireland Heritage Gardens Trust: **www.nihgt.org**;
- Perennial: **www.perennial.org.uk**;
- Royal Horticultural Society: **www.rhs.org.uk**;
- Scotland's Gardens: **www.scotlandsgardens.org**;
- Thrive: **www.thrive.org.uk**;
- Welsh Historic Gardens Trust: **www.whgt.org.uk**.

Another aspect of gardens and gardening as a hobby could include those who enjoy wildlife. Did you know that every year the RSPB (Royal Society for the Protection of Birds) holds the Big Garden Birdwatch? It is reported to be the world's largest wildlife survey. Whether you have a large garden, live in the country or town, or have access to nature reserves, you can participate. To find out more or to obtain your information pack, visit the RSPB website: **www.rspb.org.uk**.

Heritage, history and related holidays

History and our heritage is a fascinating and absorbing subject for most of us, whether knowledgeable experts or merely keen amateurs. Among the wealth of documentaries on TV, and the innumerable books and media articles, you have probably discovered your favourite period or aspect, be that social, economic, military, industrial, archaeological or genealogical. Whether you enjoy the subject as a gentle hobby, would like to take a course, or go on a special interest holiday to a historic destination, you should find information to satisfy your curiosity in this section.

As a point of interest, Heritage Help has been created by the Joint Committee of the National Amenity Societies (JCNAS) with the support of Historic England, to offer information and advice on matters related to the management and protection of local historic environments. JCNAS brings together a group of national societies interested in the historic environment of England and Wales. Seven bodies form its core membership: Ancient Monuments Society, Council for British Archaeology, Garden History Society, Georgian Group, Society for the Protection of Ancient Buildings, Twentieth Century Society and the Victorian Society. For further information see: **www.heritagehelp.org.uk**.

Other organizations that have a wealth of information include:

- Architectural Heritage Society of Scotland: **www.ahss.org.uk**;
- Battlefield Tours: **www.battlefieldtours.co.uk**;
- British Association for Local History: **www.balh.org.uk**;
- Churches Conservation Trust: **www.visitchurches.org.uk**;
- Commonwealth War Graves Commission: **www.cwgc.org**;
- English Heritage: **www.english-heritage.org.uk**;
- Federation of Family History Societies: **www.ffhs.org.uk**;
- Historic Houses Association: **www.hha.org.uk**;
- Historical Association: **www.history.org.uk**;
- Holts Tours – Battlefields and History: **www.holts.co.uk**;
- Military History Tours: **www.militaryhistorytours.co.uk**;
- National Trust: **www.nationaltrust.org.uk**;
- National Trust for Scotland: **www.nts.org.uk**;
- Northern Ireland Tourist Board: **www.discovernorthernireland.com**;
- Oral History Society: **www.ohs.org.uk**;
- Remembrance Travel (formerly Poppy Travel): **www.remembrancetravel.org.uk**;
- Society of Genealogists: **www.sog.org.uk**;
- The Cultural Experience: **www.theculturalexperience.com**.

Sport

Do you have an active or sedentary lifestyle? As discussed in Chapter 6, taking exercise becomes more important as we get older. Retirement presents the ideal opportunity to start (or spend more time) enjoying a sporting hobby. To find out what is available near to your home, your local authority recreational department, or your nearest sports or leisure centre, are sure to have details. If you want to combine a favourite sport with a holiday, you can research holidays with on-site or nearby sporting facilities quite easily. The list that follows (by no means all embracing) gives suggestions for popular sports, and includes organizations that can advise you about courses and facilities near you, and others which offer special interest holidays.

Boats and boating

Should you wish to find out whether you like the water, you can do so without a huge financial commitment. Your nearest sailing club may be able to arrange a trial sail, or you could try a water sports holiday. For further information, see New to Sailing: **www.newtosailing.com**.

If you are already familiar with life on the water, the beauty of being on a boat is that you're not on a set holiday itinerary. It's leisured, there's no rushing to the next destination, unless you want to. Whether you choose to holiday abroad or in Britain, there's loads of variety. Should you be a novice, boating is akin to travelling in a cosy floating villa, with all the comforts of home – and each day you wake up in a beautiful new destination. It's wise to plan well beforehand, such as choosing your crew with care, when afloat it's important to respect other canal users and remember to keep your boat tidy. The following websites will give you plenty of options and provide lots of information:

- Barge Cruises France: **www.bargedirect.com**;
- Beautiful Boating Holidays: **www.leboat.co.uk**;
- Blakes: **www.blakes.co.uk**;
- Drifters: **www.drifters.co.uk**;
- Hoseasons Boating Holidays: **www.hoseasons.co.uk**;
- Narrowboat Holidays Wales: **www.castlenarrowboats.co.uk**;
- Royal Yachting Association: **www.rya.org.uk**;
- Waterways Holidays: **www.waterwaysholidays.com**.

Cycling

More than 2 million people across the country now cycle at least once a week. This is an all-time high, according to British Cycling, the sport's governing body in the UK. Whether you are a 'mamil' (middle aged man in lycra), or one of the growing number of female road bikers, there is no dispute that cycling is now the third most popular recreational activity in the UK. Cycling is one of the easiest ways to fit exercise into your daily routine because it's also a form of transport. For older people it is highly recommended, as it is a non-impact sport, so doesn't put strain on the joints. It saves you money, gets you fit and is good for the environment. Whatever your level of experience, there are plenty of ways to get into the sport:

- British Cycling: **www.britishcycling.org.uk**;
- Cycling UK: **www.cyclinguk.org**;
- Road Cycling UK: **www.roadcyclinguk.com**;
- UK Cycling Events: **www.ukcyclingevents.co.uk**.

So how about a cycling holiday? There is a huge choice and what suits you will depend on your age, health, fitness and purse. Whether you choose the budget or luxury end of the market, if you haven't a lot of experience, it is sensible to choose the terrain carefully and not to be overly ambitious. Here are a few options:

- CTC Cycling Holidays: **www.cyclingholidays.org**;
- Cycle Active: **www.cycleactive.com**;
- Cycle Breaks: **www.cyclebreaks.com**;
- Hooked on Cycling: **www.hookedoncycling.co.uk**;
- Saddle Skedaddle: **www.skedaddle.co.uk**;
- European Bike Express: **www.bike-express.co.uk**.

Fishing

Fishing is the most popular participatory sport in the UK, despite the fact that non-anglers think it is boring, always raining and only old blokes do it. (There are of course many excellent female anglers.) If you can cope with the fact that when you fish, you and everything else will smell (of fish), once you have caught one, you will be totally hooked.

Fishing has many health benefits: it gives you lots of time in the fresh air, enjoying beautiful countryside and scenery, it's relaxing, you can do other things at the same time, such as read, listen to music or just think. There are many varieties of the sport: local rivers and lakes, deep sea fishing, fly fishing and much more. For more information about the sport and angling holiday providers, here are a few websites:

- Angling Trust: **www.anglingtrust.net**;
- Anglers Paradise: **www.anglers-paradise.co.uk**;
- Fishing Breaks: **www.fishingbreaks.co.uk**;
- Fly Fishing Holidays: **www.flyfishholidays.co.uk**;
- Go Fishing Worldwide: **www.gofishingworldwide.co.uk**.

Golf

Golfing is a great recreational sport that can be played by all ages, but is particularly popular with retirees. It is seen by many as a social game, and a way to get healthy as golf is an effective exercise programme. It is relaxing and can easily be enjoyed as a family sport. Golf can be a great addition to a vacation, or the sole purpose of your holiday. For those who like participating in tournaments, some of the places where these are held provide the perfect opportunity to travel and experience different cultures and exotic scenery. Should you prefer to go no further than your local area, there are municipal courses or private clubs to be found near to you. For further information:

- England Golf: **www.englandgolf.org**;
- Golf Union of Wales: **www.golfunionwales.org**;
- Golfing Union of Ireland: **www.golfnet.ie**;
- Scottish Golf Union: **www.scottishgolf.org**.

For those wanting to travel and enjoy their hobby at the same time, there are some amazing holiday destinations for golfers. From short breaks with friends, a trip to the sun with some courses nearby, or a full golf club tournament, there are destinations and vacations to suit every taste. Just a few websites to consider:

- Glencor Golf: **www.glencorgolf.com**;
- Golf Breaks UK: **www.golfbreaks.com/uk**;
- Golf Escapes: **www.golf-escapes.com**;
- Golf Par Excellence: **www.golfparexcellence.com**;
- Your Golf Travel: **www.yourgolftravel.com**.

Rambling and walking holidays

Walking is an excellent form of exercise that is accessible to almost everyone. It costs nothing, doesn't require expensive equipment and is the best form of natural exercise. It keeps you healthy, prolongs your life and improves your mental health. But in case you didn't know, there are many words to describe this pastime: walking (in the park), hiking (in the hills), rambling (across country), hill walking (in mountainous areas), fell walking (particularly in the Lake District and Yorkshire Dales – fell meaning high, uncultivated land) and scrambling (sometimes applied to mountain walking).

Some of the positive things walking does for your health:

- helping your heart and lungs work better;
- lowering your blood pressure;
- keeping your weight down;
- lightening mood;
- maintaining strong joints, muscles and bones.

A good way to start, if you are thinking of taking up walking or rambling as a hobby, is to join a small group. See the following websites for more information:

- Ramblers' Charity: **www.ramblers.org.uk**;
- Walking for Health: **www.walkingforhealth.org.uk**;
- NHS: **www.nhs.uk/Livewell/getting-started-guides/Pages/getting-started-walking.aspx**.

The choice of walking and rambling holidays is extensive. It can be a very affordable holiday if you stay in the UK, or more exotic (and expensive) should you travel abroad. There are loads of companies offering a wide range of trips. Here are just a few to help you decide what is right for you.

- ATG Oxford: **www.atg-oxford.co.uk**;
- British and Irish Walks: **www.britishandirishwalks.com**;
- Exodus: **www.exodus.co.uk**;
- Footpath Holidays: **www.footpath-holidays.com**;
- Foot Trails: **www.foottrails.co.uk**;
- HF Holidays: **www.hfholidays.co.uk**;
- National Trails: **www.nationaltrail.co.uk**;

- Rambling Tours: **www.ramblingtours.co.uk**;
- Ramblers Holidays: **www.ramblersholidays.co.uk**;
- Secret Hills Walking: **www.secrethillswalking.co.uk**;
- The Walking Holiday Company: **thewalkingholidaycompany.co.uk**;
- Walks Worldwide: **www.walksworldwide.com**.

And just one more: if you're looking for something special, why not try walking The Ulster Way? This was the brainchild of Walter Capper MBE (the Northern Ireland equivalent of Alfred Wainwright) who, in 1946, created a circular walking route taking in the six counties of Northern Ireland. This walk has since been revised and the latest route (devised in 2009) totals 625 miles (1,000 kilometres). For further information see: **www.walkni.com**.

Running

Running is a great way of getting fit: it is an excellent hobby, and a competitive sport. Running (as defined in sporting terms) is a gait in which at some point both feet are off the ground at the same time, but it can vary in speed from a slow jog to an all-out sprint. If you are thinking of taking up (or resuming) running as a hobby, you have the choice of doing it indoors (at the gym) or outdoors; by yourself as a solo activity or with a group or by joining a club. It can be done all year round whatever the weather.

Should you be a novice or veteran, running is a great way to make new friends; if you are serious, you can always engage a coach to help your performance. Considering the enormous popularity of marathon running, half marathons and other organized runs across the globe, all of which now raise millions of pounds for charity, there's no better time to consider taking up this form of exercise. For more information on clubs have a look at the following websites:

- England Athletics: **www.englandathletics.org**;
- Run England: **www.runengland.org**;
- Association of Running Clubs: **www.runningclubs.org.uk**.

There are also lots of choices if you are considering taking a running holiday. Here are just a few:

- Run the Wild: **www.runthewild.co.uk**;
- The Running Bug: **www.therunningbug.co.uk**;
- Trail Run Spain: **www.trailrunspain.com**.

Skiing

Skiing has been described as 'the best fun you can have as an adult without taking your clothes off'. Perhaps that is why it is such a popular sporting hobby. According to Norwegian archaeologists, skiing could possibly have started as far back as 4000BCE. And did you know that soldiers in mountainous regions have been using skis as a wartime mode of transport for hundreds of years? It is a terrific recreational activity and an exciting competitive winter sport. Not only is skiing good for you, there's plenty of fresh air and it is very social, particularly when you indulge in the 'apres'. Skiing and snowboarding are now accessible to everyone: whatever your level of ability, there are lots of organizations, tour operators and destinations to choose from. Here are a few:

- Crystal Ski Holidays: **www.crystalski.co.uk**;
- Disability Snowsport UK: **www.disabilitysnowsport.org.uk**;
- Powder White: **www.powderwhite.com**;
- Ski Club Great Britain: **www.skiclub.co.uk**;
- Ski Collection: **www.skicollection.co.uk**;
- Ski Solutions: **www.skisolutions.com**;
- Snow Trex: **www.snowtrex.co.uk**;
- VIP Ski: **www.vip-chalets.com**.

Swimming

Did you know that swimming has been a popular activity since before the Romans? Native Britons used swimming as a means of staying fit for the constant warfare they were engaged in during the Dark Ages. However, it is only relatively recently (mid-19th century with the coming of the railways, which enabled people to visit seaside resorts easily) that swimming developed as an accepted sport and leisure activity in England.

An obvious reason why it is important for all of us to be able to swim is that it gives us the ability to survive in water. We are often near or in water, and if that water is deeper than our height, knowing how to swim could save our life. Swimming is also one of the best forms of exercise: it builds strength and endurance and it is beneficial for the metabolism and cardiovascular system. Swimming as a hobby, whether you are a beginner or seasoned swimmer, is a great way to relax and get fit. For more information see: British Swimming: **www.britishswimming.org**.

You could, if you wish, take a swimming holiday. This is rather more than just booking a hotel or villa with access to a swimming pool. Often referred to as 'wild swimming', swimming in open water is becoming increasingly popular. There are many seas, rivers and lakes which attract adventurous people, and the following organizations can help you to find the perfect wild swimming experience for you.

- Outdoor Swimming Society: **www.outdoorswimmingsociety.com**;
- Open Water Swims: **www.openwaterswim.co.uk**;
- Strel Swimming Association: **www.strel-swimming.com**;
- Swim Quest: **www.swimquest.uk.com**;
- Swim Trek: **www.swimtrek.com**;
- Swimming without Stress: **www.swimmingwithoutstress.co.uk**;
- The Big Blue: **www.thebigblueswim.com**;
- Wild Swimming: **www.wildswimming.co.uk**.

Tennis

Tennis in some form or other has been played for thousands of years: monks, nobles and kings were avid fans of the game. The tennis court built at Hampton Court in 1625 survives to this day. According to the Tennis Industry Association some of the reasons for its popularity are because it is social, the whole family can participate, it is good for personal fitness, and it can be played all your life. Whether you want to take up tennis (or continue with it) as a hobby, or would like to enjoy playing tennis when you are on holiday, the choices are enormous. As a spectator sport it also is enormously popular, see:

- International Tennis Federation: **www.itftennis.com**;
- Lawn Tennis Association: **www.lta.org.uk**;
- Seniors' Lawn Tennis Club of Great Britain: **www.sltcofgb.org.uk**.

The key ingredients of a good tennis holiday are: good weather, a great tennis venue and exceptional accommodation. There are a number of companies who offer tennis holidays to suit your needs, whether you are a single traveller, a family or a group of friends:

- Active Away: **www.activeaway.com**;
- Annabel Croft Tennis Holidays: **annabelcrofttennis.com**;

- Discovery Tennis: **www.discoverytennistours.com**;
- Jonathon Markson Tennis: **www.marksontennis.com**;
- Lawn Tennis Association: **www.lta.org.uk**;
- Roger Walker Travel: **www.tennisholidays.co.uk**;
- Tennis in the Sun: **www.tennisinthesun.com**.

Hobbies and holidays for people with disabilities

Disabled people should have every opportunity to be as active as non-disabled people. Physical activity can make a fundamental difference to their quality of life. Facilities for people with disabilities have improved enormously over recent years, and there are some sporting organizations that cater specifically for them. If you look at the England Athletics website (**www.englandathletics.org/disability-athletics**) you will find a complete list of National Disability Sport Organizations as well as lots more useful information. Another very helpful website is the English Federation of Disability Sport, which exists to make active lives possible for the disabled. See: **www.efds.co.uk**.

If it is a holiday, rather than a sporting hobby, you are looking for, there is more good news. Affordable, accessible and enjoyable holidays for the disabled are many and varied. Airlines, hotels and resorts are providing people with disabilities or mobility issues the opportunities to travel, enjoy holidays and see the world. Specially designed self-catering units are more plentiful and of a higher standard. Also, an increasing number of trains and coaches are installing accessible loos. An elderly or disabled person seeking a holiday must explain clearly what their care needs are, not only in terms of getting to and from, but also with regard to accommodation requirements. Some people take companions/carers with them. There is masses of information available on the internet, so do take time to research carefully. Organizations that can help you include:

- Age UK: **www.ageuk.org.uk**;
- Able Community Care: **www.uk-care.com**;
- Accessible Travel: **www.accessibletravel.co.uk**;
- Disabled Holidays: **www.disabledholidays.com**;
- Disabled Access Holidays: **www.disabledaccessholidays.com**;

- Enable Holidays: **www.enableholidays.com**;
- Tourism for All: **www.tourismforall.org.uk**;
- UK Disabled Holidays: **www.disabilityholidaysguide.com**;
- Vitalise: **www.vitalise.org.uk**.

Hobbies and holidays that can be done on your own

Being single is not everyone's choice. Maybe you are on your own, widowed or divorced. For some, having to create a life outside the home for yourself is not a matter of choice. Should you be a carer for your other half, you may be unable to do things with your partner, so outside the home you are effectively single. Whatever your circumstances, you will feel the benefit if you make the effort to develop outside interests and get to know other people. All the organizations listed earlier in this chapter will help you to make new friends and enjoy companionship while taking up a leisure pursuit. Friendships will be forged while partaking in mutually enjoyable recreational activities, so it's well worth making the attempt. You should find it rewarding.

Generally speaking, getting to know new people is easier for women, as they have no difficulty talking to strangers or getting involved in social activities, new groups and hobbies. Men, however, can be either reluctant or resistant to taking the plunge. For those who fall into this category, why not become a 'shedder'? The Men's Shed movement began in Australia, as a way of creating meeting places for men, usually of retirement age, who wanted to socialize and get involved in the community. It's a great place to make friends, work on projects for the benefit of the local community or just enjoy a cuppa and a chat. There are now about 300 groups set up in the UK. For more information see: **www.menssheds.org.uk**.

When it comes to travelling there are many single people who want to see the world but are daunted by the prospect. Many people travel solo, some may be single, others not. There are companies specializing in singles holidays, tour holidays, exploring holidays and relaxing escape holidays. Singles holidays ensure safety, security and the certainty of help and support when needed. Travelling alone need not be expensive, because with single-traveller specialist firms there is no supplement to pay. There are websites that can help you find the perfect travelling companion, if you would rather not be part of an organized group; for example: Travellers Connected

www.travellersconnected.com. Or read the article 'Over 50 and tired of travelling solo? Find holiday companions' on the Silver Surfers website, **www.silversurfers.com/best-of-the-web/travel-best-of-the-web/50-tired-travelling-solo-find-holiday-companions**. This article has several useful suggestions.

Travel companies specializing in solo travel include:

- Friendship Travel: **www.friendshiptravel.com**;
- Just You: **www.justyou.co.uk**;
- One Traveller: **www.onetraveller.co.uk**;
- Solitair: **www.solitairhols.co.uk**;
- Solis: **www.solosholidays.co.uk**;
- Travel One: **www.travelone.co.uk**.

3G holidays

Did you know that in the last year more than 12.5 million people in Britain have been on a '3G' holiday? That is a trip consisting of at least three generations. New research reveals that having multiple generations holidaying together has a positive impact, enabling families to spend quality time together on vacation that they otherwise would not. Other reasons for taking such a trip can vary from a special occasion to helping with holiday expenses. Whatever your taste, you can always find a great location for a multi-generational holiday. *Mature Times* offers some top tips for 3G holidays:

- *Plan the money beforehand*: Who pays for what, whether you have a kitty system, or prefer taking turns – a conversation beforehand avoids misunderstandings later.
- *Work out the babysitting*: Discuss what you are prepared to do, how many evenings, whether you want a day off alone; plan it before you leave.
- *Cooking, shopping, chores*: It helps to agree what works best for all. Make sure everyone is involved from the youngest to the oldest and stick to the routine.
- *Respect others' privacy*: Whether that's bedtimes, bathroom usage, visiting each others' rooms: not everyone is the same, so discuss before you leave where the boundaries are and what preferences others have.

For more information on where to find suitable 3G holiday ideas and destinations, see:

- Family Adventure Company: **www.familyadventurecompany.co.uk**;
- Simpson Travel: **www.simpsontravel.com**;
- Uniworld: **www.uniworldrivercruises.co.uk**.

Home-swapping holidays

With everything now available at the press of a button, thanks to the internet, house swapping with someone across the other side of the world is easy and becoming increasingly popular. It saves money on accommodation and the bonus for those who dare to do this includes the experience of living life as a local, not a tourist. Holiday swap internet sites are on the increase, but do pay attention to the rules and conditions: some are more stringent than others. Whether you want to restrict yourself to the UK or Europe, or go global, most home swapping sites require payment of an annual subscription. If this idea appeals, have a look at:

- Exchange Holiday Homes: **www.exchangeholidayhomes.com**;
- Home Exchange: **www.homeexchange.com**;
- HomeLink: **www.homelink.org.uk**;
- Love Home Swap: **www.lovehomeswap.com**;
- Simply Home Exchange: **www.simplyhomeexchange.com**.

Travel insurance

As we age we are far more likely to have a pre-existing medical condition that needs to be declared and covered on our travel insurance. The main reason the cost of travel insurance increases for older people is that we are more likely than younger travellers to claim for health problems whilst on holiday. Medical claims are much more expensive than most other types of claim. Travel insurance is an essential safety net should anything go wrong and it's not worth taking the risk of travelling uninsured. Don't just go for the cheapest option either; it could be false economy. If you are worrying about age limits, there is some good news: the new Mature Times Travel Insurance scheme covers anyone up to the age of 115 (**www.maturetravelinsurance.co.uk**).

Top tips when purchasing travel insurance

- If you are travelling solely to Europe, *don't rely on your European Health Insurance Card for protection*, it won't cover everything.
- Adequate *personal liability cover is essential*; a minimum of around £1m is advisable.
- For safety, *medical expenses cover* should be around £2m.
- Your policy should have appropriate *cancellation and curtailment cover* in case you fall ill or cut your holiday short.
- *Don't leave arranging cover until just before you depart*, in case anything happens between booking and departure.
- If you're planning a few breaks over the next year, it could be more cost-effective to buy *annual worldwide cover*. Have a look at some of the comparison websites.
- *If you have a packaged (paid-for) bank account, check if it includes travel insurance*. Some bank accounts include a family travel policy, or winter sports cover.

For travel insurance options, here are some other websites:

- Age UK: **www.ageuk.org.uk**;
- American Express: **www.americanexpress.com**;
- Avanti Travel Insurance: **www.avantitravelinsurance.co.uk**;
- Insurance Choice: **www.insurancechoice.co.uk**;
- Laterlife Travel Insurance: **www.laterlife.com**;
- Onestop4: Travel Insurance Experts: **www.onestop4.co.uk**;
- Saga: **www.saga.co.uk**;
- Staysure: **www.staysure.co.uk**.

A cost-effective idea may be to extend any existing medical insurance you have to cover you while abroad. Then take out a separate policy (without medical insurance) to cover you for the rest of your travel needs. Two websites that provide good advice regarding the amount of cover you should be looking for in your travel insurance policy are: the Association of British Insurers: **www.abi.org.uk**; the Association of British Travel Agents: **www.abta.com**.

Another useful website to look at is Fit For Travel: travel health information for people travelling abroad from the UK – **www.fitfortravel.nhs.uk**.

When things go wrong

For complaints and assistance when things go wrong, and for the framing of a complaint, see Chapter 4.

One really important thing to remember is to make sure that when travelling you have a copy of the Consumer Council's 'Plane facts' guide in your hand luggage before leaving. See: **www.consumercouncil.org.uk/publications/plane-facts-your-essential-guide-to-air-travel**.

And for further safety, here is where you can access a portable legal adviser and translator in your pocket: **www.eccireland.ie/ecc-net-launches-new-mobile-app-to-aid-consumers-travelling-abroad**.

Compensation for lost baggage

If the airline on which you are travelling loses or damages your baggage, you should be able to claim compensation up to a maximum value of about £850 (the figure may vary slightly up or down, depending on currency fluctuations).

How to complain to an airline

If you have reason to complain about an airline and are not getting satisfaction, don't give up. Contact the Civil Aviation Authority (CAA) with full details of your complaint. The CAA can help in these circumstances.

Cancelled or overbooked flights

The Denied Boarding, Cancellation and Delay Regulation sets out a number of rules on the level and nature of compensation and assistance to be provided to passengers in the event of their being adversely affected by overbooking, flight cancellation or long delay. The regulation applies to all flights operated within the European economic area (EEA), flights departing from airports in the EEA and flights arriving in the EEA from non-member states operated by Community carriers. For full details and information on this subject, see the Air Travel Advisory Bureau, **www.atab.org.uk**, and the Aviation Consumer Advocacy Panel, **www.caa.co.uk**.

General information

Airlines

Several of the airlines offer attractive discounts to older travellers. The terms and conditions vary, with some carriers offering across-the-board savings and others limiting them to selected destinations. Likewise, in some cases the qualifying age is 60; in others, it is a couple of years older. A particular bonus is that concessions are often extended to include a companion travelling at the same time. Ask your travel agent or the airline at the time of booking what special discounts, if any, are offered.

Overseas

Many countries offer travel and other reductions to retired holidaymakers including, for example, discounts for entry to museums and galleries, day excursions, sporting events and other entertainment. As in Britain, provisions are liable to change, and for up-to-date information probably the best source to contact is the national tourist office of the country to which you are travelling. All EEA countries – as well as most rail companies in Switzerland – give 25 per cent reductions on international rail fares. These are available to holders of a Railplus Card who are purchasing international rail travel tickets, and are applicable to both first and second class travel.

Airport meet-and-greet services

With the number of 'meet and greet' parking services at UK airports on the increase, it can be hard to make a confident choice. While your vehicle is left at an airport at your own risk, the British Parking Association provides a few handy hints to follow when selecting a service:

- Is the member of staff that greets you wearing a uniform – and carrying an ID badge? If so, check the badge – does it match up with the company you think you're dealing with, in the location you're at?
- Are you doing business in a designated location – such as a stand at the airport or a kiosk in the vicinity of the airport? Not having premises is a sure-fire indication that something might not be right.

- Check where the company will be storing your car. Can they point out their storage facility? If it is off-site, which they usually are, can they tell you where it is, or show you a picture? Does the company own the storage facility?
- Ask whether the car park in which your car will be stored has the 'Park Mark'. The Park Mark® is given to car-parking facilities that have undergone an annual police assessment.

See the following websites: British Parking Association: **www.britishparking.co.uk**; Park Mark Safer Parking: **www.parkmark.co.uk**.

Tips for overseas travelling

How to book a cheaper holiday:

- Airfares tend to be lowest around *50 days ahead of departure*. Try to book in the morning; that's when airlines release tickets that were previously on hold.
- When you're hunting for tickets, remember to *keep deleting your browser history* – some websites will charge you more if you've paid them repeated visits.
- The best time to book a hotel room is *a month before your stay*. Booking any earlier isn't cheaper – in fact prices tend to be highest two or three months ahead.
- *When you're visiting a city, try to be there on a Sunday night* – it's usually the cheapest time for hotel rates.
- *Newly opened hotels* are a good bet – they tend to keep prices low in their first year to attract guests.

(Source: *The Guardian*, 4 January 2016)

- *Most important – for everyone – when organizing travel, always pay by credit card* (they give increased protection if things go wrong or a contract is broken).
- *Always check the small print of your insurance*. Going for the cheapest option can come back to haunt you under the 'what you pay is what you get' rule of life.

- *Make sure that your carrier/travel company is ATOL registered (Air Travel Organiser's Licence).* Also, ABTA have an arbitration scheme which is about as good as it gets in the absence of a travel ombudsman (lobbying point – maybe we say there should be one!). For further information, here is the link: **abta.com/go-travel/travel-clinic/arbitration-and-mediation**.
- *Pack any regular medicines you require.* Even familiar branded products can be difficult to obtain in some countries. In addition, take a mini first-aid kit with you. If you are going to any developing country, consult your doctor as to what pills (and any special precautions) you should take.
- *An overdose of sun can be painful.* In some countries it really burns, so take it easy, wear a hat and apply plenty of protective lotion.
- *Be careful of the water you drink.* Beware the water, ice, salads, seafood, ice cream and any fruit that you do not peel yourself. Always wash your hands before eating or handling food, particularly if you are camping or caravanning.
- *Have any inoculations or vaccinations well in advance of your departure date.* When flying, wear loose clothes and above all comfortable shoes, as feet and ankles tend to swell in the air.
- *To avoid risk of deep vein thrombosis*, which can be fatal, medical advice is to do foot exercises and walk around the plane from time to time. For long-haul travel especially, wear compression stockings and, another tip, unless advised otherwise by your doctor, take an aspirin before flying.

For more information and advice, see Safe Travel: **www.safetravel.co.uk**.

Chapter Ten
Taking care of elderly parents and relatives

'Ageing is an extraordinary process, whereby you become the person that you always should have been.'

DAVID BOWIE

If you happened to see a copy of *The Week*, 27 February 2016, you may have read the short obituary of Eric 'Winkle' Brown, the Second World War flying ace considered the greatest ever test pilot, who died at the age of 97. In 2014 Captain Brown was selected to be the subject of the 3,000th edition of *Desert Island Discs*, and the show's host, Kirsty Young, remarked that 'when you read through his life story, it makes James Bond seem like a bit of a slacker.' So true, but there are indeed many remarkable nonagenarians still living – HM the Queen, the Duke of Edinburgh, Sir David Attenborough, Dame Diana Athill and Baroness Trumpington, to name but a few. This chapter is in praise of the elderly and celebrates all they have achieved in their lives.

There are equally an enormous number of quips and quotes about old age. The following have unknown attributions:

'Old age isn't so bad when you consider the alternative.'

'Time may be a great healer, but it's a lousy beautician.'

'Do not regret growing old, it is a privilege denied to many.'

That last is well worth remembering if you are one of the many of us in the position of caring for an elderly person, be that a parent, relative or loved one. Old age should be a blessing, and it is more about 'being' than 'doing'; the emphasis should be on celebrating all the person represents and has done, what in their lives shaped who they are today. It is neither dreadful, nor pitiable. It is pleasant, or ought to be, because in old age there is so much that can be remembered about past events and experiences that were enjoyable and memorable.

Being old is a gift; it wasn't all that long ago that silver hair was rare. More people now live well into their 90s in a healthy and happy way, with lots of entertainment and activities in the company of friends, family and loved ones. As pensioners ourselves we gain a different appreciation of age, so looking after our elderly parents, or relatives, is something we should regard as a privilege. There are many ways in which we can contribute to their remaining years being happy, comfortable and meaningful.

Key points in this chapter

- Age UK, the national charity which campaigns for making life better for elderly people, has 'five key ambitions', where everyone in later life:
  - has the opportunities to enjoy life and feel well;
  - feels safe, comfortable and secure at home;
  - has enough money to live on;
  - can participate in society and be valued for their contribution;
  - has access to quality health and care services.

  (www.ageuk.org.uk)
- This chapter is essential reading if you have elderly parents or loved ones who will (in time) need help. The first section is all about maintaining independence for as long as possible – the most highly prized ambition of older people. It covers the ways quality of life can be preserved, via help from local authority services, and health care professionals and specialist services.
- There is a useful section on help with home repairs and adaptations, so that your loved ones can remain safely in their own home, retaining their dignity and independence.
- If you don't already know the key voluntary organizations that help the elderly, this chapter contains a list of these and how to get in touch with them. Knowledge is crucial here: it is better to do your research before it is needed than wait until a crisis occurs and then be faced with making hasty decisions.

- Elderly people are just as entitled to travel around and enjoy holidays as the rest of us, so the section on getting around and holidays for the elderly (and disabled) has lots of useful information about this.
- On the legal side, you might want to read about Lasting Power of Attorney (LPA) and when it is appropriate to draw these up. Having an LPA will safeguard your elderly relative once they cannot manage their own affairs.
- When the time comes for help, the section that covers practical help for carers is important reading. This goes on to give information on benefits and allowances and how to obtain financial assistance, if eligible.
- There is a huge amount of advice available about special accommodation for the elderly, housing options and costs. This chapter covers this area in brief and signposts where helpful information and research can be found.
- Finally, there is a section on some special problems that can afflict older people, and how to get help and assistance should this become necessary.

This chapter, which is intended to help prepare those who are likely to become carers, indicates what options and assistance there is and advises how best to obtain it.

Staying mentally and physically alert and active is something older people should try to do. Not only does it help prevent the onset of illnesses such as heart disease, it is also helpful in combating memory loss and frailty. In terms of resisting the ageing process, there is another aspect that is hugely important – the social and psychological effects of ageing. Many older people can become less interested in the world outside and lack confidence when interacting with others if there is insufficient encouragement or stimulus in their lives. The older one gets, the more important it is to maintain a positive mental attitude: as carers of the elderly it is our duty to help them fight loneliness and isolation.

In a new survey, the Campaign to End Loneliness estimates that nearly 2.5 million people over the age of 60 would not know where to go for help if they were feeling lonely. According to Age UK more than 2 million people in England over the age of 75 live alone. More worrying is the statistic that over 1 million older people say they go for over a month without speaking to a friend, neighbour or family member. Loneliness can, and does, affect anyone of any age, but there are ways to help combat this. If you are involved in looking after an older person here are some suggestions, recommended by Age UK:

- Smile – it's free and most people will respond positively.
- Offer to call in for a short visit for a cup of tea and a chat.
- Encourage their involvement in local community activities.
- Help them get out and about whenever possible – take advantage of free public transport and discounted train fares.
- If living in the country where there is limited public transport, the Royal Voluntary Service has volunteers who will provide free transport for older people with mobility issues.
- Suggest volunteering opportunities for them to help others: it will build confidence and raise morale.
- Keep in touch: the Silver Line is the helpline for older people open 24 hours a day every day of the year (see **www.thesilverline.org.uk**).

Without doubt, the most often expressed wish by elderly people is to remain independent and be able to live in their own home for as long as possible. With assistance from friends, relatives or local care organizations, many should be able to do this. If you become responsible for an elderly, frail or disabled relative, you are not alone. There are 6.5 million carers in the United Kingdom today (one in eight adults). It is estimated that there will be over 9 million by 2037. About 1.4 million people provide over 50 hours of unpaid caring per week. You are doing valuable service too, as this unpaid care saves the state £119 billion a year (Carers UK, **www.carersuk.org**).

One thing that is vital as people get older is attitude – remaining positive promotes better physical and mental health. This chapter addresses some of the issues to be faced when elderly parents or relatives need to be cared for.

Maintaining independence

There is no question about it, being able to remain independent for as long as possible, living in their own home, is hugely important for the elderly. Decent suitable housing underpins health and well-being, particularly in later life. A new report from the national charity Care and Repair England includes figures about ageing, disrepair and tenure, and reveals that poor housing costs the NHS £1.4 billion per annum. The BRE Trust is another charitable organization that looks at the impact building has on our environment. Using data collected by the English Housing Survey they report that there are over a million homes occupied by those over 55 where there is significant risk to health (such as excess cold or injury from falling on poorly designed steps). Treating such avoidable illnesses and injuries costs the NHS over £600m a year. These findings emphasize the importance of 'future proofing' the homes of the elderly so they can live safely and independently for as long as possible.

The time may come when a care home or nursing home becomes necessary. But until they are no longer safe living independently, your aged relatives will be happier if they can stay put. The local authority and your parents' doctor will be able to help in the first instance. If you can find out where help and support is available from, before you need it, you may be able to avoid emergency situations occurring where decisions have to be taken rapidly. Things to bear in mind for keeping older people safe include:

- *Home improvements*: These will help keep elderly loved ones safe all year round.
- *Front door security*: Such as fitting an extra lock and chain if security is something that worries them.
- *Fall prevention*: De-clutter walking areas and stairs and improve lighting.
- *Fire prevention*: Fit smoke alarms, at least one on each floor of the house.

For more safety tips and other useful information, go to **www.myageingparent.com**.

Local authority services

Local authorities have a responsibility to help elderly people and provide services that vulnerable people and those with disabilities may need. Approaching the GP or the adult social services department is a first step. They will be able to advise what is needed and how to obtain the required help. Your elderly relatives should be assigned a social worker, who will be able to make the necessary arrangements, or advise you on how to do this. Some of the services available include:

- practical help in the home, with the support of a home help;
- adaptations to the home, such as a ramp for a wheelchair;
- provision of day centres, clubs and similar;

- blue badge scheme for cars driven or used by people with a disability;
- advice about other transport services or concessions that may be available locally.

For full information on what services are available, see: **www.nhs.uk/conditions/social-care-and-support-guide.**

Health care and specialist services

A number of specialist helpers, employed by local authorities, are available to assist if required. The GP will help you by advising how they can be contacted:

- *Social workers* are a first point of contact if your parents need a home help, have a housing difficulty or other query.
- *Occupational therapists* have a wide knowledge of disability and can assist individuals via training, exercise or access to aids, equipment or adaptations to the home.
- *Health visitors* are qualified nurses with a broad knowledge of health matters and specialized facilities that may be required.
- *District nurses* are fully qualified nurses who will visit a patient in the home, change dressings, attend to other routine nursing matters, monitor progress and help with the arrangements if more specialized care is required.
- *Physiotherapists* use exercise and massage to help improve mobility and strengthen muscles. They are normally available at both hospitals and health centres.
- *Medical social workers* (MSWs) should be consulted if patients have any problems on leaving hospital. MSWs can advise on coping with a disablement, as well as such practical matters as transport, aftercare and other immediate arrangements. They work in hospitals, and an appointment should be made before the patient is discharged.

Council Tax

If an elderly relative has a disability, they may be able to claim a reduction on their Council Tax. They should apply to the housing benefits officer, but different councils employ different officers to deal with this; see website: **www.gov.uk** – Disabled people.

Help with home repair and adaptations

Disabled Facilities Grant

Your parents could get a grant from their local council if one of them is disabled and changes need to be made to their home. Such adaptations include widening doors and installing ramps, improving access to rooms and facilities including stair lifts or a downstairs bathroom, a suitable heating system, adjustment of heating or lighting controls. If eligible, the applicant could receive up to £30,000 in England, £25,000 in Northern Ireland and £36,000 in Wales. Disabled Facilities Grants are not available in Scotland. See website: **www.gov.uk** – Disabled people.

Home improvement agencies and handy person service providers

These are local organizations dedicated to helping older people with disabilities live in safety and dignity in their own homes. There are currently 200 home improvement agencies in England covering over 80 per cent of local authorities. Locally they may be known as Care and Repair or Staying Put agencies. The websites that will give all the information you need are:

- Foundations: **www.foundations.uk.com**;
- Care and Repair Cymru: **www.careandrepair.org.uk**;
- Care and Repair England: **www.careandrepair-england.org.uk**;
- Care and Repair Scotland: **www.careandrepairscotland.co.uk**.

Other organizations that can help include:

- Age UK: **www.ageuk.org.uk** (Age UK stairlifts, chairs and easy bathing come under the Age UK Mobility Range and are provided by Handicare; more information can be found in the leaflet 'Helping you to love your independence');
- British Red Cross: **www.redcross.org.uk**;
- Centre for Accessible Environments: **www.cae.org.uk**;
- Citizens Advice: **www.citizensadvice.org.uk**;
- Design and Manufacture for Disability: **www.demand.org.uk**;
- Disability Wales/Anabledd Cymru: **www.disabilitywales.org**;
- Disabled Living Foundation: **www.dlf.org.uk**;

- Find My HIA: **www.findmyhia.org.uk**;
- Independent Age: **www.independentage.org**;
- REMAP: **www.remap.org.uk**.

Alarm systems

Personal alarms

Personal alarms provide security for vulnerable elderly people as they know that help can be summoned quickly in the event of an emergency. It gives an elderly person independence and their family peace of mind. Some alarm systems allow people living in their own homes to be linked to a central control, or have a telephone link, enabling personal contact to be made. Others simply signal that something is wrong. Sometimes a relative or friend who has been nominated will be alerted. There is an alternative, which is a KeySafe system which can be fitted to an external wall, or inside a garage. For more information on what is available see:

- AgeUK: **www.ageuk.org.uk**;
- Callsafe: **www.callsafe.org**;
- Care Harmony Solutions: **www.careharmony.co.uk**;
- Disabled Living Foundation: **www.dlf.org.uk**;
- Saga: **www.saga.co.uk**.

Community alarms

Community alarms are also known as Lifeline, Careline, telecare or emergency monitoring services. They operate 24 hours a day, 365 days a year, giving elderly and vulnerable people the freedom to live life independently, knowing that assistance can be obtained when needed. They work via a special alarm unit connected to the telephone line, or can be activated via a pendant, which is worn round the neck or on a wristband. For further information see:

- NHS Choices: **www.nhs.uk/Conditions/social-care-and-support-guide**;
- Elderly Accommodation Counsel (now combined with Housing Care and First Stop Advice for elderly people): **www.housingcare.org**;
- Eldercare: **www.eldercare.co.uk**.

Key voluntary organizations

In addition to the services provided by statutory health and social services for elderly people living at home, there are a number of voluntary organizations that can offer help, including:

- lunch clubs and day centres;
- holidays and short-term placements;
- aids such as wheelchairs;
- transport;
- odd jobs and decorating;
- gardening;
- good neighbour schemes;
- prescription collection;
- advice and information;
- family support schemes.

You will be able to find out more via the local Citizens Advice (**www.citizensadvice.org.uk**) but the key agencies are:

- Age UK: **www.ageuk.org.uk**;
- Age Scotland: **www.ageuk.org.uk/scotland**;
- Age Cymru: **www.ageuk.org.uk/cymru**;
- Age NI: **www.ageuk.org.uk/northern-ireland**;
- British Red Cross: **www.redcross.org.uk**;
- Care Information Scotland: **www.careinfoscotland.scot**;
- Centre for Individual Living, Northern Ireland: **www.cilbelfast.org**;
- Contact the Elderly: **www.contact-the-elderly.org**;
- Disability Wales: **www.disabilitywales.org**;
- Independent Age: **www.independentage.org**;
- Royal Voluntary Service: **www.royalvoluntaryservice.org.uk**;
- St John Ambulance: **www.sja.org.uk**;
- Disability Information Scotland: **www.disabilityscot.org.uk/info-guides**.

Other sources of help and advice include:

- Civil Service Retirement Fellowship: **www.csrf.org.uk**;
- Disability Rights UK: **www.disabilityrightsuk.org**;
- Jewish Care: **www.jewishcare.org**.

Getting around

When mobility becomes an issue, quality of life is quickly diminished. For help with getting around, the facilities run by voluntary organizations just mentioned may be of assistance. Otherwise, look at these websites:

- Driving Mobility: **www.drivingmobility.org.uk**;
- London Taxicard: **www.londoncouncils.gov.uk/services/taxicard**;
- Motability: **www.motability.co.uk**.

Older drivers

By 2035 there will be 21 million older drivers on UK roads. Some elderly people may start to worry about whether they are still able to drive safely or are at risk of having an accident. LaterLife recently published an excellent article on older drivers; see: **www.laterlife.com/features/older-drivers.htm**.

Also, the AA website has helpful information for those over 70 who wish to continue safely behind the wheel. See: **www.theaa.com/public_affairs/reports/helping_the_older_driver.pdf**.

According to the AA there is no safe or unsafe age for a driver, as everyone ages differently. But older people are frailer and more likely to suffer serious injury in accidents. It is up to the individual to inform the DVLA of any medical conditions that may affect their driving. Your relative's GP should be approached to help indicate when this becomes necessary.

Driving licence renewal at 70 is now compulsory. All drivers aged 70 and over will have to re-apply for their licence every three years. There is no test or medical, but a medical declaration is mandatory. See website: **www.gov.uk/renew-driving-licence-at-70**.

Holidays

Old age may come with ailments, pains, health issues and disability, and in addition a lack of confidence about travelling away from home and being in unfamiliar surroundings. These considerations should not stop the elderly from enjoying a relaxing holiday. Perhaps all that is required for a pleasurable experience are a few helpful aids. There are a number of specialist organizations that provide holidays for people with special needs. (For the hale and hearty, see Chapter 9). Here are some websites giving advice and information for those needing special care:

- Accessible Travel and Leisure: **www.accessibletravel.co.uk**;
- Age UK: **www.ageuk.org.uk**;
- Can be Done: **www.canbedone.co.uk**;
- Disabled Holidays.com: **www.disabledholidaydirectory.com**;
- Enable Holidays: **www.enableholidays.com**;
- Holidays for All: **www.holidaysforall.org**;
- Holidays with Help: **www.holidayswithhelp.org.uk**;
- Revitalise: **www.revitalise.org.uk**;
- Richmond Retreats: **www.richmondretreats.co.uk**.

The *Disabled Travellers' Guide*, published by the AA, provides masses of information for the disabled traveller. See: **www.theaa.com/staticdocs/pdf/services/disabled-travellers-gvide.pdf**.

Lasting power of attorney

If it seems sensible for your elderly relative to set up a Lasting Power of Attorney (LPA) this has to be done before losing mental capacity, otherwise it is invalid. Before doing anything it would be wise for them to discuss the options with their family or someone they trust to see what they think and whether they can help. To find out more about mental capacity and making decisions, see **www.gov.uk/make-decisions-for-someone**.

An LPA gives someone trustworthy the legal authority to make decisions on behalf of your elderly relative. This person is known as their attorney. The person allowing the LPA to be drawn up is known as the donor. There are two types of LPA: one for *property and financial affairs* and another for *personal welfare*. It is safest to have both types. A health and welfare LPA allows others to make decisions about the donor's day-to-day care, where they live, who they should have contact with and, if desired, their choice for end-of-life care. The property and financial affairs LPA covers paying bills, collecting benefits, selling property, investing money.

The right time to draw up an LPA is while the individual is in full command of his or her faculties, so that potential situations that would require decision making can be properly discussed and the donor's wishes made clear. If an elderly person you care about is considering setting up an LPA, it is important they consult both their GP and the family solicitor, as well as members of their family. When making an LPA make sure the attorneys your parent chooses have their best interests at heart. For further information see: **www.gov.uk/power-of-attorney**.

Lasting Powers of Attorney were introduced in October 2007, replacing the old system of Enduring Powers of Attorney (EPA). An EPA created before October 2007 remains valid.

And another idea

When it comes to forward planning, many older people shrink from discussing their wishes with loved ones. But if their preferences are not known to nearest and dearest, it may be difficult when the time comes to do what is in their best interests. A helpful booklet which is available from Age UK is their *LifeBook*. This is a practical tool designed to help older people work through all the things they need, or wish, to put in order. The *LifeBook* will not only help an older person be more organized but it could also be invaluable to a family member or friend if they need to locate important information in an emergency. It is completely free and available from Age UK; see **www.ageuk.org.uk/lifebook**.

When help becomes necessary

The time may come when elderly people are no longer able to cope with running their homes and caring for themselves without a bit of assistance. There are various options, some more expensive than others. If approaching agencies, it is well worth asking friends and neighbours for personal recommendations, as this can give a lot of peace of mind. Some of the agencies listed overleaf specialize in providing temporary help, rather than permanent staff. Others can offer a flexible service and nursing care, if appropriate. Fees are normally paid by private funding but, depending on individual circumstances, public financial assistance may be available.

There are some things to bear in mind when hiring a carer:

- Should you organize home care for your elderly relative, your relative actually becomes an employer.
- Elderly people organizing care themselves also have the responsibility for checking eligibility to work in the UK and conducting a DBS check.
- Carers need clear guidelines as to documentation, medication, care plans and dietary guidance.
- There must be a contingency plan should the chosen carer fall ill or be unable to work for other reasons.

Full information and advice on this can be obtained from the National Care Line: **www.thenationalcareline.org**.

Charities such as Age UK (**www.ageuk.org.uk**) and Carers Trust (**www.carers.org**) can provide home help and domestic assistance services. The Carers Trust supports carers by giving them a break from their caring responsibilities through providing home care services. There is information on the NHS website about care services in your home: **www.nhs.uk/Conditions/social-care-and-support-guide**.

Some agencies that should be able to help include:

- Bunbury Care Agency: **www.bunburyagency.com**;
- Christies Care: **www.christiescare.com**;
- Consult Us: **www.consultuscare.com**;
- Country Cousins: **www.country-cousins.co.uk**;
- Cura Domi: **www.curadomi.co.uk**;
- Helping Hands: **www.helpinghandshomecare.co.uk**;
- Miracle Workers: **www.miracle-workers.co.uk**;
- The Care Agency: **www.thecareagency.co.uk**.

There are also lots of advertisements to be found in *The Lady* magazine (published weekly) that may be helpful. You could advertise in this if you are seeking help on a permanent basis. For some families these arrangements work well only for a while, in which case it may be necessary to consider the choice between residential care and inviting the elderly parent to live with you.

Emergency care for pets

Older people love their pets, as they give companionship, fun and can be stimulating too if they require regular outdoor exercise. When an elderly parent becomes ill, incapacitated, hospitalized or dies, leaving a beloved pet, this can cause problems for relatives. To ensure the pet continues to receive care, should something unexpected happen, the following organizations will be able to help:

- Blue Cross: **www.bluecross.org.uk**;
- Cats Protection: **www.cats.org.uk**;
- Cinnamon Trust: **www.cinnamon.org.uk**;
- Dogs Trust: **www.dogstrust.org.uk**;
- National Animal Welfare Trust: **www.nawt.org.uk**;
- Pet Fostering Service Scotland: **www.pfss.org.uk**.

Practical help for carers

The UK has 6.5 million carers. Carers Week is an annual campaign (usually taking place in June of each year) to raise awareness of caring, highlighting the challenges carers face and recognizing the contribution they make to families and communities throughout the UK. Carers Week is made up of nine charities that have joined forces to promote the role of carers in our society. For more information and to see what support is available, see: **www.carersweek.org**.

While your elderly relative is reasonably active and independent – visiting friends, able to do his or her own shopping, enjoying hobbies and socializing – the strains of caring for them may be light. However, when this is not the case, far more intensive caring may be required. Make sure you find out what help is available and how to obtain it. Earlier sections of this chapter have given some information on this. The many services provided by local authorities and voluntary agencies apply as much to an elderly person living with a family as to someone living alone. If you cannot find a solution to a particular problem you have, one of these organizations may be able to help you:

- Age UK: **www.ageuk.org.uk**;
- British Red Cross: **www.redcross.org.uk**;

- Carers Trust: **www.carers.org**;
- Independent Age: **www.independentage.org**;
- Royal Voluntary Service: **www.royalvoluntaryservice.org.uk**.

Respite care facilities enable carers to take a break from their dependants from time to time. A particularly welcome aspect of respite care is that many schemes specially cater for, among others, elderly people with dementia.

Holiday breaks for carers

Various schemes enable those with an elderly relative to go on holiday alone or simply enjoy a respite from caring. Some local authorities run fostering schemes, along similar lines to child fostering. There may be a charge, or the service may be run on a voluntary basis (or be paid for by the local authority). Some voluntary organizations arrange holidays for older people in order to give relatives a break. Different charities take responsibility according to the area where you live. Citizens Advice or your local social services department should know whom you can approach.

Another possible solution is a short-stay home, which is residential accommodation variously run by local authorities, voluntary organizations or private individuals, catering specifically for elderly people. The different types of home are described under the heading 'Retirement homes and care homes' further on in this chapter. If, as opposed to general care, proper medical attention is necessary, you should consult your parent's GP. Many hospitals and nursing homes offer short-stay care arrangements as a means of relieving relatives. The doctor should be able to help organize this for you.

Benefits and allowances

Should you have responsibility for the care of an elderly person, there are benefits and allowances available to help financially. The best place to look is on the government website, which has the latest and widest range of online public information. This is the gateway for government advice. There is a section for carers covering support services and assessments, carers' rights, working and caring, Carer's Allowance and much more. For full information see: **www.gov.uk** – Disabled people.

There is other help to be found on the NHS website: **www.nhs.uk/conditions/social-care-and-support-guide**.

Entitlements for carers

Home Responsibilities Protection

HRP was a scheme to help protect a person's State Pension. It has been replaced with National Insurance Credits for parents and carers. You may still be able to apply for HRP if you were caring for a sick or disabled person for a complete tax year before April 2010. Any HRP credits you may have had before 6 April 2010 have been converted into National Insurance Credits (up to a maximum of 22 years). You must have reached State Pension age on or after 6 April 2010 for these credits to go towards your State Pension. See: **www.gov.uk/home-responsibilities-protection-hrp/overview**.

Carer's Allowance

This is paid to anyone who is caring for someone more than 35 hours per week, who is getting Attendance Allowance or the middle or highest rate of the Disability Living Allowance care component. You are not able to be paid Carer's Allowance if you are already getting the State Pension or are working and earn over £100 per week. For further information see: **www.gov.uk/carers-allowance**.

Entitlements for elderly or disabled people

Attendance Allowance

This is an allowance paid to people 65 and over to help with personal care if they are physically or mentally disabled. It is paid at two different rates and how much the elderly person receives is calculated on the level of care needed because of their frailty or disability. For full information see: **www.gov.uk/attendance-allowance**.

Personal Independence Payment

This payment helps with some of the costs caused by long-term ill health or a disability. It has replaced the Disability Living Allowance for eligible people aged between 16 and 64. It is made up of two parts: a daily living component and a mobility component. There are two rates, standard and enhanced. For full information on the changes, and eligibility criteria, see: **www.gov.uk/pip**.

Cold Weather Payment

If your elderly relative is in receipt of certain benefits, he/she may be eligible for a Cold Weather Payment. These are made when the local temperature is either recorded as, or forecast to be, an average of zero degrees Celsius or below, over seven consecutive days. The amount paid is £25 for each seven day period of very cold weather between 1 November and 31 March. Those eligible should receive it without having to claim. See: **www.gov.uk/cold-weather-payment**.

Winter Fuel Payment

This is a special tax-free payment of between £100 and £300 to help pay heating bills for all households with a resident aged 60 and over. See: **www.gov.uk/winter-fuel-payment**.

Free off-peak bus travel

An older person's bus pass is available to people once they reach retirement age. Disabled people can also travel free on any bus service in the country. For full information on how to obtain a bus pass in England, Scotland, Wales and Northern Ireland, see: **www.gov.uk/apply-for-elderly-person-bus-pass**.

Free TV licence

Once your elderly relative reaches 75, he/she is entitled to a free TV licence. This licence covers the individual and anyone else who lives with them. It is important to apply for this whilst the person is 74 as it is not something that will be sent to them automatically. For further information see: **www.tvlicensing.co.uk**.

Financial assistance

In cases of hardship, there are charities that give financial assistance to elderly people. For many people one of the main barriers to getting help is knowing which of the many thousands of charities to approach. There are free services that help older people in genuine financial need. When seeking financial assistance, have patience and be prepared to do a lot of research. Two helpful sites are: Charity Search, **www.charitysearch.org.uk**, and Turn2Us, **www.turn2us.org.uk**.

Some organizations (amongst many others) who may be able to offer help are:

- Independent Age: **www.independentage.org**;
- Royal Agricultural Benevolent Institution: **www.rabi.org.uk**;
- SSAFA, the Armed Forces Charity: **www.ssafa.org.uk**;
- Professionals Aid Council: **www.pcac.org.uk**.

Special accommodation for the elderly

The time to start looking for appropriate accommodation for elderly parents or relatives is before they need it. A lot of research will have to be done, and there will be a better (and happier) outcome for all concerned if this process is not rushed. Whether the search is prompted by a serious medical condition, or the desire for a lifestyle change, finding the right place to move to, when living independently at home is no longer an option, can be challenging and stressful for the whole family. The earlier you make an assessment of their needs, the more choices and control you all will have.

When deciding what senior housing option will be best for your relatives, the following factors need to be borne in mind: physical and medical needs; social and emotional needs and financial needs. The loss of some level of independence can be overwhelming for many older people, bringing with it, as it often does, feelings of shame, embarrassment, fear, confusion and anger. Brainstorm with family and trusted friends, and involve their medical team. Often the older person may listen more readily to their doctor or an impartial third party.

A good place to find information about options and funding is FirstStop Advice, an independent, impartial and free service provided by the national charity Elderly Accommodation Counsel. This service is for older people, their families and carers. It aims to get elderly people the help and care they need to live independently and comfortably for as long as possible. See **www.firststopcareadvice.org.uk**.

Housing options

The following is a very brief description of the different types of housing for elderly people:

Living with family

This might at first seem the simplest option, but will the elderly relative have friends and social amenities after moving in? What would happen if the family relationship broke down? It is advisable to take legal and financial advice before moving elderly relatives into your own home, and have a written agreement about how to address disputes and how to end the arrangement should it become necessary.

Sheltered or retirement housing

This type of housing is designed to meet the needs of older people. Most schemes have a manager and communal facilities, and there are many different types of sheltered/retirement housing both to rent and to buy. There is usually a minimum age for residents, 60 or sometimes 55.

Housing with care

This is a newer form of specialist housing, sometimes referred to as extra care housing. Properties can be rented, owned or occasionally part-owned/part-rented. They are fully self-contained homes, usually with one or two bedrooms. If considering this option, if possible take your parents to visit several schemes and speak to some of the current residents.

Care homes

Deciding whether a care home is right for an elderly relative is a difficult decision which sometimes has to be made in a hurry. All care homes in England are registered and inspected by the Care Quality Commission (CQC) and must display their CQC rating throughout the home and on their website. In Wales, the inspectorate is called the Care Standards Inspectorate for Wales. In Scotland it is called the Scottish Commission for the Regulation of Care.

Some care homes provide personal care, some provide nursing care. Some older people with dementia may need a care home with an additional category of registration (DE).

First Stop provides advice and information about housing and care options for older people; see: **www.housingcare.org/downloads/kbase/3103.pdf**.

Retirement homes and care homes

Retirement homes

If your elderly relatives are able to buy or rent a retirement property from their own private means, the choice is entirely theirs. Prices and types of property vary enormously, from small flats to luxurious homes on sites with every amenity. The majority of properties are sold on a long lease (typically 125 years). It is advisable to check that the management company is a member of The Association of Retirement Housing Managers and therefore bound by its Code of Practice. If looking to rent, retirement housing and housing-with-care is provided by local authorities, housing associations and some charitable and private sector providers. Some helpful websites include:

- Retirement Home Search: **www.retirementhomesearch.co.uk**;
- Abbeyfield: **www.abbeyfield.com**;
- Anchor: **www.anchor.org.uk**;
- Girlings: **www.girlings.co.uk**;
- Hanover: **www.hanover.org.uk**;
- Jewish Community Housing Association: **www.jliving.org.uk**;
- Southern Housing Group: **www.shgroup.org.uk**.

There are charitable organizations that help particular groups of people in need. For example:

- Housing&Care21: **www.housingandcare21.co.uk**;
- Royal Alfred Seafarers' Society: **www.royalalfredseafarers.com**;
- Royal British Legion: **www.britishlegion.org.uk**;
- SSAFA, the Armed Forces Charity: **www.ssafa.org.uk**.

Care homes

Care homes offer accommodation and personal care for people who are no longer able to live independently. Some homes also offer care from qualified nurses or specialize in caring for particular groups, such as those with dementia. Care home places can be funded publicly but many people pay for their own care.

There are two main types of care homes: residential and nursing homes:

- *Residential homes* can range from small in size with a few beds, to large-scale facilities. They offer care and support throughout the day and night. Staff are on hand to help with personal care.

- *Nursing homes* offer the same type of care as residential homes but with the addition of 24-hour medical care from a qualified nurse.

There are currently over half a million older people living in residential and nursing homes in the UK. Care homes vary in cost, and fees rise depending on how complex the needs of the elderly person are. If the patient is paying their own fees in a home providing nursing care, the NHS will make a financial contribution towards the nursing care, subject to assessment.

The NHS should pay if the elderly person needs care primarily for a medical condition. Dementia is a medical condition, and so are the needs that come with it. If the elderly person is paying his/her own care home fees, they should be eligible for Attendance Allowance. Contact the Attendance Allowance helpline for a claim pack, or download a form from **www.gov.uk**.

If the NHS will not pay, then the elderly person's income and capital will be assessed to see if they have to pay all or some of the fees themselves. Other rules apply regarding treatment of the elderly person's property. The funding aspect is complex. The starting point is to see what the local authority can provide. Beyond that, careful planning is required so that best use is made of any income and assets. Further information and advice can be found at Care Quality Commission, **www.cqc.org.uk**, and SFE Solicitors for the Elderly, **www.sfe.legal**.

NHS Continuing Health Care is the name given to a package of care that is arranged and funded solely by the NHS when a patient's need for care is primarily due to their need for health care. The elderly person can receive continuing health care in their own home or in their care home, where, in addition to health care and personal care, the NHS will pay the care home fees, including board and accommodation. For more information see **www.nhs.uk/chq/Pages/2392.aspx**.

For information about care homes and nursing homes in the UK, and funding options, take a look at the following websites:

- Citizens Advice: **www.citizensadvice.org.uk**;
- Elderly Accommodation Counsel: **www.eac.org.uk**;
- Registered Nursing Home Association: **www.rnha.co.uk**;
- United Kingdom Home Care Association Ltd: **www.ukhca.co.uk**;
- Friends of the Elderly: **www.fote.org.uk**;
- Independent Age: **www.independentage.org**;
- Jewish Care: **www.jewishcare.org**;
- Action on Elder Abuse: **www.elderabuse.org.uk**;
- Relatives and Residents Association: **www.relres.org**.

Some special problems

Elderly people can suffer from special problems that cause great distress. Families do not necessarily talk about these and they may be unaware of what services are available. Practical help and sometimes financial assistance may be obtainable, so it is worth doing some research.

Falls

One in three people over the age of 65 have a fall each year. Across the UK every year 1.2 million people end up in A&E after a fall, costing the NHS £1.6 billion. Bone loss slowly increases as part of the ageing process but falls can be prevented if the correct action is taken. The Chartered Society of Physiotherapists has published a guide called 'Get up and go', which provides exercises to improve strength and balance and tips on how to fall-proof your home. For more information see: **www.csp.org.uk/publications/get-go-guide-staying-steady**.

Hypothermia

Living in a cold home significantly increases the risk of death during the winter months. Approximately 24,000 more people die in England and Wales between December and March than at other times. Damp is another danger to health. In cold weather the risk of hypothermia is greater: those most at risk are people with dementia, who may not be able to recognize the symptoms of hypothermia or recognize when they are cold. Age UK produces a useful guide on how the elderly can keep warm in winter, 'Winter wrapped up'. See: **www.ageuk.org.uk/health-wellbeing/keeping-your-body-healthy/winter-wrapped-up/preparing-for-winter**.

Elderly people should automatically receive the annual tax-free Winter Fuel Payment (mentioned earlier in this chapter) to help with heating costs. See: **www.gov.uk** – Winter Fuel Payment.

Incontinence

More than 3.2 million people over 65 in the UK suffer from urinary incontinence, and 6.5 million people of all ages are affected by some form of bowel problem. Many do not talk about this or seek help because of embarrassment and they often think nothing can be done. In the case of an elderly person, the doctor should always be consulted. Bladder and bowel problems can often be cured, or at least alleviated, by proper treatment, so contact your GP if you have any concerns about bladder or bowel function.

Malnutrition

Malnutrition and malnourishment are common occurrences in the elderly. The digestive tract is important to our health and elderly people should be aware of how to eat and drink to get the most out of their digestion. People who have difficulty in moving about may not bother to go into the kitchen to get a meal or a drink. Malnourishment leads to hypothermia and dehydration. Drinking enough fluids is as important as eating properly. The elderly should make a conscious effort to drink water, even if they don't feel thirsty. They should have three small meals a day, even if it is only a bowl of porridge or soup. Staying mobile by walking every day will help to keep their joints moving.

Dementia

It is well known that dementia is on the rise – because people everywhere are living longer. Last year's *World Alzheimer Report* estimated that the number of people with the condition, currently 46.8 million, will almost double in the next 20 years. Dementia costs the national economy £26 billion per year. The most common type of dementia is Alzheimer's disease, and dementia is the illness most feared by people over the age of 55, who are understandably concerned about losing their memory and identity. Despite the fact that this is a frightening and confusing illness, planning for the future will make life easier to bear and a positive attitude is vitally important.

The Alzheimer's Society suggests the following simple 'lifestyle tweaks' to help reduce the risk of the disease:

1. *Get active.* There's evidence that regular exercise will prevent dementia more than any other measure.
2. *Eat Mediterranean style.* Pile on the veg, fruit, fish, olive oil and nuts.
3. *Keep up with the check-ups.* Diabetes and high blood pressure increase the risk of dementia.

Should your elderly relative have been diagnosed with dementia there are some treatments available that can delay progression of some forms of the disease. Clinical signs are characterized by progressive cognitive degeneration, together with a decline in the ability to carry out common daily tasks and behavioural changes.

The British Association for Music Therapy trains therapists to work with people living with dementia to help maintain their quality of life and care. Music therapy is an established psychological clinical intervention to help dementia sufferers. To find out more: **www.bamt.org**.

The Alzheimer Show, in association with the Alzheimer's Society, takes place each year in London. It is the UK's only dedicated exhibition and conference for families and professionals caring for someone with dementia (**www.alzheimersshow.co.uk**). The Alzheimer's Society has masses of information and advice for carers and reminds us that people with dementia are still people. We should treat them with respect and dignity, be a good listener and communicator and remember that little things mean a lot. For more information see Alzheimer's Scotland, **www.alzscot.org**, and Alzheimer's Society, **www.alzheimers.org.uk**.

Chapter Eleven
No one is immortal

'The fear of death follows from the fear of life. A man who lives fully is prepared to die at any time.'

MARK TWAIN

Preparing for the end of life is something few of us are comfortable thinking or talking about, whether it is our own life or that of a loved one. This is particularly so while we (or they) are happy, healthy and enjoying good quality of life. It might seem morbid to encourage people to prepare for death, but it is the only certainty in life – we are all going to die at some point. A little preparation and a few basic arrangements, well ahead of the event, could save endless amounts of angst amongst family and friends when death finally occurs. Doesn't this just make sense?

According to Compassion in Dying:

> Seventy per cent of us want little or no medical intervention at the end of life; fifty three per cent believe family can make healthcare decisions on behalf of a loved one; and only four per cent of us have made our treatment wishes known in an Advance Decision.
>
> (Source: **compassionindying.org.uk**)

Making your wishes known and getting your affairs in order well ahead is neither gloomy nor unhealthy: quite the reverse. It is prudent, sensible and unselfish. Being prepared will also allow more quality time with loved ones, particularly when those precious final weeks or days come. It is helpful and will relieve family and care givers at a particularly difficult time lots of strain and stress. Tough discussions and decisions are often not so difficult once the subject is broached. Once you have done so, you can then concentrate on living and enjoying each day as if it could be your last.

Many people find it enormously helpful to have openly talked about end of life related issues in plenty of time. Conversations will differ depending on when and with whom such things are being discussed. If you have reservations about airing such matters, commit them to paper instead. Maybe you are good at making lists, perhaps you have had your 'bucket list' prepared for years and are steadily working your way through it. If so, start writing down all your thoughts and wishes regarding end of life planning, but make sure you tell an appropriate person where this information is located.

Key points in this chapter

This chapter is vital reading for anyone undertaking pre-planning for their end of life. Not everyone wants to think far ahead, but there are a number of matters you should consider attending to as a first priority.

- The first section is all about making your will, and how you can go about it. It also gives some pointers on the Laws of Intestacy and why making a will can save everyone pain and anguish.
- Inheritance Tax is an issue for a growing number of people; it is flagged here but covered fully in Chapter 3.
- Funeral planning is another important factor. You probably already know whether you want to be buried or cremated, but where do you want your funeral to be held?
- There is a section on dealing with a death, some information on the state benefits and tax which may help alleviate some of the unknowns and possible money worries.

Read this chapter so that you can take the initiative and set out your wishes now. Then with these arrangements in hand you can get on with the rest of your life, knowing that when the time comes your loved ones will be aware of what you wanted and be spared making difficult decisions.

The NHS website gives general advice on end of life planning: **www.nhs.uk/planners/end-of-life-care**. Here are other good websites for information and advice on the same subject:

- Dying Matters: **www.dyingmatters.org**;
- Final Fling: **www.finalfling.com**;
- Good Funeral Guide: **www.goodfuneralguide.co.uk**;
- Say it Once: **www.sayitonce.info**;
- Age UK: **www.ageuk.org.uk**.

Everyone deserves as 'good end of life' as possible. If we've spent years trying to live well, shouldn't we make an effort to die the same way? When considering advance decisions, the important thing is not to become emotional, but to get organized and be ready to communicate. As part of the preparation people often explore their thoughts, feelings and preferences regarding some of the following issues:

- making a will;
- organizing your finances;
- drawing up a Lasting Power of Attorney;
- preparing your end of life care plan, including:
  - where you wish to be cared for;
  - advance decision to refuse treatment (do not resuscitate (DNR) form);
  - organ and tissue donation;
  - planning your funeral;
- ensuring all key documents are readily accessible.

You can include in your advance care plan anything that is important to you. Talking openly to trusted friends, family, your GP, other health care professionals or spiritual advisers can be helpful. It is essentially a matter of making sure everyone who needs to know does understand your wishes and intentions, and that your wishes are unambiguous, clearly recorded and easily retrievable when they are needed.

Wills

Apparently 61 per cent of adults in the United Kingdom have not made a will. More worryingly, over one in ten people in the UK have never thought about doing so. According to **unbiased.co.uk**, the South West is the most prepared region in the country, with more than half of the people surveyed saying they have already made a will. People are now living longer, hence the need to protect money and assets so they can be passed on to heirs is even more important.

Your will lets you decide what happens to your money, property and possessions after your death. Making a will can also ensure you don't pay more inheritance tax than you should. Having a will is essential if you live with an unmarried partner, have divorced, remarried, or need to provide for someone with a disability. The importance of making a will cannot be overstressed.

You can write your will yourself, but legal advice is thoroughly recommended, to make sure your will is interpreted the way you wanted. Your will needs to be formally witnessed and signed to make it legally valid. If at any time you wish to update your will, this must be done officially, by means of a codicil. If your circumstances change (death of a loved one, or new family members) you should make a new will.

Laws of intestacy

When a person dies without leaving a valid will, or the will has been lost, the government will decide who inherits their estate (possessions, property and money) according to the laws of intestacy. Without a will there is no guarantee the deceased person's wishes will be carried out, or that their estate will go to those they intended. Only married or civil partners (actually married at the time of death) and some other close relatives can inherit under the rules of intestacy. Children might inherit, but not necessarily the amount intended. An unmarried partner and stepchildren have no rights. A husband, wife or civil partner does not automatically get the whole of the estate. Possessions, including the home, may have to be sold to split the proceeds between the heirs. If the deceased has no partner or children, more distant relatives inherit. If there are no relatives, the state gets the whole lot.

Making a will

It is never too early to make a will, but it is frequently left too late. There are several different types of wills:

- a *single will* relates to an individual;
- *mirror (or joint) wills* are designed for couples who have the same wishes;
- a *property trust will* places the estate into trust for beneficiaries;
- a *discretionary trust will* allows trustees to decide what is best at the time of your death.

There is no 'one size fits all' answer to deciding which sort of will is best. Specialist advice is essential and researching your circumstances (personal and financial) will reveal what kind of will is right for you. When making a will, it is sensible to enquire as to the costs and make sure you get the right advice. Your will should be stored carefully where the relevant people can find it. Review it every few years, or sooner if your situation changes. If you get divorced, this doesn't automatically revoke your will, but if you re-marry this automatically revokes an existing will. It is also important to update your will so that dependants (such as new grandchildren) are not excluded.

There are several ways of making a will: doing it yourself, asking a bank to help you, using a professional will-writing practitioner or a solicitor.

Doing it yourself

If you have very simple circumstances, you can obtain 'template' will forms from stationers, which can be completed and filled in at home. There are also online DIY wills, which can be searched for. You must be over 18, and have the mental capacity to make a will. Some useful information can be found on **moneysavingexpert.com**, Family and health, Cheap and free wills.

Banks

Some banks offer a will-writing service. If you do not have a family solicitor, you can ask if your bank will help. They can advise on wills and the administration of estates. They can introduce clients to a solicitor and keep a copy of the will – plus other important documents – in their safe, which avoids the risk of them being mislaid. If asking them to draw up your will for you, make sure that you can choose your own executor, as sometimes banks charge a lot for this service.

Professional will-writing specialists

A will-writing service can be cheaper than using a solicitor, and more reliable than a DIY will. If considering this option make sure the will-writing service is accredited. There are online services where you visit a website and answer questions about your will. A will writing service could be a good choice if you understand the basics of how wills work, you wish to pay less than a solicitor would charge and your estate is not complex. To find an accredited will-writing service see the Society of Will Writers, **www.willwriters.com**, and the Institute of Professional Will Writers, **www.ipw.org.uk**.

Solicitors

Asking a solicitor to draw up your will for you is usually the most expensive option. But if your estate is complex using a solicitor can save a lot of stress. Depending on where you live, a single will drawn up by a solicitor costs on average around £250, joint wills for couples cost upwards of that. If your affairs are complex the cost will be higher. If you do not have a solicitor, ask friends for a recommendation, or ask Citizens Advice. The Law Society can also provide you with names and addresses; see: **www.lawsociety.org.uk**.

Age UK Legal Services offers legal advice and support. This service is available free of charge to anyone of retirement age: **www.ageuk.org.uk**.

Executors

An executor is the person you appoint in your will to be responsible for handling your estate and making sure your wishes are carried out after you die. It is usual to appoint more than one executor. They may have to decide when to sell your property so that those who inherit get the most money. They are also responsible for making sure the right amount of Inheritance Tax, Capital Gains Tax or Income Tax gets paid. It is important to choose your executors with care, since the job involves a lot of work and responsibility. The person must be over 18, have been informed of the decision and agreed to take on the role. Choosing a professional and impartial executor will incur charges, so bear this in mind if you appoint your solicitor, your accountant or your bank.

The following steps, if taken, will make your executor's job easier:

- list where important documents such as wills, bank accounts and share certificates are stored;
- get regular valuations of your assets;
- appoint more than one executor to share the workload;
- ensure your will is up to date and safely stored;
- be specific with your bequests – even for items of sentimental value.

(Source: *Saga Magazine*, January 2015)

Inheritance Tax

Many people, if asked, say what happens to their estate after they've died doesn't matter as they won't be there to worry about it. For some, the prospect of Inheritance Tax will not arise because the value of their assets is not high enough. However there are many for whom this tax could be a problem. To help avoid some issues, make sure there is a valid will, a list of assets and their current value, any life insurance policies are written into trust, and any substantial gifts are made in good time. The most important thing is to take proper financial advice – it could save thousands of pounds in the future. For detailed information see Chapter 3.

Provision for dependent adult children

A particular concern for parents with a physically or mentally dependent son or daughter is what plans they can make to ensure his or her care continues when they are no longer in a position to manage. This is a complex area and there are no easy answers. Each case varies according to the severity of the disability or illness, the range of helpful voluntary or statutory facilities locally, and the extent to which they, as parents, can provide for their child's financial security in the long term. While social services may be able to advise, parents thinking ahead might do better to consult a specialist organization experienced in helping carers in this situation in order to explore the possible options available to them. Useful addresses are Carers UK, **www.carersuk.org**, and Carers Trust, **www.carers.org**.

Parents concerned about financial matters such as setting up a discretionary trust or making alternative provision in their will should consult their solicitor or accountant.

Money and other worries – and how to minimize them

It is quite usual for people to disregard forward planning until some important lifestyle change occurs, such as the death of a parent or sibling, or the birth of a first child. It is only then that they get a mortality jolt, and start thinking, 'Is it me next?', and other 'what ifs'. Anyone with a family should consider – and review from time to time – the following two things: life insurance and mortgage protection. Most banks and building societies urge home-owners to take out mortgage protection schemes. If you die, the loan is paid off automatically and the family home will not be repossessed. Banks also offer insurance to cover any personal or other loans. This could help a family to avoid being left with debts.

Funeral plans

Taking the worry out of funeral costs is something everyone should consider, because funerals are getting more expensive. According to funeral planner Dignity, the average cost of a funeral has increased by about 60 per cent over the last seven years, in 2014 the cost being around £3,500, and this is expected to rise to around £4,500 by 2019. 'Pay now – die later', as it is known in the industry, is big business in the UK and is estimated to be worth over £500 million a year. Nearly ten per cent of funerals in the UK are now funded by pre-paid plans.

One of the key benefits of funeral plans is that they are guaranteed to cover the costs of the agreed funeral arrangements, regardless of any future rise in price. Pre-pay funeral plans can be bought in two main ways: from a funeral plan provider or from a local funeral director. Payment is flexible, most providers allow a one-off payment in advance, or the option to pay in instalments over 12 to 120 months. Before you take out a funeral plan, do check what's included. Cremation fees tend to be cheaper than burial fees, so if you opt for a cremation funeral plan that fully guarantees third party costs, that is better cover than funeral plans for burials. Plan providers can register with the Funeral Planning Authority (FPA). You can find a list of registered plan providers at: **www.funeralplanningauthority.com**.

There are other ways to help offset funeral costs: by saving in an ISA for your funeral, taking out whole-of-life cover, or home burial – unusual, but legal. You can be buried in your own garden; however, this could affect the value of your property should it be put up for sale in the future. If you or your partner are on low incomes or receive benefits and need help towards the cost of a funeral, there is a government subsidy available. Be aware that this may have to be repaid from any money tied up in the deceased's estate. See: **www.gov.uk** – Bereavement benefits.

For information on funeral plans see the following websites:

- Age UK: **www.ageuk.org.uk**;
- Co-operative Funeral Care: **www.co-operativefuneralcare.co.uk**;
- Dignity: **www.dignityfunerals.co.uk**;
- Golden Charter: **www.goldencharter.co.uk**;
- Golden Leaves: **www.goldenleaves.com**;
- Perfect Choice: **www.perfectchoicefunerals.com**.

Dealing with a death

When someone dies there are many people to be informed, including many companies and organizations, often at a time of great personal distress. You may find it helpful to make a list of all the people who need to be informed (either by letter or telephone) and work through it gradually over the coming days. Don't be afraid to ask family members and friends to help. This is an emotional time, but there are some important things that have to be done first, to comply with the law.

If someone dies at home, you should first *call the family doctor and nearest relative* immediately. If the death was expected the doctor will give you a medical certificate showing the cause of death. If the person dies in hospital, the medical certificate and formal notice will be issued by the hospital.

If someone *dies unexpectedly*, or the family doctor has not seen the person within 14 days of death (28 days in Northern Ireland), *the death is reported to the coroner.* They may call for a post-mortem or inquest. In these circumstances the funeral may need to be delayed.

You must *register the death* with the Registrar of Births, Marriages and Deaths for the district where the death occurred. This must be done within five days (eight days in Scotland). You will then get the documents you need for the funeral. How you register a death differs depending on your circumstances and where you live in the UK. The government website gives information on this.

You can use the Tell Us Once service (**www.gov.uk/after-a-death/organisations-you-need-to-contact-and-tell-us-once**) to report a death to most government organizations in one go. (This service is not available in Northern Ireland or certain local authorities in England.) You do not need to deal with the will, money and property straight away.

Some useful websites that give detailed information and practical advice on what to do after a death are:

- Age UK: **www.ageuk.org.uk**. The Age UK booklet *When Someone Dies* is full of practical information and is available free on request;
- Bereavement Advice Service: **www.bereavementadvice.org;**
- Money Advice Service: **www.moneyadviceservice.org.uk**.

Experiencing the loss of someone close through death is an inevitable part of life, but that does not make it any easier when we experience it, even when the death was expected. This can be even more difficult if circumstances mean that practical changes have to be made, such as moving house. Should this be the case, the bank manager should be notified as soon as possible, so that help can be given until the estate is settled. Adjusting to life without the person takes time, usually more than we realize. Receiving direct mail bearing the name of the deceased is often painful and unnecessary. To avoid this, contact The Bereavement Register, **www.thebereavementregister.org.uk**, who will be able to help.

State benefits and tax

There are some extra financial benefits for widowed people, most of which take the form of a cash payment: Bereavement Payment, Bereavement Allowance and Widowed Parent's Allowance. These have replaced the former Widow's Benefits, as all benefits are now payable on equal terms to men and women alike. To find out more information see: **www.gov.uk** – Bereavement benefits. You will be given a questionnaire (BD8) by the registrar when you register the death. It is important that you complete this, as it acts as a trigger to speed up payment of your benefits.

- *Bereavement Payment* is a tax-free lump sum of £2,000, paid as soon as people are widowed, but only if their spouse or civil partner paid National Insurance contributions and they were not entitled to a State Pension when they died, or the widow/widower was under State Pension age when they died.
- *Bereavement Allowance* is paid if the widow is over 45 but under State Pension age and doesn't have any dependent children. This is paid for up to a year.
- *Full-rate Bereavement Allowance* is paid to widowed people between the ages of 55 and 59 inclusive. Age-related Bereavement Allowance is for younger widows or widowers who do not qualify for the full rate. Bereavement Allowance is normally paid automatically once you have sent off your completed form BB1, so if for any reason you do not receive it you should enquire at your social security office. In the event of you being ineligible, owing to insufficient NICs having been paid, you may still be entitled to receive Income Support, Housing Benefit or a grant or loan from the Social Fund. See website: **www.gov.uk** – Bereavement benefits.
- *Widowed Parent's Allowance* is paid to widowed parents with at least one child for whom they receive Child Benefit. The allowance is usually paid automatically. If for some reason, although eligible, you do not receive the money, you should inform your social security office.
- *War Pensions*: If your late spouse or civil partner served in the armed forces, you may be entitled to help. Contact the Service Personnel and Veterans Agency for more information: **www.veterans-uk.info**.

Retirement pension

Once a widowed person reaches state retirement age, he or she should receive a state pension in the normal way. An important point to remember is that a widow or widower may be able to use the late spouse's NICs to boost the amount he or she receives. See leaflet RM1, 'Retirement – a guide to benefits for people who are retiring or have retired'.

Problems

Both pension payments and bereavement benefits are dependent on sufficient NICs having been paid. Your social security office will inform you if you are not eligible. If this should turn out to be the case, you may still be entitled to receive Income Support, Housing Benefit, Council Tax Benefit or a grant or loan from the Social Fund. If you are unsure of your position or have difficulties, ask Citizens Advice, which will at least be able to help you work out the sums and inform you of your rights. See website: **www.citizensadvice.org.uk**.

Particular points to note

Most widowed people's benefits are taxable. However, the £2,000 Bereavement Payment is tax-free, as are pensions paid to the widows or widowers of armed forces personnel. Widowed people will normally be able to inherit their spouse's additional pension rights, and, where applicable, all widowed people are entitled on retirement to half the graduated pension earned by their husband or wife.

Women in receipt of a widow's pension who remarry, or live with a man as his wife, lose their entitlement to the payment unless the cohabitation ends, in which case they can claim it again. If a woman is aged over 60, the fact that she is living with a man will not affect her entitlement to a retirement pension based on her late husband's contribution record. Widows and widowers of armed forces personnel whose deaths were a direct result of their service are now entitled to keep their armed forces attributable pension for life, regardless of whether they remarry or cohabit.

Tax allowances

Widows and widowers receive the normal Single Person's Tax Allowance of £11,000 (2017) and, if in receipt of Married Couple's Allowance, are also entitled to any unused portion of the allowance in the year of their partner's death.

Organizations that can help

People deal with bereavement in various ways. For some, money problems seem to dominate everything. Help is sometimes available from benevolent funds linked to a spouse's, civil partner's or your own past employment. *A Guide to Grants for Individuals in Need* is a publication kept by most libraries and well worth browsing. A local advice agency, Charity Search (**www.charitysearch.org.uk**) helps older people in financial need receive support from a variety of charitable sources. Or consult Turn2us (**www.turn2us.org.uk**).

For others, the hardest thing to bear is the loneliness of an empty house. For older people who have been part of a couple for decades, widowhood creates a great gulf where for a while there is no real sense of purpose. Many widowed men and women go through a spell of feeling enraged against their partner for dying. Talking to other people who know the difficulties from their own experience can be a tremendous help. The following organizations provide an advisory and support service: Cruse Bereavement Care: **www.cruse.org.uk** and Samaritans: **www.samaritans.org**.

Many professional and other groups offer a range of services for widows and widowers associated with them. These include the Civil Service Retirement Fellowship: **www.csrf.org.uk** and The War Widows Association of Great Britain: **www.warwidows.org.uk**.

Many local Age UK groups offer a counselling service. Trade unions are often particularly supportive, as are Rotary Clubs, all the armed forces organizations and most benevolent societies.

USEFUL RESOURCES AND CONTACTS

Benefits advice

Advice NI (Northern Ireland), tel: 0800 988 2377, website: **www.adviceni.net**.

Age UK, tel: 0800 169 2081, website: **www.ageuk.org.uk**.

Age Cymru, tel: 0800 022 3444, website: **www.agecymru.org.uk**.

Age NI, tel: 0808 808 7575, website: **www.ageni.org**.

Age Scotland, tel: 0800 470 8090, website: **www.agescotland.org.uk**.

Citizens Advice, online advice, or to find your local office in England, Wales and Northern Ireland: **www.citizensadvice.org.uk**; for Scotland: **www.cas.org.uk**.

Entitled To, to identify which benefits you may be eligible for: **www.entitledto.co.uk**.

Government benefits adviser: **www.gov.uk/benefits-calculators**.

Independent Age, advice line: 0800 319 6789, website: **www.independentage.org**.

Money Advice Scotland, tel: 0141 572 0237, website: **www.moneyadvicescotland.org.uk**.

Turn2us, to identify potential sources of funding for those facing financial difficulty: **www.turn2us.org.uk**.

Debt

Citizens Advice, online advice, or to find your local office in England, Wales and Northern Ireland: **www.citizensadvice.org.uk**; for Scotland: **www.cas.org.uk**.

Debt Advice Northern Ireland, tel: 0800 043 0550, website: **www.debtadvicenorthernireland.co.uk**.

Money Advice Service – Debt Test, tel: 0800 138 7777, website: **www.moneyadviceservice.org.uk**.

Money Advice Scotland, tel: 0141 572 0237, website: **www.moneyadvicescotland.org.uk**.

National Debtline, tel: 0808 808 4000, website: **www.nationaldebtline.org**.

Step Change Debt Charity, tel: 0800 138 1111, website: **www.stepchange.org**.

Disabilities

Age UK, tel: 0800 169 2081, website: **www.ageuk.org.uk**.

Age Cymru, tel: 0800 022 3444, website: **www.agecymru.org.uk**.

Age NI, tel: 0808 808 7575, website: **www.ageni.org**.

Age Scotland, tel: 0800 470 8090, website: **www.agescotland.org.uk**.

Action for Blind People, a charity providing practical help and support. Contact through the RNIB Helpline: 0303 123 9999, website: **www.actionforblindpeople.org.uk**.

Action on Hearing Loss (formerly RNID) provides advice and support for people who are deaf or hard of hearing, helpline: 0808 808 0123, website: **www.actiononhearingloss.org.uk**.

Attendance Allowance, helpline: 0345 605 6055.

Carer's Allowance Unit, tel: 0345 608 4321, website: **www.gov.uk/carers-allowance-unit**.

Citizens Advice, online advice, or to find your local office in England, Wales and Northern Ireland: **www.citizensadvice.org.uk**; for Scotland: **www.cas.org.uk**.

Disability Benefits Centre, website: **www.gov.uk/disability-benefits-helpline**.

Independent Age, advice line: 0800 319 6789, website: **www.independentage.org**.

Pension Credit, tel: 0800 99 1234, website: **www.gov.uk/pension-credit**.

Personal Independence Payment, tel: 0345 850 3322, website: **www.gov.uk/pip**.

Winter Fuel Payment Helpline, tel: 03459 15 15 15, website: **www.gov.uk/winter-fuel-payment**.

Energy-saving advice and grants

Citizens Advice consumer helpline: 0345 404 0506, website: **www.citizensadvice.org.uk**.

Energy Saving Trust, tel: 0300 123 1234, website: **www.energysavingtrust.org.uk**.

National Energy Action, a national charity that helps people on low incomes to heat and insulate their homes, tel: 0191 261 5677, website: **www.nea.org.uk**.

NEST (Wales Fuel Poverty Scheme), tel: 0808 808 2244, website: **www.nestwales.org.uk**.

Home Energy Scotland (SCARF), tel: 01224 213 005, website: **www.scarf.org.uk**.

Affordable Warmth Scheme (Northern Ireland Housing Executive), tel: 03448 920 900, website: **www.nihe.gov.uk**.

Warm Homes Scheme Northern Ireland, tel: 0808 278 9970, website: **www.homeserveheating.co.uk**.

Funeral and Inheritance Tax planning

Bereavement Register, tel: 0800 082 1230, website: **www.the-bereavement-register.org.uk**.

National Association of Funeral Directors, tel: 0121 711 1343, website: **www.nafd.org.uk**.

National Society of Allied and Independent Funeral Directors, tel: 0345 230 6777, website: **www.saif.org.uk**.

For Inheritance Tax advice

HMRC Probate and Inheritance Tax, helpline: 0300 123 1072, website: **www.hmrc.gov.uk/inheritance-tax**.

Society of Trust and Estate Practitioners, tel: 020 3752 3700, website: **www.step.org**.

To register a death and advice on what to do afterwards

To register a death in England and Wales: **www.gov.uk/register-a-death**; in Scotland: **www.nrscotland.gov.uk/registration/registering-a-death**; in Northern Ireland: **www.nidirect.gov.uk/articles/registering-death**.

The Department for Work and Pensions carries out eligibility checks on surviving relatives to see what benefits they are entitled to: **www.gov.uk/bereavement-payment/eligibility**.

To obtain a copy of the booklet 'When someone dies' (a step by step guide to what to do) published by Age UK, tel: 0800 169 2081, website: **www.ageuk.org/moneymatters**.

To obtain a copy of the government booklet 'What to do after a death': England and Wales: **www.gov.uk** – Death and bereavement; Scotland: **www.scotland.gov.uk**; Northern Ireland: **www.nidirect.gov.uk**.

Principal Probate Registry: in England and Wales – information and advice on dealing with an estate and contact details for local probate registries, Probate and IHT helpline: 0300 123 1072, website: **www.justice.gov.uk/courts/probate**; in Northern Ireland, Probate Office, tel: 028 9072 4678, website: **www.courtsni.gov.uk/en-gb/services/probate/pages/probateinformation.aspx**; in Scotland, Registers of Scotland, tel: 0800 169 9391, website: **www.ros.gov.uk**.

Tell Us Once Service provides government information about bereavement benefit: **www.gov.uk/after-a-death/organisations-you-need-to-contact-and-tell-us-once**.

Health and health care

Help with Health Costs, tel: 0300 330 1343, website: **www.nhs.uk/NHSEngland/Healthcosts**.

Free prescriptions and other health benefits in the UK – free leaflet, HC11 'Help with health costs', from your GP or pharmacies: **www.nidirect.gov.uk/get-help-covering-health-costs**.

In Scotland, Northern Ireland and Wales prescriptions are free.

For Scotland: free booklet HCS2 'Help with health costs': **www.scotland.gov.uk/Publications**.

Prescription prepayment certificates (England), tel: 0300 330 1341, website: **www.nhsbsa.nhs.uk/HealthCosts/2131.aspx**.

Health Scotland provides information to promote healthy living for people living in Scotland, tel: 0800 22 44 88, website: **www.healthscotland.com**.

Holidays

European Health Insurance Card, to apply pick up a form at the Post Office or tel: 0300 330 1350, website: **www.gov.uk/european-health-insurance-card**.

House and home

Local domestic energy assessors, see EPC Register: **www.epcregister.com**.

Energy Saving Trust has a network of Energy Efficiency Advice Centres and offers free, impartial, expert advice to help consumers reduce their energy use, save money and help the environment, tel: 0300 123 1234, website: **www.energysavingtrust.org.uk**.

Home Energy Scotland, tel: 0808 808 2282, website: **www.energysavingtrust.org.uk/scotland**.

To find an independent surveyor/valuer

Royal Institute of Chartered Surveyors: **www.rics.org/uk**.

For protection

The Property Ombudsman scheme provides an independent review service for buyers or sellers of UK residential property in the event of a complaint. To fill in a consumer enquiry form: **www.tpos.co.uk**.

Help for the elderly

Elderly Accommodation Counsel, tel: 0800 377 7070, website: **www.eac.org.uk**; or **www.firststopadvice.org.uk**.

Independent Age advice line, tel: 0800 319 6789, website: **www.independentage.org**.

Royal Society for the Prevention of Accidents promotes safety and prevention of accidents at work and in the home, and provides information on home safety, tel: 0121 248 2000, website: **www.rospa.com**.

Telephone Preference Service registration line, tel: 0345 070 0707 or register online at: **www.tpsonline.org.uk**.

Home improvement agencies

England – Foundations, tel: 0300 124 0315, website: **www.foundations.uk.com**.

Wales – Care and Repair Cymru, tel: 02920 674 830, website: **www.careandrepair.org.uk**.

Scotland – Care and Repair Forum Scotland, tel: 0141 221 9879, website: **www.careandrepairscotland.co.uk**.

Northern Ireland – Fold Housing Association, tel: 028 9042 8314, website: **www.foldgroup.co.uk**.

Help for tenants

Association of Retirement Housing Managers, tel: 020 7463 0660, website: **www.arhm.org**.

Leasehold Advisory Service, tel: 0207 832 2500, website: **www.lease-advice.org**.

Landmark Leasehold Advisory Services Ltd specializes in providing legal services to residential leaseholders of England and Wales: **www.landmarklease.com**.

Department for Communities and Local Government, for advice on leasehold legislation and policy, tel: 0303 444 0000, website: **www.gov.uk/government/organisations/department-for-communities-and-local-government**.

Independent financial advice

To find an independent financial adviser

Unbiased.co.uk: **www.unbiased.co.uk.**

Chartered Institute for Securities and Investment: **www.cisi.org.**

Personal Finance Society: **www.thepfs.org/yourmoney/find-an-adviser.**

Financial Conduct Authority, tel: 0800 111 6768, website: **www.the-fca.org.uk.**

Financial Ombudsman Service, tel: 0800 0234 567, website: **www.financial-ombudsman.org.uk.**

Financial Services Compensation Scheme, tel: 0800 678 1100, website: **www.fscs.org.uk.**

MyLocalAdviser: **www.mylocaladviser.co.uk.**

Society of Later Life Advisers, tel: 0333 2020 454, website: **www.societyoflaterlifeadvisers.co.uk.**

To find a stockbroker

London Stock Exchange: **www.londonstockexchange.com.**

Wealth Management Association: **www.thewma.co.uk.**

To find equity release providers

Equity Release Council (incorporating SHIP standards), tel: 0844 669 7085, website: **www.equityreleasecouncil.com.**

To find a tax adviser

Chartered Institute of Taxation, tel: 0207 340 0550, website: **www.tax.org.uk.**

Insurance

Association of British Insurers, tel: 020 7600 3333, website: **www.abi.org.uk.**

Association of Medical Insurance Intermediaries, tel: 01736 740491, website: **www.amii.org.uk**.

ABI/BCIS Residential Rebuilding Costs calculator on the RICS website, to check whether you have enough buildings insurance: **www.rics.org**.

Car Pages, to check a car's insurance group: **www.carpages.co.uk**; or CTC: **www.checkthatcar.com**.

British Insurance Brokers Association, to find an insurance broker, consumer helpline: 0370 950 1790, website: **www.biba.org.uk**.

Legal

To find a solicitor

Law Society, tel: 0207 320 5650, website: **www.lawsociety.org.uk**.

Law Society of Scotland, tel: 0131 226 7411, website: **www.lawscot.org.uk**.

Law Society of Northern Ireland, tel: 028 9023 1614, website: **www.lawsoc-ni.org**.

Civil Legal Advice, to check whether you are eligible for legal aid and free legal advice from qualified legal advisers, tel: 0345 345 4345, website: **www.gov.uk/civil-legal-advice**.

Solicitors for Independent Financial Advice, the trade body for solicitor financial advisers. Its membership now also includes accountancy IFAs as members, tel: 01372 721 172, website: **www.sifa.co.uk**.

Legal Ombudsman, for complaints about a legal adviser, tel: 0300 555 0333, website: **www.legalombudsman.org.uk**.

Making a will

Institute of Professional Will Writers, tel: 0345 257 2570, website: **www.ipw.org.uk**.

Power of Attorney

Office of the Public Guardian (England and Wales), registers Lasting Powers of Attorney and helps attorneys carry out their duties, tel: 0300 456 0300, website: **www.gov.uk/government/organisations/office-of-the-public-guardian**.

Office of the Public Guardian, Scotland, tel: 01324 678 300, website: **www.publicguardian-scotland.gov.uk**.

Office of Care and Protection, Northern Ireland, tel: 028 9072 4732, website: **www.courtsni.gov.uk**.

Leisure

Free digital TV channels

Freeview: **www.freeview.co.uk**.

Freesat, tel: 0345 313 0051, website: **www.freesat.co.uk**.

Free bus travel

England and Wales, your local council or: **www.gov.uk/apply-for-elderly-person-bus-pass**.

Scotland, your local council or: **www.transportscotland.gov.uk/public-transport/concessionary-travel**.

Northern Ireland, your local council or: **www.nidirect.gov.uk/free-and-concessionary-bus-and-rail-travel**.

Cheap rail and coach travel

Rail travel in the UK, buy a Senior Railcard from rail stations or some travel agents, or tel: 0345 3000 250, website: **www.senior-railcard.co.uk**.

Voyages-sncf.com (was Rail Europe): **uk.voyages-sncf.com**.

National Express, tel: 08717 81 81 81, website: **www.nationalexpress.com**.

Money

Money Advice Service, for information and advice on money matters: 0800 138 7777, website: **www.moneyadviceservice.org.uk**.

To trace lost savings: get a claim form from British Bankers Association, tel: 0207 216 8800, or Building Societies Association, tel: 0207 520 5900, or National Savings & Investments, tel: 0500 007 007, or, for full information on how to claim, see: **www.mylostaccount.org.uk**.

Unclaimed Assets Register, to trace lost investments, tel: 0844 481 81 80, website: **www.uar.co.uk**.

Internet comparison sites:

www.comparethemarket.com;

www.confused.com;

www.gocompare.com;

www.moneyfacts.com;

www.moneysupermarket.com;

www.which.co.uk/switch;

www.uswitch.com.

Pensions

State Pension forecasting: **www.gov.uk/state-pension-statement**.

For all matters relating to the State Pension, Pension Credit and how to apply see: **www.gov.uk/contact-pension-service**.

State Pension claim line: 0800 731 7898.

Pension Credit helpline: 0800 99 1234.

International Pension Centre, if you live abroad, tel: 0191 218 7777, website: **www.gov.uk/international-pension-centre**.

To check your State Pension age: **www.gov.uk** – State pension.

Pension Tracing Service, tel: 08000 271 300, website: **www.pension-tracing-service-uk.co.uk**.

Pensions Advisory Service for any help understanding your pension rights, tel: 0300 123 1047, website: **www.pensionsadvisoryservice.org.uk**.

Pensions Ombudsman, tel: 0207 630 2200, website: **www.pensions-ombudsman.org.uk**.

Pension Protection Fund (PPF), tel: 0345 600 2541, website: **www.pensionprotectionfund.org.uk**.

Money Advice Service has comparison tables, if you wish to shop around for an annuity, see 'annuity and pensions comparison tables', tel: 0800 138 7777, website: **www.moneyadviceservice.org.uk**.

Service Personnel and Veterans Agency Service, to claim a war widow or widower's pension, tel: 0808 1914 218, website: **www.gov.uk/government/organisations/veterans-uk**.

Society of Later Life Advisers, tel: 0333 2020 454, website: **www.societyoflaterlifeadvisers.co.uk**.

Savings and investments

To find a credit union

Association of British Credit Unions Ltd, tel: 0161 832 3694, website: **www.abcul.org**.

Ace Credit Union Services, tel: 029 2067 4851, website: **www.acecus.org**.

Scottish League of Credit Unions, tel: 0141 774 5020, website: **www.scottishcu.org**.

UK Credit Unions, tel: 01706 214 322, website: **www.ukcu.coop**.

To compare savings accounts

Money Advice Service, tel: 0800 138 7777, website: **www.moneyadviceservice.org.uk** – Comparison tables.

To find out about investment funds

Unit trusts and open-ended investment companies: Investment Association, tel: 020 7831 0898, website: **www.theinvestmentassociation.org**.

Investment trusts: Association of Investment Companies, tel: 0207 282 5555, website: **www.theaic.co.uk**.

Life insurance funds: Association of British Insurers, tel: 0207 600 3333, website: **www.abi.org.uk**.

Ethical investments: Ethical Investment Research Service, tel: 0203 752 5750, website: **www.eiris.org**.

To report suspected investment scams

If you spot a scam or have been scammed, report it and get help. Contact Action Fraud, the UK's National Fraud and Cyber Crime reporting centre, tel: 0300 123 2040, website: **www.actionfraud.police.uk**, or contact the police in your area.

Tax

Free help with tax problems if your income is low

Tax Aid, for help with a tax problem if HMRC can't sort it out, tel: 0345 120 3779, website: **www.taxaid.org.uk**.

Tax Help for Older People, tel: 0845 601 3321 or 01308 488 066, website: **www.taxvol.org.uk**.

For tax help and advice

Association of Taxation Technicians, tel: 0844 251 0830, website: **www.att.org.uk**.

Association of Chartered Certified Accountants, tel: 0141 582 2000, website: **www.accaglobal.com**.

Chartered Institute of Taxation, tel: 0207 340 0550, website: **www.tax.org.uk**.

Institute of Chartered Accountants in England and Wales, tel: 020 7920 8100, website: **www.icaew.co.uk**.

Chartered Accountants Ireland, tel: 00353 1 637 7200, website: **www.charteredaccountants.ie**.

Institute of Chartered Accountants of Scotland, tel: 0131 347 0100, website: **www.icas.com**.

HMRC, for local enquiry centres, see: **www.gov.uk/government/organisations/hm-revenue-customs**. For your local tax office, see your tax return, other tax correspondence or check with your employer or scheme paying you a pension.

Adjudicator's Office, for information about referring a complaint. The adjudicator acts as a fair and unbiased referee looking into complaints about HMRC, including the Tax Credit Office, the Valuation Office and the Office of the Public Guardian and the Insolvency Service, tel: 0300 057 1111, website: **www.adjudicatorsoffice.gov.uk**.

If you have received an HMRC-related phishing/bogus email, forward it to the following email address and then delete it: **phishing@hmrc.gsi.gov.uk**.

HMRC helplines

Income Tax: 0300 200 3300.

National Insurance: 0300 200 3500.

Capital Gains Tax: 0300 200 3300.

Self-Assessment: 0300 200 3310.

Tax Credit: 0345 300 3900.

Volunteering

To find out about how to volunteer across the UK

REACH: **www.reachskills.org.uk**.

Volunteer Now (Northern Ireland): **www.volunteernow.co.uk**.

Volunteer Scotland: **www.volunteerscotland.net**.

Volunteering England: **www.volunteeringengland.org.uk**.

WCVA – Wales Council for Voluntary Action: **www.wcva.org.uk**.

Leading volunteering organizations

British Red Cross: **www.redcross.org.uk**.

Citizens Advice: **www.citizensadvice.org.uk**.

Lions Clubs UK: **www.lionsclubs.co**.

Royal Voluntary Service: **www.royalvoluntaryservice.org.uk**.

Checks for volunteering

Disclosure and Barring Service, tel: 0300 0200 190, website: **www.gov.uk** – Disclosure and barring service.

Work

To find out about rights at work

Advisory, Conciliation and Arbitration Service, tel: 0300 123 1100, website: **www.acas.org.uk**.

Labour Relations Agency (Northern Ireland), tel: 028 9032 1442, website: **www.lra.org.uk**.

Jobcentre Plus (Great Britain), tel: 0345 608 8545, new applications helpline: 0800 055 6688, website: **www.gov.uk/contact-jobcentre-plus**.

Jobs and Benefits Office (Northern Ireland), tel: 0300 200 7822, website: **www.nidirect.gov.uk/contacts/jobs-benefits-offices-jobcentres**.

National Careers Service (UK), tel: 0800 100 900, website: **nationalcareersservice.direct.gov.uk**.

Skills Development Scotland, tel: 0141 285 6000, website: **www.skillsdevelopmentscotland.co.uk**.

Careers Wales, tel: 0800 028 4844, website: **www.careerswales.com**.

Professional Contractors Group, tel: 0208 897 9970, website: **www.pcg.org.uk**.

Recruitment and Employment Confederation, tel: 020 7009 2100, website: **www.rec.uk.com**.

To register a new business

HMRC, newly self-employed helpline: 0300 200 3500, website: **www.gov.uk/government/organisations/hm-revenue-customs/contact/newly-self-employed-helpline**.

Companies House, tel: 0303 1234 500, website: **www.gov.uk/government/organisations/companies-house**.

Organizations providing free or subsidized help

Government resources

The government's online resource for businesses: **www.gov.uk**. National Enterprise Network, for regional help: **www.nationalenterprisenetwork.org**.

Northern Ireland Business Information: **www.nibusinessinfo.co.uk.**

Scotland: **www.mygov.scot.**

Business Wales: **www.business.wales.gov.uk**.

Other resources

StartUp Britain, an initiative of the Centre for Entrepreneurs, will help you find information about starting a business and contains offers and discounts available to new business start-ups: **www.startupbritain.org**.

The Prince's Initiative for Mature Enterprise has merged with Business in the Community and addresses the growing unemployment issue of the over 50s: **www.bitc.org.uk**.

INDEX

Note: page numbers in *italic* indicate tables.

100 Things I Wish I'd Known About Diabetes 145
2017
  anniversaries 2–3
  top five wishes of pensioners for 3

accountants 64, 156–59
  chartered 67, 74–75, 98, 155, 156, 157, 161, 176
  professional bodies for 94–95
Advisory, Conciliation and Arbitration Service (ACAS) 172
Age UK 28, 231–32, 241, 242
  advice on 'fitter feet' 138
  and boosting bone health 146
  counselling services 264
  funeral plans 260
  Legal Services 258
  and number of people in England over age of 76
    living alone 231
  Staying Safe 115
  website 115, 138
  'Winter wrapped up' guide to keeping warm 250
alarm systems *see also* your home
  personal and community 236
  security 115
  smoke 233
alcohol 121, 122, 126, 127, 128, 139, 143, 144
    see also health
Altmann, Baroness 179
Alzheimer's Society
  and Alzheimer Show 252
  'lifestyle tweaks' 251
annuities 34–36
  obtaining 35–36
  and other options 35
  types of 34–35
art and antiques
  Association of Art and Antique Dealers 117
  British Antique Dealers' Association 117
articles (on)
  '"Extreme green" homes where energy costs £1 per day' (*Daily Telegraph*, 2016) 111
  'How to spot a bad physician' (*The Oldie*, 2014) 134
  length of British tax code (*The Guardian*, 2015) 53
  older drivers ((LaterLife) 238
  saving by switching energy suppliers (*The Sunday Times*, 2016) 109
  'Should you switch to a Junior ISA?' (www.moneysavingexpert.com) 45
  tax legislation in the UK (*Daily Telegraph*, 2009) 53
arts and culture 202–06
  arts and crafts: organizations 202
  creative arts 202
  cultural holidays 202–03
  festivals 203–04
  film 204
  museums 204–05
  music: opera, ballet and concerts 205
  theatre 205–06
  TV and radio audiences 205

baby boomers 4, 102
bad debts 152
banks (and) 32, 37–38, 44, 45, 48, 51, 96, 106, 170 *see also* National Savings and Investments (NS&I) *and* scams/scammers
  British Bankers Association 273
  business accounts 177
  as executors 268
  interest on accounts 57, 79
  loan insurance 259
  offshore accounts 73
  services 96
  will-writing services 257
BBC *Crimewatch Roadshow* 115
BBC *Rip Off Britain* 100
Becket, M 46
benefits (and) 28–29
  for help with eye problems 137
  housing 119, 120 *see also* council tax
  Pension Credit 29
  Turn2Us 29
  Universal Credit 134
Birtles, J (MoneyMagpie.com) 119
bonds 48–50
  gilts 48
  corporate 49
  investment 49–50
Branson, R 148, 151
British Insurance Brokers Association 117, 173
British Insurers, Association of 117, 132
    see also long-term care insurance
British Red Cross 190, 235, 237, 242
Brown, E 229
budget for the year (example) *12*
budgeting and finances *see* planning for the future, money and your life
business
  at home 178
  names 176
  plans 178

Campaign for Better Transport 206
Capper, W (MBE) 217
care *see also* carers *and* elderly parents and relatives
  and nursing agencies 199
  respite 243
carers 243–44, 252
  allowance for 244

holiday breaks for 243
and Home Responsibilities Protection (HRP) 244
Carers Trust 187, 241, 243, 259
Carers UK 187, 232, 259
charities
Action on Hearing Loss 138, 266
British Heart Foundation 144, 189
Cancer Research UK 144, 189
Diabetes UK 145, 189
Elizabeth Finn Care 28
Tax Aid 56, 77, 276
Tax Help for Older People (TOP) charity 56, 76, 276
Charity Search 245, 264
children, investing for (in) 44–46
Child Trust Fund (CTF) 45
Children's Bonds 45–46
children's savings account 44
Help-to-Buy ISA 45
Junior ISA 45
pension 46
useful reading for 46
Chiropodists and Podiatrists, Society of 138 *see also* Age UK
Citizens Advice Bureau (CAB) 56, 99, 119, 183–85, 243, 257
volunteer roles 184–85
volunteer training 185
Civil Service Retirement Fellowship 238, 264
clutter, clearing 118–19
and Clear Your Clutter Day 118
coach and rail holidays (and) 206–07
coach operators 206–07
rail travel safety and tour operators 207
Companies House 82, 87, 98, 167–68, 176, 177
company pension schemes 21–23
auto-enrolment 23
questions on 23
types of 21–22
career average 22
final salary 21–22
group personal pension 22
money purchase 22
complaints and 'how to complain' 97–99
The Complete Guide to Letting Property 118
council tax 119–20
benefit 120
disputes 120
exemptions from 120
cruising holidays 207–09
on cargo ships 209
top tips for 208
websites for 208–09
Cruse Bereavement Care 264

The Daily Telegraph Tax Guide 2016 77
death, preparing for (and) 253–64
Compassion in Dying 253
end-of-life planning 254–55
funeral plans (and) 259–61
legal requirements 261
practical advice 261
registration of death 261
minimizing money and other worries 259
organizations that can help 264
provision for dependent adult children 259
state benefits and tax 262–66
bereavement allowance 262
bereavement payment 262
full-rate bereavement allowance 262
and points to note 263
problems 263
retirement pension 263
tax allowances 264
war pensions 262
widowed parent's allowance 262
wills (and) 255–58
bank will-writer services 257
doing it yourself 257
executors 258
inheritance tax 258 *see also* tax
laws of intestacy 256
professional will-writers 257
solicitors 257
types of 256–57
definition(s) of
tax avoidance (HMRC) 54
tax evasion (HMRC) 54
dementia 243, 247, 248, 249, 250, 251–52
dentists/dentistry 136, 139
health plans 139
websites for 139
Diabetes UK 145 *see also* health: common disorders
and *100 Things I Wish I'd Known About Diabetes* 145
Disabled Facilities Grants 235
Disabled Travellers' Guide 239
Disclosure and Barring Service (DBS) checks 183, 199
discrimination in employment 171
Dudley, B 179

Einstein, A 1
Eisenhower, General 148, 153
the elderly, special accommodation and options for 246–52
care homes 247, 248–49
nursing 249
residential 248
websites for 249
housing with care 247
living with family 247
retirement homes 248
sheltered or retirement housing 247
and special problems 250–52
dementia 251–52 *see also* Alzheimer's Society *and subject entry*
falls 250
hypothermia 250
incontinence 250
malnutrition 251
the elderly (and) *see also* AgeUK
Silverline 232
statistics and surveys on 231–32
elderly parents and relatives (and) 229–52
accommodation *see* the elderly, special accommodation for
benefits and allowances for elderly and disabled people 243–45 *see also* carers

elderly parents and relatives (and) *continued*
attendance allowance 244
cold weather payment 245
free off-peak bus travel 245
free TV licence 245
personal independence allowance 244
winter fuel payment 245, 250
care services and agencies 240–41
Council Tax reduction 234
Disabled Facilities Grant 235
emergency care for pets 242
financial assistance from charities/organizations 245–46
getting around for older drivers/driving licence renewals 238
holidays 239
home improvement agencies/handy person service providers 235–36
key voluntary organizations for 237–38
lasting power of attorney (LPA) 239–40
Lifebook (Age UK) 240
local authority services 233–34
loneliness and isolation 231–32
maintaining independence and safety (via) 232–36
alarm systems – personal and community 236
health care and specialist services 234
help with home repairs and adaptations 235–36
practical help and holiday breaks for carers 242–43 *see also* carers
provision of necessary care 240–41
energy bills, reducing (by) 109–11
buying an eco-home 111
smart meters 110
switching supplier 109
tips for 110–11
and useful organizations 111
useful websites/magazines for 110
England Care Quality Commission (CQC) 247
Enterprise Investment Scheme (EIS) 67
equities and other investments 39–44
Enterprise/Seed Enterprise Investment Schemes 43–44
individual savings account (ISA) 43
investment trusts 41
Lifetime Individual Savings Account (LISA) 43
ordinary shares listed on the London Stock Exchange 42–43
other tax incentives for interest and dividends 44
unit trusts and OEICs 40–41
equity release 29–30
Equity Release Council 30, 271
eyesight and blindness, associations and information for 137

FALCON (Fraud And Linked Crime Online) Organized Crime Command 85
Federation of Small Businesses 171
financial advisers 26
and independent financial advisers (IFAs) 36, 92–93, 177
financial assistance 231, 241, 245–46, 250
Charity Search 245, 264
Financial Assistance Scheme (FAS) 28
Turn2Us 29, 245
Financial Conduct Authority (FCA) 26, 51, 52, 93–94
Financial Ombudsman Service (FOS) 26, 51, 100, 117
top tips on financial predators and fraud 89–91
1. are they regulated? 90
2. 'out of the blue' 90
3. vishing and smishing 90
4. passwords, PINs, chip-and-PIN 91
5. internet shopping 91
6. keeping up to date with your finances 91
Financial Planning, Institute of 36
Financial Services Compensation Scheme (FSCS) 15, 26, 32, 38, 39, 51, 90, 94, 271
First Stop advice on housing and care 236, 247
Foreman, G 13
franchising 169–70 *see also* starting your own business
and the British Franchise Association (BFA) 170
the future, your money and your life *see* planning for the future, money and your life

Genders, D 77
'Get up and Go' (falls prevention guide, CSP) 129
Go Away Great Britain: The Oldie's Guide to Britain Through Its Festivals 203
Gorvett, M (and) 20, 21–22
five pension tips 15–16
tips on savings 31
grandparents
help for 140–41
investing for grandchildren 44–46
outstanding examples of 201–02
role of 200–01
Grandparents Plus website 141
Guide to Freelancing (IPSE) 175
A Guide to Grants for Individuals in Need 264
Guide to Taking Your Pension 35

health (and) 121–47 *see also* health insurance; key points; long-term care insurance *and* National Health Service
accident prevention (and) 129–30
falls 129
'Get up and Go' guide 129
aches, pains, abnormalities 130
and symptoms needing medical investigation 130
alcohol (and) 128
NHS Change4Life drinks checker 128
support/organizations for drinkers 128
common disorders *see* health: common disorders
complementary and alternative medicine 136–37
websites for 136–37
depression 141
disability 147 *see also* elderly parents and relatives
eyes 137
feet 137–38
food safety 127–28
and prevention of poisoning – NHS suggestions 127–28
healthy eating 125–26

hearing and specialist organizations 138
income protection 133
keeping fit 123–24
keeping healthy in the heat 126–27
organized activities and websites 124–25
personal relationships 140–41 *see also* grandparents
screening and assessment options 133
sleep/insomnia 138–39
and tips for a good night's sleep 139
website advice on 139
smoking and support organizations 129
teeth 139 *see also* dentists/dentistry
top tips for achieving healthy retirement 123
useful websites 123
health: common disorders 141–47
aphasia 142
arthritis 142
asthma 142–43
back pain 143
blood pressure 143
cancer 143–44
chest and heart diseases 144
constipation 145
diabetes 129, 137, 145, 251 *see also* Diabetes UK
migraine 146
osteoporosis and menopause problems 146–47
stroke 147
and FAST 147
health insurance (and) 130–32
being a private patient without insurance 131
choosing a scheme 131
medical tourism 132
private medical insurance (PMI) organizations 131
Health and Safety Executive 171
Health Services Ombudsman (England) 136
Heritage Help: Joint Committee of the National Amenity Societies (JCNAS) 212
Historic England 212
HM Revenue and Customs (HMRC) 36–38, 55–57, 63, 71–77, 86, 90, 149–50, 152, 156–62, 166, 167, 175 *see also* income tax *and* tax
definitions of tax avoidance and evasion 54
helpline for newly self-employed 166
mistakes by 64–65
'Private Residence Relief' (helpsheet 283) 67
Stamp Duty Land Tax (SDLT) 107
'tax trap': HMRC regulation number 35 (IR35) 160–61, 175
hobbies and holidays 200–28 *see also* key points
arts and culture 202–06 *see also subject entry*
coach and rail holidays 206–07 *see also subject entry*
cruising 207–09 *see also subject entry*
for the disabled 220–21
education at home: books, libraries and reading groups 209–10
gardens and gardening 211
general information on
airlines 226
airport meet-and-greet services 226–27
overseas travel 226, 227
heritage, history and related holidays 211–12
holiday complaints and assistance *see subject entry*
home-swapping holidays 223
important issues: ABTA, ATOL registration, health, insurance *and* money 227–28
learning holidays 210
solo – for singles 221–22
sports 213–20 *see also* sport/sporting holidays
three-generation (3G) holidays 222–23
and travel insurance/top tips for 223–24
Hodgkinson, L 118
holiday complaints and assistance 225
cancelled or overbooked flights 225
compensation for lost baggage 225
complaining to an airline 225
Holmes Jr, O W 53, 55
home improvement agencies/handy person service providers 235–36
How the Stock Market Works 46
Hyde, M 53

income, protecting (in event of illness or death) 177
income tax (and/on) 21, 30, 57–58, 62–64, 258 *see also* tax
income free of tax 60–61
income received gross 63
investments 62–63
mis-sold PPI compensation 'interest' 64
mistakes by HMRC 64
reclaiming tax on savings income 63
savings 62
self-assessment dates/tax tip 65
Independent Age 243
advice guides and website 11
Independent Professionals and the Self Employed, Association of (IPSE) 161
Individual Savings Account (ISA) 30
Inheritance Tax and wills (and) 68–75
help in dealing with a tax investigation 71–75
key aspects (as of summer 2016) of 2015 Budget 69–71
tax tips for 68, 70
tax treatment of trusts 71
insurance 115–17 *see also* health insurance; life assurance policies *and* long-term care insurance
advice on 117
and British Insurance Brokers Association 117, 173
brokers 96, 131, 172–73, 177
buildings 116
contents 116–17
income protection 133
policies for business risks 177
professional valuations for 117
for small businesses 172–73
travel 224
intellectual property 176
Intellectual Property Office 170, 176
investing 31–33
general strategy for 33
and sources of investable funds 33
tips for 31–32
and types of investment 32
IT systems and support 178

key points (for)
care of elderly parents and relatives 230–31
death 254
health 122
hobbies and holidays 201
pensions, savings, financing retirement 14–15
planning for the future 2
preparing for death 254
starting your own business 148–49
Super Saturday, scams and complaints 78–79
tax 55–56
working for others: volunteering and paid work 180–81
your home 102–03

The Lady 199, 241
Lasting Power of Attorney (LPA) 231, 239–40
Laterlife website 192, 224
Law Society 95, 257
Lawrenson, D 32, 173
leasehold advice (from)
Association of Retirement Managers (ARHM) 108
Leasehold Advisory Service (LAS) 108
Leasehold Valuation Tribunal (LVT) 108
legislation: The Companies Act 168
Lewis, M 35–36
website 100
Lewis, P 110
libraries, using 209
life assurance policies 46–48
alternatives to surrendering 48
options: without profits, with profits *or* index-linked 47
traded endowment policies (TEPs) 48
whole-life, term *and* endowment 46–47
limited liability company/limited company (and) 167–68
approval of company name 168
Certificate of Incorporation 167
directors' responsibilities under The Companies Act 168
registration with Companies House 167
The Little Book of Big Scams 100
locksmiths: safety and security tips from Master Locksmiths Association 114–15
long-term care insurance (and) 132–33
A Brief Guide to Long Term Care Insurance: Choosing the Right Option for You 132
critical illness insurance 132
hospital care cash plans 133

marketing
loyalty 117
promotion strategy 178
and selling 178
Mature Times 202, 207, 222, 223 *see also* travel insurance
Migraine Trust 146
money comparison websites: www.moneysavingexpert.com 79
Moules, J 175
Music Therapy, British Association for 251

National Accident Helpline 130
National Care Line 241
National Employment Savings Trust (NEST) 23
National Federation of Occupational Pensioners (NFOP) 28
National Health Service (and) 133–36
the 111 service 130, 134
changing your GP 134
Choices website 136
choosing a GP 133–34 *see also* articles
complaints 135–36
Continuing Health Care 249
going into hospital 135
help with NHS costs 134–35
Low Income Scheme 134
Patient Advice and Liaison Service 136
prescriptions 135
websites 135
National Insurance (NI)
Contributions (NICs) 17, 158, 160
credits 244
Disabled Facilities Grant 235
records/contributions 18, 171
National Savings and Investments (NS&I) 36–37
Children's Bonds 37, 45–46
easy-access savings accounts 36
fixed interest savings certificates 36
Income Bonds 36
index-linked savings certificates 36
Pensioner Bonds 37
Premium Bonds 37
nonagenarians 229
Northern Ireland 101, 110, 112, 174, 176, 205, 211, 212, 217, 235, 237, 245, 261
healthcare in 135
Law Society of 95
and the Ulster Way 217

Ogunlaru, R 175
Old and Wealthy – End of the Golden Years (ITV, *Tonight*, 2016) 4
The Oldie 203
Ombudsmen *see also* Scotland
consumer/Ombudsman Services 98 , 100
Health Services (England) 136
Legal Services 95
Pensions 27–28, 52
Property Ombudsman Service 100
Public Services (Wales) 136

paid employment (and) 191–93
searching for 191–93
tips for your job search campaign 193
Palmer, K 111
Pension Credit 17, 29, 119, 120, 135, 266
Pension Protection Fund (PPF) 28, 52
pensions 6, 177 *see also* State Pension *and* State Pension entitlement
pensions, savings and financing retirement (and/with) 13–52, 177
alterations in operation and taxing of 'defined contribution' 13–14
annuities 34–36 *see also subject entry*
benefits, help by claiming 28–29 *see also* benefits
defined contribution pensions 19–26 *see also* company pension schemes
and 2014 Budget 'pensions liberation' 19–20
Lifetime Individual Savings Account (LISA) 25

minimum retirement age for 26
self-invested personal pensions (SIPPs) 24–25
and small pension pots 25
equities and other investments 39–44 *see also subject entry*
equity release 29–30
fixed interest securities: gilt-edged and permanent interest-bearing shares (PIBS) 39
general investment strategy 33
help and advice (from/on) 26–28 *see also* Pensions Advisory Service
Pensions Ombudsman 27–28
previous schemes 26–27
trustees/managers 27
importance of pensions and investment planning 15–16
investable funds, sources of 33
investing for your grandchild 44–46 *see also* children, investing for
investor protection 51–52
long-term lock-ups 46–51 *see also* bonds; life assurance policies *and* structured products
National Savings and Investments (NS&I) 36–37 *see also subject entry*
predators and pensions liberation fraud 26
protection for pension scheme members 28
savings as part of retirement planning 30–33 *see also* investing
top five pension tips (Gorvett) 15–16
understanding your State Pension entitlement *see* State Pension entitlement
variable interest accounts 37–38
fixed term 38
high interest savings 38
instance access savings 38
Pensions Advisory Service 27
Pensions Ombudsman 27–28, 52
personal relationships 122, 140–41
organizations for help/advice on 140
planning for the future, money and your life (and) 1–12 *see also* key points
balancing the books 9–10
budget (example) *12*
doing the sums for 5–6, 11
estimating expenditure (on) 7–9
food and drink 7
household and property 7–8
leisure 8
sundries 9
travel 8
estimating income 6–7
the 'grey pound' 5
how to go about it 10–11
increasing retirement income 11
pre-retirement 4–5
websites for 5

The Rebel Entrepreneur: Rewriting the Business Rulebook 175
red tape 53, 171, 173, 178
redundancy 192 *see also* paid employment
money 33
payments 61
Redundancy Help 192
reports (on)
best places to live in Britain (BBC) 101
housing and the elderly (Care and Repair England) 232
A New Vision for Older Workers: Retain, Retrain, Recruit (UK) 179
The Stiglitz Report: Reforming the International Monetary and Financial Systems in the Wake of the Global Crisis 101
wealth of the over 50s (Centre for Economics and Business Research) 5
wealth of the over 50s (Saga) 5
Working Lives (Aviva, 2016) 191
World Alzheimer Report 251
research on
heart health (Sirco) 144
hospital admissions for constipation (*Mature Times*) 145
how the over 50s see old age (*Mature Times*) 121
life satisfaction and happiness (Office for National Statistics, 2015) 1
respite care 183, 243
Reuvid, J 175
Royal Institution of Chartered Surveyors' Building Cost Information Service 116
Royal Society for the Prevention of Accidents (ROSPA) 113, 129
Royal Voluntary Service (RVS) 181, 186, 187, 232, 237, 243, 277
Russell, J 53

Saga Magazine 191, 258
Samaritans 141, 190, 264
savings (through) 79–81
bank account upgrades/switching 79
cash back and air mile credit cards 80
checking direct debits 80
consumer ombudsman for utilities, phone, internet and property 81
estate agent fees 80
insurance discounts on renewals 80
lost premium bonds/NSI investments 80
overpaying your mortgage 80
Property Ombudsman – estate and letting agents 81
TV and broadband bundles 80
utilities 80
scams/scammers (and) 81–94
advance fee fraud 83
advice from FOS 89–92 *see also* Financial Ombudsman Service
advice on scam mail (from)
FALCON 85
'Sterling' fraud prevention team 85
www.thinkjessica.com 85
credit and bank card cloning or snatching 84–85
email scammers 86–87
five tests for staying safe from 82–83
The Little Book of Big Scams 88
online fraud 87–89
protecting yourself from 81–83
reporting 85
romance scams 84
surprise prize-ballot win 83–84, 85
telephone cold calls and Telephone Preference Service (TPS) 86
the worst passwords 89

Scotland (and) 112, 135, 174, 205, 211, 235, 237, 245, 261
accountants in 176
Alzheimer's Scotland 252
Law Society of 95
Scottish Commission for the Regulation of Care 247
Scottish Public Services Ombudsman 136
Seed Enterprise Investment Scheme 43, 67
SERPS 17, 18 *see also* State Pension entitlement
Silver Surfers 222
Smith, A E 150
Smith, G 72–74
Smith, S 11, *12*
sole traders 72, 149–50, 158–59, 160, 161, 165–66, 176
solicitors 96, 98, 99, 167, 168, 169, 170, 175, 176, 240, 257–59, 272
Solicitors for the Elderly (SFE) 249
Solicitors for Independent Financial Advice (SIFA) 95
Solicitors Regulation Authority 95
Soul Trader: Putting the Heart Back Into Your Business 175
sport/sporting holidays 213–19
boats and boating 213
cycling 214
fishing 214–15
golf 215
rambling and walking 216–17
running 217
skiing 218
swimming 218
tennis 219
Start Up and Run Your Own Business 175
starting your own business (and) 148–78
alternative ways of 168–70
buying a business 168–69
franchising 169–70
checklist for 175–78
as different from employment 151
help, advice and training (from) 174–75
adult education centres 174
Association of Independent Professionals and the Self Employed 175
Business is Great 174
business start-up websites 175
Federation of Small Businesses 175
government resources 174
solicitors 175
Start-up Britain 174
insurance/package insurance 172–73
marketing tips *see* starting your own business: marketing tips
operational and other issues 170–72
employing staff: legislation, discrimination *and* disputes 171–72
inventions and intellectual property 170
licences 170
permissions 171
paperwork 155–57
basic bookkeeping 156
accountants 156–57
planning (and) 152–55
income and expenditure forecast (stage 3) 155
learning why businesses fail 152–53
market research (stage 2) 154–55
objectives (stage 1) 153–54
practical and emotional tips for 155
property investment 173
secret ingredient for 150–51
step-by-step guide to starting a small business 149–50 *see also* HMRC
tax and National Insurance (and/for) 158–62 *see also* tax
IR35 regulation 161
limited companies 160–61
partnerships 160
sole traders 158–59
and tax-deductible expenses 159
VAT flat-rate scheme 162
VAT registration 161–62
trading formats 165–68
limited company 167–68
partnership 166–67
sole trader 165–66
useful reading for 175
starting your own business: marketing tips 162–65
advertising 164
agencies 164
awards 164
business alliances 165
discounts and offers 163
flyers and business cards 163
learning when to say 'no' 164
personal contacts and networking 163
sponsorship 164
testimonials 164
your own website and/or social media 162–63
State Pension 6, 14, 15–16, 29, 56, 191, 262–63, 274
State Pension entitlement (and) 16–19, 20, 23, 26, 180, 244
early retirement 18
obtaining pension forecast 18
SERPS 17, 18
sources of help and advice on 19
top-up/S2P 18
step-by-step guide to starting a small business 149–50 *see also* HMRC
stockbrokers 96–97
structured products 50–51
deposits 50
investments 50–51
study on productivity and flexibility of older workers (Age UK) 180
Stuttaford, T 134 *see also* articles
Successful Property Letting: How to Make Money in Buy-to-Let 32, 173
Sugar, Lord A 165
Super Saturday, scams, complaints (and) 78–100 *see also* complaints; key points *and* scams/scammers
adviser, types of 94–97
defeating over-charging by making savings *see* savings (through)
further reading for 100
professional advisers 92–94 *see also* financial advisers

surveys (on)
housing and the elderly (English Housing Survey) 233
loneliness in the elderly (Campaign to End Loneliness) 231
personal relationships (Relate) 140

table: example budget for the year *12*
tax (and) 53–77 *see also* council tax; HM Revenue and Customs (HMRC); income tax *and* value added tax (VAT)
allowances 58–59
Blind Person's 59, 137
Married Couple's 59, 264
Personal 6, 58, 62
for same-sex partners 59
for widowed partners 59, 264
avoidance/evasion 54–55, 72, 150, 152
Bereavement Payment 263
Capital Gains Tax (on) 21, 30, 39, 66–68, 258
assets not subject to 66–67
selling a family business 68
your home 67
-deductible expenses 159
evasion 150, 152
failure in dealing with 152
further information on 76–77
help with the complications of 56
income free of 60–61
Inheritance Tax 20, 67, 68–75, 258 *see also* Inheritance Tax and wills
IR35 (HMRC) 160–62, 175
PAYE 160, 171
Pensions Death Tax 20
rebates 65–66
record keeping: obligations and deadlines 177
relief 60
retiring abroad (and) 75–76
double tax agreement 76
Statutory Residence Test 76
on savings and investments 62
self-assessment 56–57
tips on
inheritance tax and wills 68
investments 62, 63
joint accounts 63
ownership of two homes 67
reclaiming tax on savings income 63
savings 62
shares 63
useful reading on 77
Thomson, J 179
Thynne, J 118
Tips for Meanies: Thrifty Wisdom from The Oldie 119
Tolley's Tax Guide 53
top tips for
3G holidays 222
buying travel insurance 224
choosing financial advisers 93
cruising 208
dealing with email scammers 87
fraud and scams – trust your instincts 92
free online security advice 89
healthy retirement 123
home repairs and improvements 111–12
job search campaigns 193
keeping safe from telephone cold calls 86
paying by credit card/dealing with online fraud 89
staying safe from scammers 83, 84
trade and professional associations 176
travel (and)
Air Travel Advisory Bureau (ATAB) 225
websites 225
travel insurance 223–24
Mature Times 223
top tips 224
websites for 224
Turn2us 264

The Ultimate Guide to Grandparenting 200
University of the Third Age (U3A) 200–01
useful resources and contacts (for) 265–79
benefits advice 265
debt 265–66
disabilities 266
energy-saving advice and grants
funeral and Inheritance Tax planning 267
Inheritance Tax advice 267
health and health care 268–69
holidays 259
house and home 269–70
independent financial advice 271
insurance 271–72
legal: finding a solicitor; making a will *and* Power of Attorney 272–73
leisure: cheap rail and coach travel, free bus travel and free digital TV 273
money 273–74
pensions 274–75
registering a new business 278–79
registration of death/advice 268
savings and investments, and suspected scams 275–76
tax 276–77
volunteering 277
work/rights at work 278

value added tax (VAT) 68, 75, 107, 112
flat-rate scheme 162
obligations 177
registration 161–62
venture capital trusts (VCTs) 44, 61, 67
voluntary work (for/with) 185–90 *see also* Citizens Advice
animals 186–87
armed and ex-services 187
bereavement 188
children and young people 188
choosing the right kind of 185–86
conservation 188
and Disclosure and Barring Service (DBS) check 183
the elderly 187
families 189
health and disability 189
heritage 189
long-term and overseas volunteering 190–91
opportunities for 181–83

voluntary work (for/with) *continued*
politics 190
social welfare 190
websites for 186

Wales (and) 174, 176, 205, 206, 211, 212, 213, 215, 237
bus passes 245
Care Standards Inspectorate for Wales 247
Disability Wales 235
Disabled Facilities Grant 235
home improvement agencies in 235
NHS 135
Public Service Ombudsman 136
Volunteering Wales 186
War Widows Association of Great Britain 264
The Way I See It: Rants, Revelations and Rules for Life 165
Wealth Management Association 97
'Why does the UK have the longest tax code in the world?' (*The Guardian*, 2015) 53
working for others 179–99 *see also* paid employment *and* voluntary work
Citizens Advice 183–85
employment ideas for 194–99
caring for others 199
consultancy and contracting 194–95
house sitting 198–99
interim management 195
market research 197
non-executive directorships 195–96
paid work for charities 197
public appointments 196–97
teaching and tutoring 198
tourism and travel jobs 198
training opportunities: open and flexible learning 194
volunteering opportunities 181–83 *see also* voluntary work
Working for Yourself: An Entrepreneur's Guide 175
World Oral Health Day 139

Young, K 229
your home (and) 101–20 *see also* key points
benefits and taxes 119–20 *see also* benefits *and* council tax
caravans/mobile homes 108–09
earning money from 117–19
by clearing clutter 118–19
energy bills *see* energy bills, reducing
and equity release 29–30
fall-proofing tips 129
future proofing 103
home security 114–15
insurance 115–17 *see also subject entry*
buildings 116
for flood-prone areas 116
contents 116–17
living in leasehold 108 *see also* leasehold advice
moving to a new home 105–08
abroad 106–07
counting the cost of 107
pros and cons for 105–06
and removals 107–08
using the Property Ombudsman scheme 107
park mobile homes 109
retirement housing/sheltered accommodation 109
safety (and) 113–14
DIY and garden 114
gas leaks 13–14
medicines and chemicals 114
tips from ROSPA 113
security 114–15 *see also* locksmiths
staying put (and) 104–05
buying the property next-door 104
converting your garage 105
extending your property 104
structural repairs and improvements 111–13
tips on safety, efficiency and cost-effectiveness 111–12
useful websites on structural work 112–13
Youth Hostels Association (YHA) 204